# Winemaking in Style

## Gerry Fowles

This book is copyright under the Berne Convention.
All rights are reserved.
Apart from the purpose of private study, research or review.
as permitted under the Copyright Act 1956,
no part of this publication may be reproduced
stored in a retrieval system or transmitted in any form
without prior permission of the copyright owner.

© Gerry Fowles 1992

ISBN 0-9517173-1-6

Manuscript prepared by Professor Gerry Fowles using
Ventura Publisher plus HP Laserjet IIID
Cover photograph by Norman Weston, Woodley
Printed by Flowprint Ltd., Warren Row, Berks.
for Gervin Press.

# Contents

| Chapter 1 | Introduction | 3 |
|---|---|---|
| Chapter 2 | Background to Winemaking | 7 |
| Chapter 3 | Introduction to Home Winemaking | 15 |
| Chapter 4 | Selection of Ingredients | 22 |
| Chapter 5 | Processing Ingredients | 46 |
| Chapter 6 | The Must | 62 |
| Chapter 7 | Special Techniques | 76 |
| Chapter 8 | The First Gallons | 83 |
| Chapter 9 | Country Wines | 96 |
| Chapter 10 | Wines with Style | 123 |
| Chapter 11 | Bacteria, Moulds and Yeasts | 154 |
| Chapter 12 | Acids in Wine | 168 |
| Chapter 13 | Carbohydrates and Sweeteners | 181 |
| Chapter 14 | Colour of Wines | 191 |
| Chapter 15 | Cloudy Wines | 201 |
| Chapter 16 | Fining and Filtering | 213 |
| Chapter 17 | Curing Faults | 223 |

# Chapter 1
# Introduction

*"Come,come, good wine is a familiar creature if it be well used; exclaim no more against it". Iago (Othello)*

The grape is the king of winemaking ingredients, of course, and as early as the Sixth Century BC folk living in Northern Iran and Iraq made good use of the grapes growing wild there as a source of food. They appreciated the sugar content which provided a much sought after source of energy. It seems likely that the first wines were made in these regions quite by accident, as a consequence of "natural" or "wild" yeast bringing about a fermentation of the sugar in the grapes. No doubt the product was tasted and the effect of the "wine" noted.

The delights of the beverage would have been appreciated, but it is unlikely that the wine would have been other than the crudest "plonk". Even so the news of this elixir would have spread and over the next centuries both grape growing and winemaking became established in Egypt and subsequently throughout the Eastern Mediterranean.

Storage of the wines must have been a real headache, though, since the wines would become oxidised quite quickly in the warm climate, and suitable containers just didn't exist. The new goatskins used to hold water hardly matched up to today's vats made from oak or stainless steel, and corked bottles were still centuries away!

Although grapes formed the basis for wines, other sugar-containing fruits would have fermented in much the same way, and we can speculate that early alcoholic beverages might have been around in other parts of the world. The history of winemaking from fruits other than grapes is less well documented, but in Europe generally, and in the UK in particular, country folk have long made wine from fruits such as apples, blackberries, elderberries and gooseberries. They also made use of less obvious ingredients including grain and vegetables, but had to provide the sugar source in addition; sugar was expensive, so honey was often used.

I have a number of books that were published in the early nineteenth century and all of them give recipes for a number of fruit wines. Some of the recipes talk about fermentation, and some add unspecified ale yeast, while others seem to rely on the addition of brandy or wine for much of the alcohol. In *The British Guide*, published in 1808 by Nuttall, Fisher and Dixon, and compiled by "AN EXPERI-ENCED GENTLEMAN", the recipe for blackberry wine makes no reference to either fermentation or yeast, and there is no addition of brandy. By contrast, the elderflower recipe is much closer to some of the recipes to be found in relatively modern (but ill-informed) winemaking books. The recipe is as follows:

"Take thirty pounds of good sugar, twelve gallons of water, and boil them half an hour, skimming it well all the time. Let it stand till milk warm; then put in three spoonfuls of yeast, and, after it has worked awhile, add two quarts of flowers, picked from the stalks, and stir it every day, till the fermentation is ceased. Then put it into a clean cask, bung it close up, let it stand two days, and then bottle it off."

A somewhat later book (1830), "The Cabinet Cyclopædia", compiled by the Rev. Dionysis Lardner, "assisted by EMINENT LITERARY AND SCIENTIFIC MEN", contains a Vol.I by Michael Donovan, a Professor of Chemistry, no less, to the Company of Apothecaries in Ireland. This unlikely combination gives a very interesting account of fermentation. The account describes how grape juice, left to itself becomes muddy, increases in temperature and generates a bubbling noise owing to the breaking of minute air bubbles at the surface. It is said that the whole appears not only to boil but it tends to boil over. On account of this resemblance to boiling the process is called "fermentation" from *fevere*, to boil. It goes on to say that the material which settles to the bottom of the vessel possesses the property of exciting fermentation in certain other substances not spontaneously disposed to such a change.

These observations are interesting since although as early as 1680 yeast cells had been observed in fermenting beer by Antonie van Leeuwenhoek, who used a primitive microscope, it wasn't until 1836-7 that the relationship between yeast cells and alcoholic fermentation was firmly stated. And it was the 1860s and 1870s before the classic studies of Pasteur settled the role of yeast in fermentation beyond question.

Wines made by amateurs in the first half of the this century tended to be very sweet and sometimes seemed very alcoholic. I say seemed very alcoholic, since the effect was obvious, but the choice of ingredients and the methods by which the wines were made could well mean that the wines were not necessarily of a particularly high ethyl alcohol content. Often wines made from grain or vegetables would contain relatively high levels of "higher" alcohols or "fusel oil", and it would be these substances that would produce the hang-over! Typical of its kind would be Grandmother's Wheat and Raisin brew. The protein content of the ingredients acted as a source of nutrient for the yeast and at the same time produced the unwanted higher alcohols. We shall go further into this in the next chapter.

The yeast used by most amateurs before say 1950 would have been bakers' yeast. This type of yeast produced a lot of froth and vigour but was unable to ferment out the very high levels of sugar many of the early recipes called for. Hence the formation of over-sweet wines. Such yeast can give wines of acceptable quality, of course, but a lot of care has to be taken to avoid the wines taking on a "yeasty" character, and few winemakers today would knowingly use a "bread" yeast, when excellent true wine yeasts are available.

I have to confess though that my earliest experience of winemaking was of this old-fashioned type. My mother had an annual autumn ritual of making potato wine. She boiled up the potatoes with sugar and lemon juice, placed the strained solution into an earthenware bowl and added the Bakers' yeast - fresh, of course, and spread on a piece of toast! The fermenting liquor was covered with a piece of butter muslin to keep out the flies, but once the fermentation stopped the cloudy "wine" was poured into bottles and loosely corked. After a few days the corks were banged in firmly, leaving the wine on the sediment. The bottles were kept in a cool place (the cupboard under the stairs) until Christmas, when they would be opened with due ceremony.

I well remember those early days, since at the tender age of eight I found my way into this store cupboard, and drank two whole bottles of the nectar. As a consequence I spent the next two days in bed - but whether as a punishment or a necessity I don't recall.

It was some twenty years later that I tried out the gentle art of winemaking for myself. By now it was the early fifties, and the amateur movement had begun to grow. Sugar was available again after the wartime rationing, and Wine Circles began to spring up. For the first time, perhaps, a little science began to creep into amateur winemaking. Although Bakers' yeast still dominated the scene, Grey Owl started to produce proper wine yeasts either as slopes or as liquid suspensions. These yeasts were expensive and had to be handled carefully, but they were worth the trouble, and soon the amateurs were making wines of real quality, at a fraction of the price of their commercial equivalents.

The open earthenware vessels had now largely gone (indeed people were beginning to realise that some vessels had a lead glaze and shouldn't be used), and glass "demijohns" or suitable plastic vessels became the order of the day. We realised the importance of cleanliness, and the need to keep our wines safe from the ravages of microbial attack and aerial oxidation. The winemaking movement had come of age, and it was now possible for us to make quality wines in the style of commercial wines. We could make aperitifs, table wines (red, white or rosé), heavier "quaffing" wines (called "social wines"), and true dessert wines.

Predictably, a home-brew industry built up, and before long it provided us with prepared ingredients such as concentrated grape juice. And to cater for the impatient winemaker, who wanted to make a wine that could be drunk in as short a time as possible, the "kit" wine emerged. A package deal was offered that enabled the winemaker to produce a drinkable alcoholic beverage in a surprisingly short period. The early kits aimed for three weeks, then 14 days and finally ten days.

These kits introduced people to the making of wines, and many moved on to using fresh fruit etc. and made wines of greater character. The best kits certainly produce drinkable wines, but in my view they take the fun out of winemaking, and they will not usually produce other than fairly basic wines. I believe that much better wines can be made from fresh ingredients, if care is taken in selecting and processing the fruit etc. so as to get a balanced "must" with the proper level of acidity, nutrients and sugar. And the flavour and aroma are likely to be better, too.

The aim of this book, which is a successor to my best selling *"Straightforward Winemaking"*, is to provide enough information for the winemaker so that wines of real quality can be made. The first part fills in the background on the principles of winemaking, the equipment needed, the choice and processing of the ingredients, and the adjustment of the must.

The second part of this book then shows how to develop recipes to produce wines in different styles. This section will give balanced recipes for wines in the more obvious commercial styles. In addition it will give recipes for country-style wines where the need is for a wine in which a particular flavour dominates.

The final section covers the more technical aspects of winemaking. It has chapters on micro-organisms (bacteria, moulds and yeasts), acidity, carbohydrates and sweeteners, wine colour, cloudy wines, fining and filtering and curing faults.

# Chapter 2
# Background to Winemaking

## Chemical aspects

At its simplest level the winemaking process is one in which sugar is changed into ethyl alcohol and carbon dioxide gas, thanks to the action of yeast. Thus the air bubbles reported by Professor Michael Donovan (see Introduction) were in reality carbon dioxide.

The overall equation for the process is

$$C_6H_{12}O_6 = 2C_2H_5OH + 2CO_2$$

glucose -> ethyl alcohol + carbon dioxide

This simple relationship was established as long ago as 1815, by Josephe Gay-Lussac, who was professor at the Sorbonne, but it was a grossly over simplified view of the chemical change taking place, of course, since the process is now known to be one involving many stages, each involving one or more enzymes. As we noted in the introduction to this book, yeast cells were found in fermenting wort by the Dutch scientist Antonie van Leeuwenhoek. The developments taking place in the 1830's saw the first published work on the relationship between fermentation and yeasts, the yeasts being called Zuckerpilz. These ideas about the nature of the fermentation were rejected by the leading scientists of the day, unfortunately, and in particular the famous organic chemist Justus Liebeg ridiculed the whole concept. And so it wasn't until Louis Pasteur published his famous treatises, Etudes sur le Vin (1866) and Etudes sur le Biere (1876) that the role of yeast cells was properly recognised, and Liebeg's objections rejected.

Returning to the fermentation process, it is now known that the first stage involves the breakdown of any sucrose present into a 50:50 mixture of fructose and glucose. This mixture is already present in grape juice, but other fruits may contain sucrose, and it is sucrose that is added when additions of cane or beet sugar are made to the must. It is an enzyme called invertase that brings about the breakdown. This enzyme is found in the yeast cell between the outer cell wall and the membrane. Thus the sucrose passes through the wall of the yeast cell, and then is processed by the enzyme into the smaller molecules of fructose and glucose. Whereas the larger sucrose molecule cannot get through the membrane into the inside of the cell, this is possible for both fructose and glucose.

Once the fructose and glucose are formed then they move through the membrane into the inside of the cell and then fermentation starts; but since this fermentation is carried out in the absence of freely available oxygen (air), then the yeast has to get the energy it needs by breaking down the fructose and glucose into ethyl alcohol and carbon dioxide. The more technical description of the process is that under anaerobic conditions (i.e. no air) the monosaccharides (i.e. fructose and glucose) are metabolised.

The next stages are very complicated and involve a whole collection of enzymes and mineral salts.

The breaking down of the sugars, or glycolysis, normally goes by way of the so-called *Embden-Meyerhof-Parnas* pathway. Magnesium and phosphorus are both essential as well as the enzymes, as the fructose and glucose both breakdown into compounds containing only three carbon atoms. The subsequent biochemical sequence involves the formation of pyruvic acid, then acetaldehyde and finally ethyl alcohol. Although this is the main route taken, it can sometimes be blocked. In particular, if there is a fair amount of sulphur dioxide present then this combines with the acetaldehyde and stops the formation of ethyl alcohol. When this happens then an alternative pathway is taken leading to the formation of glycerol (glycerine).

As if this wasn't complicated enough, there are other processes involved, albeit to a minor degree. These lead to the formation of such by-products as higher alcohols, esters, lactic acid and succinic acid. All these detailed processes are fascinating to professional oenologists, whose studies often unravel some of the mysteries that still baffle most of us. The practical winemaker then sifts the new evidence and adjusts his methods to improve his wines still further.

For most amateur winemakers, all of this biochemistry may seem a little deep, and I will leave out further detailed discussions. In the remainder of this book, the detailed science will be reduced to a minimum, but relevant recent ideas will be incorporated into the methods described whenever possible. Readers with an insatiable thirst for more scientific and technical details are referred to the list of more technical books given in the appendix. My own technical book, *Winemaking Science*, which is scheduled for 1994, should help make the material a little more digestible.

# Commercial winemaking.

## Preparing the must.

To start with, let us ignore the question of the variety of grape and simply talk about black grapes and white (green) grapes, although it has to be appreciated that it is the variety of grape that is mainly responsible for the character, taste and bouquet of the wine. The skins of the grapes contain desirable flavour and bouquet enhancing substances, together with phenolic compounds (often referred to loosely as tannin) which give the wine an astringent and mouth-puckering taste. These phenolic compounds also serve the role of "guardian", helping to reduce the tendency for the wine to become oxidised at the slightest opportunity.

The skins of black grapes contain much higher levels of phenolic compounds than do the skins of white grapes, and in addition they contain anthocyanins that give a red colour to the wine. This colouring material is normally found only in the skins, the juice of the black grapes being virtually colourless. An illustration of this is the use of the juice of black Pinot noir grapes in the production of quality Champagne.

Grape seeds and stems are very rich in phenolic compounds, but we can have too much of a good thing, and the usual practice is to remove the stems from the grapes and to crush the grapes carefully so as to avoid damaging the seeds which would add an unwanted degree of astringency to the wine. The de-stemming is carried out by suitable machinery before the grapes are sent to the crusher. The crushing is done by machine in all but the oldest wineries, but treading the grapes is still practised for part of the crop in various wineries. One such example is with some of the port producers, where a part of the crop is crushed by bands of men and women from the winery. It is a splendid sight to see a dozen or so folk stomping up and down with the deep red juice reaching well up their thighs. This apparently primitive crushing method avoids any damage to the seeds and brings out the maximum amount of colour without reducing the grape skins to a fine pulp.

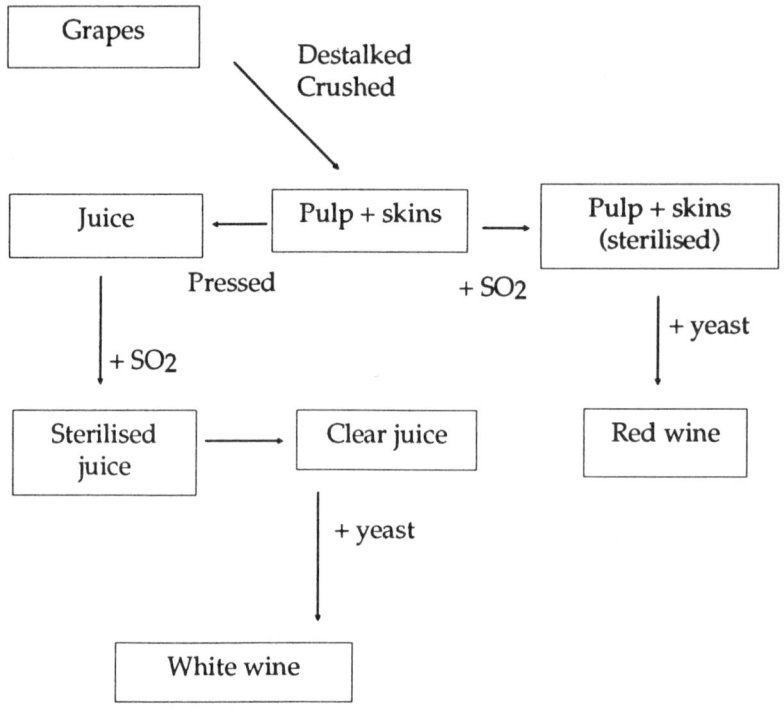

**Grape wine production scheme**

When white wine is to be made, the crushed grapes are pressed very carefully so as to remove the skins and other solid matter. This pressing ensures that excessive amounts of phenolic compounds are not transferred to the juice. In some areas the skins, either wholly or in part, are allowed to remain with the juice for the first part of the fermentation since it is believed by these winemakers that the skins contain flavour enhancing substances which results in the finished wine having more character and greater depth of flavour. Unfortunately leaving the skins in the must can lead to the production of an unstable wine and the occasional formation of off-flavours.

Grapes contain enzymes (phenoloxidases) that will cause the grape juice to go brown if oxygen (air) is present, and so precautions have to be taken to prevent this browning from taking place. It is for this reason that sulphur dioxide, or its salt potassium metabisulphite, is added to the grapes at the time they are being crushed. The sulphur dioxide reacts with the oxygen and stops the process. Besides this antioxidant property, sulphur dioxide also has the ability to kill bacteria and yeasts, so any such micro-organisms found on the surface of the grapes will be destroyed.

The grape juice, now referred to as the "must", is then allowed to stand overnight so that any solids in suspension can settle out. The clear juice is then syphoned (racked) off from the sludge at the bottom of the vessel. When relatively delicate white wines are being made, it is now common practice to make the juice as clear as possible, by either filtering or fining it, or by means of a centrifuge. This is done since winemakers have found that wines made from such clarified juice are much less likely to develop off-flavours or turn brown at a later stage.

## The fermentation.

The clarified juice will have lost a lot of the sulphur dioxide that was added, and it will not be in a high enough concentration to destroy the wine yeast which is then added. This added yeast will be one of the newer "active dried wine yeasts" that have been made available to commercial winemakers for the past decade or so. Suitable selections of these commercial yeasts are now available to amateur winemakers in quantities sufficient for making say five gallons. It should be pointed out that some wineries do not add such yeast starters but rely on the "natural" yeast to be found on the surfaces of their winemaking equipment. Contrary to popular opinion the equipment is the source of the yeasts rather than the skins of the grapes - recent research has shown that the bloom of grapes contain almost none of the yeast strains that produce worthwhile wines. When the wineries are of long standing, special yeast flora may well have become established, and excellent, and even great wines are made, but elsewhere the result is likely to be the worst sort of plonk, rich in acetic acid and ethyl acetate! I mention this since there are still some amateur winemakers who rely on whatever yeasts nature may have provided on the surfaces of the many fruits we use for our winemaking. My advice is to use a decent wine yeast of established quality.

The fermentation is carried out in a suitable container, with the temperature kept below 20°C if possible. The lowish temperature has been shown to give wines with a desirable young fruity character. These days the container will be made from fibre glass or stainless steel (for wealthy wineries aiming for the best), although some less well equipped establishments may still use concrete or tile-lined vats. It must be appreciated that during the fermentation a lot of heat will be generated, and unless there is some provision for cooling the fermenting liquor the temperature in the vat may rise to the high 20's or even higher, with a consequent reduction in quality. In the simplest systems, the tanks are cooled by running a stream of cold water over them, while the larger wineries will have cooling coils immersed in the wine.

When the must is fermenting vigorously a great deal of carbon dioxide gas will be released and to a large extent this will protect the must from oxidation by air. But open vats are not permitted since this exposes the must to the perils of attack

A typical small modern winery in Northern Portugal

by the bacteria that will always be around any winery. A large fermentation lock or trap is used to protect the must; this lock is filled with water or a solution of sulphite which allows the carbon dioxide gas to pass through but prevents air or bugs getting back into the container. Once the initial fermentation is over and there is no further emission of carbon dioxide gas, then the wine settles down and spent yeast cells and any other solid material are deposited on the bottom of the container. The clearing wine is then racked or pumped into a clean fresh container, a little sulphur dioxide is added to protect it, and then nature takes over and the wine gradually clears. The clarification can be speeded up by fining or filtering, as we shall see shortly.

The production of red wine differs in that the grape skins are not removed. The yeast is added to the grape juice, plus pomace and skins, and the fermentation allowed to proceed for four to seven days before the skins are removed. The time allowed for the fermentation period on the skins varies according to the grape variety and the style of wine being made. If the fermentation period is too long, then although this extracts a lot of colour it also takes out excessive amounts of "tannin", which gives us a wine with a great deal of astringency. Such a wine will need keeping for quite a few years to allow the tannin level to drop and to let the wine mellow. Not all wines benefit from such a treatment since it can be that by the time the tannin level becomes acceptable to the palate the fruitiness will have disappeared.

Shorter periods "on the pulp" will give somewhat paler wines, which can be drunk fairly soon because of the relatively low tannin level. Typical of such wines will be Beaujolais, which make use of the Gamay grape. A fair amount of colour will be extracted quite quickly, but the tannin level will be only about half of that found in a good Bordeaux red (claret), and the youthful, full-of- fruit wine can be drunk with pleasure without a long maturation period.

Sparkling wines such as Champagne are usually white wines, although some rosé sparklers are made, and sparkling red wines appear to be getting more popular. The method of making the sparkling wine involves first making the base wine, of whatever colour is required, clarifying it, and then adding more sugar (usually in the form of grape juice) and more yeast. Since the base wine is likely to be fairly acidic and contain some 12% or so of alcohol, the added yeast finds itself in a rather unfriendly environment. This secondary fermentation stage as it is called, which takes place either in the bottle or in large sealed tanks, needs a yeast that is alcohol tolerant, and this means one of the *Saccharomyces* strains (a Champagne yeast!).

The secondary fermentation puts the sparkle into the wine, because of the dissolved carbon dioxide gas. When this stage is complete, the bottles are inverted in stages and the yeast persuaded to settle down into the neck of the bottle. The bottles are then chilled, and the plug of frozen wine and trapped yeast is removed carefully. The headspace is then topped up with more dry wine (for a dry sparkling wine) or grape juice (for a sweeter wine) and re-corked with the famous Champagne cork.

## Choice of yeast

The vintner has to choose a strain of yeast that will bring out the best from his grapes. For table wine production a yeast is selected that will ferment fairly quickly to the required 11-12% alcohol level, and which will settle out firmly without delay, thus making racking a simple task. With red wines a typical selected yeast might be one of the Montrachet Burgundy strain of *Saccharomyces cerevisiae*, since this copes well with the fermentation over the usual temperature range of 18-25°C. As we have seen, white wines by contrast give the best results at a lower temperature, so strains are selected that will ferment at say 12-15°C, and produce the required ester balance.

We shall look in much more detail at wine yeasts in Chapter 11.

## Clarification and maturation

Turning again to the finished table wine, this has to be treated such that it becomes star-bright. This means either fining or filtering, or both in the case of white wines, although reds normally clear without such treatment. Excess of protein has to be removed from the wine since otherwise it may form unwanted hazes and unsightly flocculent deposits later on. The protein removal is achieved by adding bentonite. This is a clay material (technically an aluminium silicate) that combines with protein and removes it. Other clarifying agents such as gelatin, isinglass and silicic acid may be used to remove both haze-making particles that are already making the wine murky and substances that may produce hazes after the wine has been stored for some time. Filtering is also an important weapon in producing a stable clear wine. Red wines are less likely to need clarification and usually fall clear spontaneously.

We shall look at the implications of fining and filtering, and the methods available to the amateur in some detail in Chapter 16.

We have seen that white wines are particularly prone to oxidation. For this reason they must be protected and sulphur dioxide is added before they are fined or filtered. At the bottling stage, white wines are usually treated of between 50 and 100 mg/litre of sulphur dioxide. In my view this level of sulphiting is unlikely to cause problems, but there is an ever increasing pressure on commercial wine-makers to keep the sulphur dioxide to a minimum. This is fine provided it does not go too far. Thus while the smell of some cheaper white plonks may be dominated by the objectionable stench of "sulphite", there is the alternative problem of getting an oxidised wine if the sulphur dioxide is omitted. Personally I prefer a wine that retains its clean fruity taste and smell, thanks to the discrete use of sulphur dioxide, rather than one that has developed the distinctive acetaldehyde nose of a "cheap British Sherry".

Long periods of maturation are inappropriate for most of the lighter white wines, which are best drunk quite young, although heavier whites such as classic white Burgundies need several years to develop fully, and a period in an oak barrel works wonders in most cases. The effect of cask storage is to add a delicate note of oak to the wine and a general smoothening out. Too much oak, though, and a vanilla taste takes over. Really full-bodied sweet white wines such as Sauternes invariably benefit from a fairly lengthy period in bottle.

Red wines also benefit from cask ageing, for it is during such a period that various complex processes take place. These include polymerisation of anthocyanins and phenolics, and a remarkable rounding of the wines.

# Chapter 3
# Introduction to Home Winemaking

## Changes from commercial winemaking

The most obvious change is one of scale. Thus whereas the smallest commercial winery will be talking in terms of hundreds of litres of must being handled, and bigger wineries will deal with many thousands at a time, the average enthusiastic amateur winemaker makes 5 to 10 gallon batches of wine at a time, and many winemakers will limit themselves to one gallon brews (4.5 litres). The 5 gallon (say 20 litre) batch is ideal for enthusiasts since it is the sort of quantity that can be handled fairly easily, and it gives us 25 to 30 bottles of wine at a time. This way we can make plenty for our own needs and still be generous to our friends. If we go for the smaller one gallon batches, we will get only a maximum of six bottles from each container, and this is a very modest yield if the wine turns out to be particularly good. A further point in favour of the larger production unit is that wine in 5 gallon lots is less likely to be spoilt if a small amount of air gets into it.

However, many winemakers, especially those just starting out, and perhaps the older readers who may find five gallons of wine too heavy to handle, prefer to make one gallon lots; in any case, in the early days it will be much easier to acquire the smaller fermentation vessels. For these reasons all the recipes given later in this book will be to make 4.5 litres (one gallon) of wine. Any reader who wishes to make larger quantities should simply multiply the amounts given by the appropriate number.

An even more important change is that most of the time we shall be making wine from ingredients other than grapes, and this means using a recipe that gives the right balance. Thus in the last chapter we looked briefly at the commercial winemaking methods and saw that the yeast converted the sugar into alcohol. What must be appreciated is that grape juice is pretty well the ideal base in which yeast can thrive and carry out the sugar-alcohol conversion. Occasionally there may be problems with over-acid grapes, and in poorer seasons the sugar level in the juice will be less than ideal. Moving now to the amateur scene, we have to consider whether fruits such as apples for instance are lacking in some respect.

First of all we must think about the level of sugar in the juice. A rough guideline is that 10% of sugar will produce 6% of alcohol, so that for a table wine containing 12% alcohol by volume, we shall need to make sure that the must contains around 20% of sugar. It doesn't matter whether the sugar is that found naturally in the fruit etc. or whether it is added as granulated sugar (cane sugar and beet sugar are both pure sucrose and equally acceptable to the yeast). The guideline I have given (10% sugar - 6% alcohol) assumes that all of the sugar is changed into alcohol, thus giving us a dry wine. Later on we will look into the best way of sweetening up wines. One thing is certain. No yeast can cope with massive concentrations of sugar, and even the most voracious of yeasts will cry "enough" if the sugar level gets above 30%. For the one-gallon enthusiasts, who are still uneasy with grams and litres, 10% of sugar corresponds to a pound of sugar in one gallon of must; hence under no circumstances should more than three pounds of sugar be used for making a gallon of wine. At this level, under otherwise ideal conditions, a suitable yeast will produce some 18% of alcohol! You are most unlikely to get more than this, although we will return to the subject later when we consider different strains of yeast.

Now the yeast is a "plant", being a member of the fungi family. And like all plants it needs good conditions if it is to flourish and do its job well. Besides sugar levels, the yeast will be sensitive to acidity and nutrients. Think of the yeast rather like you would lime-hating plants. In other words the yeast needs acid. We will discuss just how much and which acid in the next few chapters.

Equally important is the provision of nutrients. As every gardener knows, plants need nitrogen, phosphate and potash, together with a lesser amount of magnesium, and much smaller amounts of other minerals. Yeast too needs these mineral salts. If we use adequate quantities of fruit in our musts then it is more than likely that enough of these minerals will be present, but this will not be the case if attempts are made to make simple flower wines for instance. Nutrient supplements will be needed in such cases, and acid additions as well. Besides the minerals, yeast will need other vitamins etc. to grow properly and to produce good wine. We will look into these problems later on.

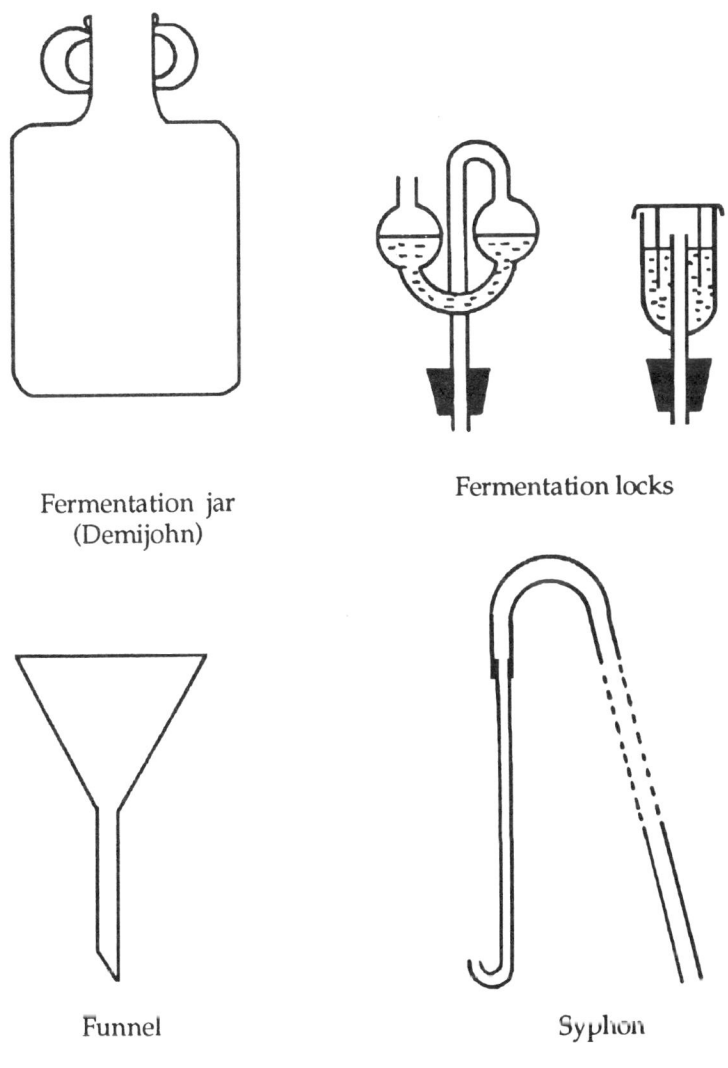

Figure 3.1 Basic winemaking equipment

# Equipment needed.

In the early stages it is best to keep the equipment to a minimum, and to avoid making purchases that may turn out to be expensive "white elephants". The equipment I am going to recommend is the basic bare minimum for making one gallon (4.5 litre) batches of wine. It is assumed that readers will have access to simple items of kitchen equipment such as scales and teaspoons. To ensure continuing domestic harmony I strongly recommend readers to buy items such as sieves and stirring spoons etc. The following list is the basic minimum for making one gallon batches of wines from either juices and solid fruits.

> Primary fermentation vessel (bucket or brewing bin)
>
> Gallon jars (demijohns)
>
> Nylon flour sieve
>
> Long-handled plastic or wooden spoon
>
> Syphon tube
>
> Fermentation traps
>
> Large funnel
>
> Small funnel
>
> Bottle brush
>
> Plastic teaspoon

There is one general, and very important point I must make. Wine picks up off-flavours very easily, so all the equipment must be made from materials that will not contaminate the wine. Metals must be kept out of the wine at all costs (unless you have really high quality stainless steel). Hence we will normally use either plastic or glass equipment; a wooden spoon is an exception, but it will need sterilising properly.

**Fermentation vessel.** If the wine is being made from juices only, then all the early operations can be done in the demijohn, but if solid fruit, pulp etc. is involved, then we need a wide mouthed container such as a bucket to hold our ingredients for the first few days. The container is normally made from food-grade plastic. If you are near a home-brew shop, pay it a visit and invest a modest sum in a white plastic brewing bin, complete with fitting lid. Such containers are easy to use and clean, and most importantly will have been made from plastic that will not add a taint to your wine. The alternative is a new white polythene or polypropylene bucket. Although the colouring substances used in plastics are normally harmless, I suggest that you play safe and avoid using brightly coloured buckets.

You may be lucky enough to lay your hands on a suitable second-hand plastic jar or wide-mouthed bottle. This will be satisfactory provided the container has been used to hold foodstuffs. But do not use any plastic vessel that has been used to hold chemicals etc., and don't use any plastic vessel that has been used for holding any strongly tasting or smelling substance. The taste and smell gets into the plastic and is almost impossible to remove.

A final word or warning about fermentation vessels concerns the earthenware crocks that you may find lying around in junk shops and the like. Many of these earthenware containers will be unsuitable, and may well have a lead glaze; the wine or fruit juice will strip off the lead glaze giving you a toxic wine! If you are sure that the glaze is a salt one, and provided that the glaze is not badly crazed, then the container can be used. But if there is any doubt about the container, don't use it.

**Gallon jars (demijohns).** These jars can be obtained from any home-brew shop. They can be obtained too from anyone buying cider in bulk or from a kindly cafe proprietor who gets his fruit juices etc. in such vessels. Increasingly though, fruit juices come in fairly lightweight plastic bottles. These are quite satisfactory for holding fermenting must for fairly short periods - say two to three weeks - but should not be used for storing wine; they allow air to get into the wine and so the wine will deteriorate. A point to bear in mind is that the glass used for making the gallon demijohns will not take kindly to sudden heat changes. If you pour boiling water into such glass jars they will shatter!

**Nylon flour sieve.** This is a very valuable item for straining off the larger pieces of pulp and so on. Buy one that has a diameter of around six inches (say 16 centimetres). A sieve of this size will fit nicely into the top of the larger funnel (g). Nylon is ideal because it can be cleaned easily and stands up to chemical sterilants very well.

**Long-handled spoon.** This can be made of plastic or wood, but I believe that plastic is much better since it is sterilised more easily than wood. But make sure that the spoon you buy is fairly substantial and does not bend under the slightest pressure in hot water. For convenience a spoon with a handle some 12 inches or so long is the most suitable. Such a spoon can be immersed deep into the must for stirring.

**Syphon tube.** The wines have to be racked or syphoned off from sediment at various stages, and for this purpose a simple length of plastic tubing is used. Normally the end of the tube that goes into the wine is fitted with a U-tube of glass, so that when suction is applied to the tube there is no direct "suck" on the sediment, which would disturb it. Personally I use a really long glass U-tube attached to the plastic tubing, the long arm being of sufficient length to reach to the bottom of a demijohn. The rigidity of the glass helps to keep the tubing in position during the racking and makes it less likely that the sediment will be disturbed.

Another type of glass attachment has a sealed end and a hole in the side; once again this ensures that there is no strong suction directly affecting the sediment. I have suggested using plastic tubing for the flexible part of the syphon because it is transparent, and you can see just where the wine has reached when you first suck it up. It is also easy to clean and sterilise. Rubber tubing can be used if plastic is not available, but then I suggest adding a short length of glass tubing to the end that is sucked, so that the initial filling of the tubing by mouth suction is easy. Whatever tubing is used I suggest using tubing of say one centimetre in internal diameter. Anything much smaller will give a very slow racking speed.

We will discuss the best way of using the syphon tube later on (page 84).

**Fermentation traps.** As the illustration shows, these traps are typically a U-tube with two bulbs in it. The trap is partly filled with water or a dilute solution of sodium metabisulphite. Carbon dioxide gas released during fermentation can escape by bubbling through the water barrier, but the fermenting must or wine is protected from the outside atmosphere. The open end of the tube is lightly plugged with a little cotton wool. This stops the odd inquisitive fly from committing suicide on the trap liquid. These simple traps can be made from either glass or plastic. Glass is more easily broken but it can be sterilised if necessary by boiling, whereas plastic traps cannot be treated in this way.

**Funnels.** I find it best to have two funnels, one small and one large. The exact sizes are not important, but for the smaller one I suggest a diameter of say 10 centimetres (4 inches), and for the larger one a diameter of 20 centimetres (4 inches). The large funnel is useful for pouring large amounts of liquid from one vessel to another, while the smaller one, which has a much narrower stem will be very useful for pouring liquids into narrow necked containers such as wine bottles. Plastic funnels, being virtually non-breakable, are probably the best ones to get, but they do get stained rather badly and they can be easily scratched, giving tiny grooves that will harbour stains and micro-organisms unless they are cleaned properly. Personally I use a large plastic funnel and a smaller glass one.

**Bottle brush.** Wine bottles used by amateurs will normally be second-hand ones. They must be thoroughly cleaned, both inside and out. Chemical cleaners help to loosen up old residues of wine and the occasional mould growth, but there is nothing quite so effective as a good bottle brush used with a little detergent. Purchase a brush that will go through the neck of the wine bottle without difficulty, but which has a good stiff set of bristles that will really get to work on the sides and bottom of the bottle. More on bottle preparation later, when we come to discuss the making and handling of the first gallon!

**Plastic teaspoon.** Ideally I recommend that you get one of the sets of plastic spoons used in the kitchen. Both the teaspoon and the half teaspoon are very useful for measuring out small amounts of solutions. The larger spoons are valuable when the 5 gallon batches of wine are being made.

In later chapters we will discuss the best way of using these various bits of equipment effectively. We shall consider also the use of one or two more elaborate pieces of equipment such as an hydrometer.

# Chapter 4
# Selection of Ingredients

## Introduction

What is it we look for when we are considering what to make the wine from? All too often it is something cheap, or free, or something that we have too much of in the garden and for which there is no other obvious use. It is for this reason that I am often asked for a recipe for green tomato wine, for instance! But why on earth should we make wine from such unpromising material? It has no sugar worth mentioning and certainly no desirable flavour.

I well remember the occasion just after my first winemaking book had appeared, when I came across this problem. I had walked into a home-brew shop in the South West, hoping to persuade the proprietor to put a few copies of my book on his shelves. The person in front of me asked for a book with a recipe for onion wine, and rather foolishly I butted in and asked him why he was making wine from onions. "Oh", he said, "I have a garden full of onions and I don't know what else to do with them". My comment was that he might find the flavour unacceptable in his wine. "That's alright", he replied, "I've been told that if you leave the wine for two years the onion taste will go". I replied that if he left the onions out he wouldn't have to wait for two years before drinking the wine. "That's a good point, I'll take your advice," he replied, "I shan't need a book after all". The man running the home-brew shop was a little peeved with my interruption, because he did have a book (it shall be nameless) with just such a recipe, and he had lost a sale. And, not surprisingly, he wasn't interested in my book either!

But the point of the story is that while in principle you can literally make wine from anything, provided that the must contains sugar, acid, nutrients and yeast, there is no point in adding an ingredient unless it adds something to the must that is needed. Thus we look for sugar, acidity and nutrients from our ingredients, and we leave out ingredients that can cause unnecessary problems such as starch hazes.

Perhaps the most important things of all are aroma and flavour - we want the wine to have a decent smell and taste. To some extent aroma and taste are a matter of opinion; bananas for instance have a very distinctive and strong flavour, and while this is much appreciated by some folk, others avoid the strong flavour like the plague.

Later in this chapter I shall suggest the sorts of wine that I have found best suited to particular ingredients. While I believe that my choices are sound ones, it must be appreciated that I am merely giving my opinions and not putting down firm rules. The final decision on what fruits are best for say a medium-dry rosé wine is yours to make!

**First of all sugar.** Generally speaking, the ingredients we are likely to use will not contain enough sugar to produce a wine with the required level of alcohol. Thus if we want to make a table wine with an alcoholic strength of 11 - 12%, we shall have to start with a must that contains around 18 to 20% of sugar, or about two pounds of sugar in a gallon of must, and it is only with grapes or 100% bananas that we can meet this requirement. We shall see just what sugar levels are to be found in the ingredients a little later on, but as a rough guide we can anticipate that most fruits will give 5 - 10% of sugar, grain just 1 - 2%, vegetables very little apart fromcarrots and parsnips (after they have experienced a period in cold weather), and flowers virtually none. This means that all the recipes will need additional sugar.

This additional sugar is usually ordinary granulated sugar - and it doesn't matter whether the sugar comes from cane or beet. There is no virtue in buying expensive invert sugar, because this contains a fair bit of water and will not ferment any quicker (see the chapter on yeasts). Avoid using more strongly-flavoured sugars such as Demerara or such syrups as Golden Syrup and molasses.

**Turning to acid,** we have to decide just how much should be in the must, and if we have to add any more we have to choose which acid to use. We shall look at this matter in more detail later (Chapter 12) but for the moment let us assume that we need somewhere between 4 and 6 grams per litre (expressed as tartaric acid). Whereas grapes contain a mixture of malic and tartaric acids, many of our country fruits will be rich in citric acid. For all practical purposes this will not matter in most instances, but I do recommend that any extra acid that is needed should be added as tartaric acid. The reasons for this are that tartaric acid is the least likely to be attacked by bacteria, and it is the acid that can often be removed in part simply by chilling the wine. All fruits contain acid, but there is almost none in flowers, grain or vegetables. All the recipes given in this book have been worked out so as to give a sensible level of acidity. We shall return to the more technical aspects of acidity later (Chapter 12).

**Nutrients** are an essential requirement of the must if the fermentation is to be successful. As we have seen, like all plants, yeasts require fair amounts of the major minerals (containing magnesium, nitrogen, phosphorus and potassium), plus some minor minerals and a range of "growth factors". Grape juice is an ideal medium for the yeast because it nearly always contains roughly the right amount of these essential nutrients. Other fruits are pretty good in this respect, provided enough fruit is used in the recipe. Flowers by contrast provide virtually no nutrients - their sole contribution is aroma (and possibly colour). Grain and root vegetables contain quite a lot of nutrients, but the nitrogen is present in the form of protein, and the yeast has to struggle to extract it. In so doing an unwanted by-product (higher alcohols, or fusel oil), may be formed. Thus when a must is prepared which does not contain a fair measure of fruit, adjustments have to be made and nutrients added.

## Classes of ingredients

For convenience we can group ingredients under the five headings:-

>Fruit
>Vegetables
>Grain (cereals)
>Flowers
>Others

We will look at each of these in turn to see what the commoner ingredients have to offer us. I have put in tables of data summarising the levels of sugar (Table 4.1) and acid (Table 4.2) likely to be present in "ripe" fruit. Tables 4.3, 4.4, 4.5, 4.6 and 4.7, contain respectively information about the amounts of sugar and acid found in dried fruit, canned fruit, fruit juice, cereals and vegetables. Readers should consult my data book **MUST** for more detailed information.

Table 4.1 Sugar content of fruits*

| Fruit | Total sugar (%) | Fructose | Glucose | Sucrose | Sorbitol(%) |
|---|---|---|---|---|---|
| Apple |  |  |  |  |  |
| cooking | 8-10 |  |  |  |  |
| domestic crab | 12-14 | 55 | 20 | 25 | 0.5 |
| eating | 10-13 |  |  |  |  |
| Apricot | 6-7 | 10 | 20 | 70 | - |
| Banana | 18 | 20 | 40 | 40 | - |
| Bilberry | 5-7 | 55 | 40 | 5 | - |
| Blackberry | 5-6 | 50 | 45 | 5 | 0 |
| Blackcurrant | 7-8 | 55 | 35 | 10 | - |
| Cherry |  |  |  |  |  |
| black | 11-13 |  |  |  |  |
| morello | 9-11 | 55 | 40 | 5 | 1.4 |
| red | 9-11 |  |  |  |  |
| white | 10-12 |  |  |  |  |
| Cranberry | 3-4 | - | - | - | - |
| Damson | 8-10 | 35 | 55 | 10 | 1.0 |
| Elderberry | 10-13 | 45 | 45 | 10 | - |
| Gooseberry |  |  |  |  |  |
| culinary | 4-6 | 45 | 45 | 10 | - |
| dessert | 8-9 |  |  |  |  |
| Grape | 15-22 | 50 | 50 | 0 | - |
| Grapefruit |  |  |  |  |  |
| juice | 6 | 30 | 30 | 40 | - |
| Greengage | 10-12 | 20 | 40 | 40 | 1.0 |
| Hawthorn berry | 3 | 50 | 50 | 0 | - |
| Lemon juice | 1-2 | 55 | 30 | 15 | - |
| Lime juice | 3-4 | 50 | 50 | 0 | - |
| Loganberry | 4-6 | 40 | 55 | 5 | - |
| Medlar | 10-11 | - | - | - | - |
| Melon | 5-6 | - | - | - | - |
| Mulberry | 8 | 45 | 55 | 0 | - |
| Nectarine | 12-13 | - | - | - | - |
| Orange | 9-10 | 25 | 20 | 55 | - |
| Passion fruit | 6 | - | - | - | - |
| Peach | 8-9 | 10 | 10 | 80 | 0.9 |
| Pear | 9-11 | 10 | 20 | 70 | 2.0 |
| Pineapple | 12 | 10 | 20 | 70 | - |
| Plum |  |  |  |  |  |
| culinary | 6-8 | 20 | 55 | 25 | 2.0 |
| Plum |  |  |  |  |  |
| dessert | 9-11 | 15 | 40 | 45 | - |

Table 4. 1 (contd.)

| Fruit | Total sugar (%) | Fructose | Glucose | Sucrose | Sorbitol (%) |
|---|---|---|---|---|---|
| Pomegranate | 11-14 | 45 | 50 | 5 | - |
| Quince | 7-9 | 70 | 25 | 5 | - |
| Raspberry | 6-7 | 40 | 40 | 20 | - |
| Redcurrant | 5 | 45 | 55 | 0 | - |
| Rhubarb** | 1 | - | - | - | - |
| Rose hip | 8-10 | - | - | - | - |
| Rowanberry | 8-10 | 50 | 45 | 5 | 3-6 |
| Sloe | 5 | 45 | 55 | - | - |
| Strawberry | 5-6 | 40 | 40 | 20 | - |
| Tangerine | 7-8 | 20 | 15 | 65 | - |
| Whitecurrant | 5-6 | - | - | - | - |

Principal sugars (% of total)

\* The values given are typical of those to be found for ripe fruits; there may be some variation between varieties. Where no information appears to be available this is shown by means of a dash (-).

\*\* Rhubarb is included here although strictly speaking it is a vegetable rather than a fruit.

Table 4.2 Acid content of fruits

| Fruit | Total acidity (% as tartaric) | Citric | Malic | Tartaric | Minor acids (less than 5% unless stated) |
|---|---|---|---|---|---|
| Apple |  |  |  |  |  |
| cooking | 0.9-1.4 | - | 90 | - | Quinic (5%) |
| eating | 0.4-0.9 | - | 90 | - | Shikimic in peel |
| Apricot | 1.1-1.3 | 25 | 75 | - | Quinic |
| Banana | 0.3-0.4 | 20 | 70 | - | - |
| Bilberry | 0.9-1.0 | 90 | 10 | - | Quinic;shikimic |
| Blackberry | 0.9-1.3 | 50 | 50 | - | - |
| Blackcurrant | 3.0-4.0 | 90 | 10 | - | Oxalic |
| Cherry | 0.4-0.6 | 10 | 90 | - | - |
| Damson | 2.0-2.4 | - | 90 | - | Quinic |
| Elderberry | 0.8-1.3 | 85 | 15 | - | Quinic;shikimic |
| Gooseberry | 1.4-2.0 | 50 | 50 | - | Shikimic;oxalic |

| | | | | | |
|---|---|---|---|---|---|
| Grape | 0.4-1.3 | - | 20 | 80 | - |
| Grapefruit juice | 2.0 | 95 | 5 | - | |
| Greengage | 1.0-1.4 | - | 90 | - | Quinic |
| Hawthornberry | 0.35 | - | 90 | - | - |
| Lemon juice | 4.0-4.5 | 95 | 5 | - | - |
| Loganberry | 1.5-2.5 | 80 | 20 | - | - |
| Mulberry | 0.4-0.5 | - | - | - | - |
| Orange juice | 0.8-1.1 | 90 | 10 | - | - |
| Peach | 0.5-0.8 | 25 | 75 | - | - |
| Pear | 0.2-0.4 | - | 90 | - | - |
| Pineapple | 0.8-1.3 | 80 | 20 | - | - |
| Plum | 1.4-1.7 | - | 95 | - | Quinic |
| Pomegranate | 1.5 | 90 | 5 | - | Oxalic |
| Quince* | 0.7-1.2 | - | 100 | - | - |
| Raspberry | 1.4-1.6 | 75 | 25 | - | - |
| Redcurrant | 2.0-2.5 | 85 | 15 | - | Succinic;oxalic |
| Rhubarb | 1.0-2.0 | - | 80 | - | Oxalic (12%) |
| Rose hip | 0.7-0.9 | - | - | - | - |
| Sloe | 1.3-1.5 | - | 90 | - | - |
| Strawberry | 0.6-1.5 | 90 | 10 | - | Succinic;quinic |
| Tangerine juice | 1.0-1.5 | 90 | 10 | - | - |

* The data is for the true quince, not the Japonica quince.

We will make use of this information when we come to devise good recipes for the different styles of wine (see Chapters 9 and 10).

Table 4.3  Acid and sugar content of dried fruit

| Fruit | Acid content (% as tartaric) | Sugar content (%) |
|---|---|---|
| Apricot | 4 | 40-50 |
| Banana | 1 | 60 |
| Currant Raisin Sultana | 2 | 65-70 |
| Date | 1 | 65 |
| Fig | 2.5 | 50-55 |
| Peach | 1 | 50-55 |
| Prune | 1.3 | 45-50 |

Table 4.4 Acid and sugar content of canned fruit*

| Fruit | Acid content (% as tartaric) | Sugar content (%) |
|---|---|---|
| Apricot | 0.5 | 28 |
| Peach | 0.3 | 23 |
| Pear | 0.2 | 20 |
| Pineapple | 0.17 | 20 |

* The values given are for the contents of the can, including the syrup. The syrup used in canning usually contains around 20% of sugar, although some fruits are canned in natural juice and will have lower levels of sugar.


Table 4.5 Acid and sugar levels of commercial fruit juices (UK)

| Juice | Acid content (% as tartaric) | Sugar content (%) |
|---|---|---|
| Apple | 0.5-0.8 | 10-11 |
| Grape (white) | 0.5-0.8 | 16-18 |
| Grapefruit (unsweetened) | 1.4-1.7 | 7-9 |
| Orange | 0.9-1.1 | 9 |
| Pineapple | 0.7-0.9 | 12-13 |

# Fruit

Let us consider each of the commoner fruits in turn, first "white" and then "black" and comment as appropriate on such matters as the choice of variety, method of collection, and the chemical constitution.

The more technical aspects of both acids and sugars is left until later (see Chapters 12 and 13), but it is worth commenting briefly that all three of the sugars listed ferment equally well, with most yeasts fermenting glucose rather more quickly than fructose. Should any sugar be left unfermented then it is likely to be fructose which is about twice as sweet as glucose. I have listed sorbitol, which is sold in pharmacy shops as diabetic sugar, since it occurs in just a few fruits. It is not used by the yeast and so remains in the wine to give it a slight residual sweetness.

The acid content of each fruit is summarised in the column headed total acidity, and listed as the tartaric acid equivalent; this will be explained fully later (see page 171).

There is a general "rule" I follow with only one or two exceptions that I will mention as we go along. The rule is to use ripe fruit, not under-ripe or over-ripe. Thus the little green apples that fall from the trees prematurely should be added to the compost heap, and the "bargains" of over-ripe fruit on offer in markets at the end of the day should be left well alone. And fresh fruit should be used rather than dried or canned whenever possible.

## "White" fruits

**Apple.** In my view, apples are one of the best ingredients for making white wines, and I find them suitable as a major part of the must ingredients for all types of white and rosé wines; but they do not have quite enough depth of flavour to be the major ingredient for heavy dessert types of wine. I also find apples very useful as part of the make-up of a must for lighter, fruitier red wines (in the Beaujolais mode).

First of all, what varieties of apple should we use. I hesitate to be too dogmatic about this because while I have my own favourites, these may not be available to all readers. But to start with I recommend using a mixture of cooking and eating apples, with several varieties of each if possible. Bramley Seedlings are splendid for apple pies, but they are very acidic and their aroma is not the most suitable for making apple wine. By all means include some Bramleys, but don't overdo it. My heartfelt advice is to leave out "wild" crab apples, since these are likely to be over-acid and usually have an unwelcome aftertaste of "phenolics". John Downie crabs are fine, and I find them particularly good for inclusion in recipes for medium-sweet wines, where their golden colour and extra sugar will be appreciated.

The levels of acid and sugar given for apple juice in Table 4.5 refers to juices packaged for supermarkets etc. in one-litre cartons or bottles. If you juice your own apples and use a mix of varieties then it will have a similar composition. Delicious varieties contain less acid (usually 0.3-0.4%). Newton Wonder and Worcester Permain apples give juice with sugar levels somewhat below the average while the top end of the sugar range is found with juice from Cox's Orange Pippins and Laxton's Fortune.

Pick the apples if you can, rather than use fallers, but in any case wash the fruit well to remove the grime that collects on the surface of the fruit even in country districts. Throw away any badly bruised apples, or cut out the bruised portions. I will return to the processing of the apples in the next chapter, and limit my comments here to simply saying that for table wines we will get the best results if we use only the juice.

**Apricot.** One problem we face is that it is often difficult to obtain really ripe fresh apricots. All too often the fruit is imported under-ripe, and rather lacks flavour. Where this is a problem I suggest using dried apricots. But buy the best grade available, and remember that dried apricots contain a lot of acid and have a pretty intense flavour. This means that only relatively small amounts of dried apricots should be used in the must, which is just as well when we see just how expensive the best quality fruit can be.

Personally I feel that the flavour of apricots makes them best suited for making sweet and dessert wines, although drier wines can benefit by the inclusion of small amounts of dried apricots in the must.

**Banana.** Bananas are rich in sugar and contain only modest levels of acidity, and this combination should make them ideal candidates for extensive use in winemaking. But as I commented earlier, they have a very distinctive flavour, and this can overwhelm the wine if too many are included in the must. The fruit must be really ripe as indicated by the skins beginning to turn black. If bananas are not quite ripe they will still contain a fair amount of starch, which can cause hazes. The fruit should be skinned and only the pulp used. I mention this because some old recipes suggest boiling up the bananas, skins and all, and using the extract for winemaking. What wasn't appreciated by the authors of such recipes is that banana skins contain one or two substances that are harmful to our health.

Bananas have a reputation for adding body to a wine and for helping the wine to drop clear. While there is some substance to these suggestions, the case is usually considerably overstated. I recommend limiting the use of bananas in dry and medium-dry wines (which are normally not too heavy in fruit) to the pulp of one medium sized banana per 4.5 litres of must. The heavier dessert wines can tolerate larger amounts, as we shall see.

**Citrus fruits.** I have grouped together all the citrus fruits since they have much in common. In every case I recommend that only the juice be used. The pith of all citrus fruits is pretty bitter and should be omitted from the must; a possible exception is when an aperitif wine is being made, since this type of wine can take a little bitterness. Grapefruit juice should be kept for aperitif wines, and lemon and lime juices should be used in moderation. Many old recipes included the juice of lemons or oranges as the source of acid, but the recipes were flawed since they did not specify the amount of juice - the fruit does differ in size! As I mentioned earlier, I prefer using tartaric acid when extra acid is needed by the must.

Orange juice can be used in its own right as one of the major sources of flavour, and in such cases a little zest from the skin of suitable oranges adds a little extra aroma. I tend to use oranges, or related fruit such as clementines, tangerines etc. in my sweeter wines.

**Gooseberry**. This has a long history of use in winemaking in this country, and there are many reports of how sparkling wines made from the "hairy grape" were added to, or took the place of commercial wines. Apart from apples and grapes, gooseberries are the best of the ingredients available to us for making quality white table wines. The flavour is very suitable for inclusion of the fruit in recipes for wines of the Burgundy, Chablis and Sancerre styles. In my experience, a lot of misleading information has been given to winemakers about how to get the best out of the fruit. In particular it is often said that unripe green gooseberries should be used for dry wines and dessert gooseberries for sweeter wines. The second part of this statement is true, but under no circumstances should really unripe green gooseberries be used for winemaking. All the fruit should be reasonably ripe.

The varieties that are best for culinary purposes tend to make the best dry white wines, provided the fruit is not too unripe. I find *Careless* and *Keepsake* varieties excellent for this purpose. If these varieties are allowed to get really ripe, then they are also fine for dessert wines, although I prefer *Leveller* if it is available. *Whinham's Industry* is a lovely dessert gooseberry with red fruits, and moderate amounts can be used in white dessert wines, since the red colour tends to go to an acceptable golden-orange as the wine ages.

A point of some importance is that the berries must be sound. Avoid using berries that have split open because they are likely to be full of bacteria that are unwelcome in the must. Some varieties of gooseberry are prone to mildew, which in extreme conditions forms a firmly attached "skin" on the berries. If the berries are only slightly affected then the worst ones can be rejected and with patience the unwanted patches on the berries can be scraped off at the washing stage. We shall consider the best way of processing the fruit in the next chapter.

**Grape.** I often say that if I could stroll through the fields and pick ripe Riesling grapes then that would probably be the only ingredient I would use for making most of my white table wines. Unfortunately nature is not considerate enough to provide me with such luxuries. Accordingly we have the choice between using imported grapes, homegrown grapes, grape juice, grape concentrate and dried grapes (i.e. sultanas etc.).

Each Autumn, wine grapes are imported from Italy and Spain, and can be purchased at the International Market near Heathrow airport. Winemakers in other parts of the UK are served by enterprising importers who organise an annual "grape run". These imported wine grapes make reasonable wines, but they are fairly expensive. Alternatively the local market may sell trays of grapes quite cheaply at the end of the day, but it must be appreciated that these grapes are usually of varieties intended for eating rather than winemaking. Such grapes are very useful as part of the recipe, and should be used together with apples and gooseberries to give of their best. *Thompson Seedless* grapes are especially valuable in this respect.

Gardening enthusiasts may wish to grow their own grapes and should obtain plants from vineyards rather than garden centres if they want to get the most suitable varieties. The commonly grown *Brant* grape gives black, rather acidic berries that are full of seeds. I no longer bother to net mine, but let the birds have a feast. The point is that berries from this grape give only mediocre wines. Grapes grown in greenhouses, such as the *Black Hamburg*, are best eaten. On their own they make only a somewhat insipid wine, but when added to other fruits are a valuable asset.

Grape concentrate is a useful standby, especially red grape concentrate. But be cautious. Concentrates are often diluted with glucose syrup or some form of sugar. There is no point in buying such mixtures at grape concentrate prices, and it should be appreciated that glucose syrup contains some unfermentable sugars, so that the wines they produce will have some residual sweetness. Another point is that the origin of the concentrate should be established from the label. If the label does not tell you about the country of origin then be warned that it may not be from one of the better sources.

If I want a prepared white grape juice I prefer to use cartons or bottles of juice rather than buy concentrate. If the juice you buy has not been made from concentrate (read the label) then it is likely to have a rather better colour and aroma. Whether you are using concentrate or juice, do not buy really old stock; use up your supply in the year you bought it.

**Greengage** (and "green" plums). These are not my favourite fruits for winemaking since they can give rise to wines with hazes that are almost impossible to clear, and they take a long time to become drinkable. As with all "plums", do not use fruit that oozes with gum. This plum gum is one of the possible causes of haze.

**Peach.** Really ripe fresh peaches can make a really splendid wine, particularly one that is on the sweet side. I use such fruit in my heavier white dessert wines. But do make sure that the fruit is ripe. We shall look at how best to process peaches in the next chapter, but I should mention now that if the fruit is properly ripe then the skins will peel off very easily indeed if the fruit is first plunged into boiling water.

Since peaches are obviously seasonal, and are available at bargain prices for only a very short period, there is some merit in using canned peaches for round the year winemaking. The flavour is good and processing required minimal.

**Pear.** Pears are valuable fruits for winemaking if used together with several other fruits. They are rich in sugar and low in acid. This means that fair quantities can be incorporated into the must without raising the acid level too much. Personally I prefer to use pears rather than bananas to give my wine "body", but I am choosy about which variety I use. I do not recommend using *Williams* since they contribute a marked "pear drop" aroma. Most other varieties are acceptable. I suggest extracting the juice for white wines but using the chopped up fruit for red wines; pears add no red colour of course, but in addition to the body they provide tannin from the skins and a measure of fruitiness.

**Pineapple.** Fresh pineapples are not very easy to handle, since it is necessary to cut off all the outside skin before processing the pulp and juice, but they are well worth the trouble if they are on special offer. But remember that pineapple flavour is very obvious, and will take over the wine if used in substantial amounts. Make sure that the pineapples are not past their best!

It is rather more practical for us to use either the canned pineapple, or easier still to use the juice. Generally speaking the juice is likely to have been prepared from concentrate, but it still retains a good aroma and flavour. For all practical purposes in calculating the amounts of acid and sugar present, treat pineapple juice as apple juice. Because of the flavour intensity of the juice I recommend limiting the amount used to half a litre for 4.5 litres of must. If you decide to try out the canned fruit I suggest that you buy the pulp rather than chunks or rings. It is cheaper and has a good flavour.

**Quince.** Here we are talking about the true quince, *Cydonia oblonga*, rather than the Japonica quince, a distant relative belonging to the *Chaemomeles* family. The true quince hails from Mesopotamia, and it has been said to be the original "apple" that tempted Adam in the Garden of Eden; it was also the favourite fruit of Aphrodite, the Goddess of Love. With that sort of reputation it is hardly surprising to find that the fruit has a very distinctive aroma and taste. It has a lot of pectin, but the acidity, at around 1%, is only slightly higher than that found in the apple. Because of the intensity of aroma, only 200 grams or so of the fruit is needed for 4.5 litres of must.

The Japonica quince is much less valuable. The aroma is quite pleasant, especially if the fruit is allowed to ripen fully, and kept in store for a few weeks. But the acid level is very high, being around 5% By all means add the odd piece of fruit to your must if you wish, but do not use too much.

**Rhubarb.** I have included this as a fruit, even though technically it is a vegetable. The sticks of rhubarb must be picked quite young if we are to get the best flavour; older fruit really isn't worth bothering with. It is an easy ingredient to grow in our gardens, and I strongly recommend that you obtain a crown or two of *Champagne Early* or of the later *Victoria* variety. Only the juice should be used, after extraction from the petioles. And be warned that the leaves contain substantial amounts of the poisonous oxalic acid. There are numerous accounts of ill-informed people using the leaves as a substitute for spinach, and suffering as a consequence.

**Whitecurrant.** This is not a fruit I use a lot in my winemaking because it contains a fair amount of tannin which is not wanted in white wines. I use the fruit when making my red wines, where the tannin and the fruitiness are welcome.

## Red/black fruits

**Bilberry and blueberry.** The bilberry is not found naturally in all parts of the UK, but enthusiasts gather the berries from moorlands in both the West Country and in the north. It is a back-aching job but rewarding since the berries make a splendid wine. Travellers passing through the Vosges region, en route to Alsace, should tarry a while in the mountains and pick a few pounds of berries from the bountiful crops. Alternatively, a visit to one of the local markets there may be repaid with supplies of ready-picked berries.

Gardeners may prefer to grow one of the blueberry varieties that crop well. These berries make a good wine, but in the early stages of post fermentation the wine still has an alarming purple-blue colour. This drops out as the wine matures. A tip for the non-gardening types is to visit the local freezer shop, since there is often a good supply of frozen blueberries imported from New Zealand. Failing that, health stores and the like may stock imported bottled blueberries from Poland.

Once upon a time, dried bilberries were readily available in home-brew shops, and at a reasonable price, but now they are very difficult to come by and outrageously expensive when you can find them.

**Blackberry.** This is one of the two or three principal fruits used by home winemakers for making red wines. They have a lovely flavour and a good level of nutrients. In fact a simple recipe based on just three pounds of berries to the gallon, plus two pounds of sugar and the necessary water, will produce a simple, pleasant, fruity wine without fail. There are several excellent cultivated varieties, such as the *Himalayan Giant*, which is extremely vigorous and gives good yields of rather acid fruit. *Oregon Thornless* is one for folk like me who try to avoid the really thorny bushes.

Most of the time we pick the free fruit of the hedgerows and woodlands, of course, and we have to take what varieties nature has provided. There are all types of fruit, ranging from huge juicy berries with a gorgeous flavour, to smaller, harder berries with fairly high levels of acidity. I try to avoid the latter. A general guideline is to pick the fruit on a fine day when there has been little opportunity for the growth of a lot of mould. I am wary of bushes growing around fields just in case the farmer has been spraying his fields in recent days, and I never pick berries that grow on really busy highways. Such berries will be likely to have suffered exposure to the exhaust fumes of passing cars. Even if the fumes were all from unleaded petrol, the taste would be very unpleasant.

Blackberries can be used to make virtually all types of wine, but I recommend using them together with other fruits such as elderberries, since this introduces a measure of welcome complexity. Moreover, blackberries on their own often give a wine which develops an orange tinge as it ages. Bearing in mind that all the fruits required for the must may not ripen at the same time, I should remind winemakers that blackberries freeze very well, and do not deteriorate significantly when stored in the freezer for six months or so. But more about freezing in the next chapter.

**Blackcurrant.** This fruit is particularly useful for adding a commercial note to dry red table wines. However, we must not overdo a good thing, because a few blackcurrants will add quite enough flavour. It must be remembered, too, that blackcurrants are very acidic, so that too generous an allocation to the must will result in the wine having a sharp (acid) taste. As with blackberries, blackcurrants freeze well. As gardeners will know, the *Boskoop Giant* variety crops well and gives large sweet berries. These days, the many pick-your-own establishments grow blackcurrants for those of us who merely want the fruit and do not enjoy the trials and tribulations of growing it.

There are several blackcurrant syrups available, which can be used as part of the must; one well-known variety is Ribena. This is not just blackcurrant concentrate, though, but contains a lot of added sugar. And a point to watch is that some of the syrups may have added stabilisers, which will hinder the yeasts and can cause the fermentations to stick before all of the sugar has been metabolised. My advice is to check the labels of such syrups, and of all processed juices and fruits for this matter, to make sure that there are no stabilisers present. A little sulphur dioxide (as sodium metabisulphite or a similar salt) won't matter, since the yeast will be able to cope with it. But avoid ingredients containing benzoate or sorbate, both of which will remain unchanged in the must and may inhibit the fermentation.

**Cherry**. Cherries are out for most of us because they are expensive to buy, but really ripe black cherries do add quality to a wine, especially a dessert one. They have the advantage of containing rather low levels of acid, so that a lot of fruit can be added to the must of a dessert wine to be without raising the acid too much. Personally I do not use Whiteheart cherries in my winemaking, but stick to the black ones. *Morello* cherries are excellent for cooking and preserving, but they are "sour", and for the best results should be used in moderate amounts in the must. Of course the Morello cherries are splendid for making liqueurs, especially if care is taken to reduce the acidity a little.

**Cranberry**. The cranberry (*Vaccinium Macrocarpon*) is closely related to the blueberry. While it can be grown quite easily in this country, it is not often found in fruit gardens. Most of us know it through the use of cranberry sauce as an adjunct to our Christmas turkey, and the berries can now be found in many freezer stores. I have used both the frozen berries and the juice, but I found that the wine took on a somewhat unpleasant bitter/astringent note. My advice is to leave this fruit to the turkey; there are much nicer fruits to use for our winemaking.

**Damson/black plums**. The comments I made about greengages and "green" plums also apply to other plums, of course, and to some extent to damsons. Make sure that you are getting the true damson rather than the so-called damson plums, because the latter have much less flavour. I am very fond of damsons and use them in fairly small amounts in my red table wines and red desserts. They tend to be fairly acidic, even when really ripe, so keep this fruit as a relatively minor part of the total fruit mix. I should mention that damsons can be used to make an excellent liqueur, along the lines of sloe gin (see my *Straightforward Liqueur Making* ).

**Elderberry**. This fruit is perhaps the most important one that we have for making our red wines. Like the gooseberry, the elderberry has long been used for making wines, and there are many stories of how commercial wines have been topped up with elderberry wine to improve their colour and taste; the addition also reduces the cost too. And until recently it was believed that some of the Portuguese winemakers in the north of the country regularly used elderberries in their wines. Elderberries also have a strong reputation for health giving properties, and older herbal books are full of ideas for cures that elderberries might bring about. Way back in the 17th century, a Dutch physician, Dr. Boerhaave, was so convinced of the virtues of the elder that he raised his hat every time that he passed a bush!

While most of us take reports of the medicinal merits of various plants with a certain scepticism, there is some recent scientific work that suggests that elderberries really do have therapeutic properties. The evidence from California is that a chemical called quercetin is a powerful anticancer agent; and quercetin is found in substantial amounts (in combined form) in elderberries. Since a glass of wine a day is now believed to reduce the chance of heart attacks, there is perhaps a good case to be made for drinking a glass of elderberry wine a day!

Elderberries are plentiful most years, but care should be taken in selecting the berries. I have a simple three-part check, namely look, squeeze and taste. First of all I look for the bush or tree that is well loaded with really black berries; if some of the bunches still contain green berries, or even berries just turning black, then I reckon that much of the fruit on the tree is still under-ripe and I leave it alone. If the berries look good, then I squeeze a few. What I am looking for are berries that are full of really dark red juice. If the juice is pale or distinctly orange in tint, then I reject those berries. Once I am satisfied with the look of the berries, and the colour of their juice, then I eat a few. If I don't like the flavour then the berries are rejected.

This routine may seem a little fussy, but it does mean that I get wines of high quality, and not wines that have unpleasant aftertastes. Naturally I pick the elderberries in their bunches and take them home before I strip off the berries. There are many ways of carrying out the stripping, ranging from the simple plucking of a berry at a time to using a fork or some fancy tool for speeding up the stripping. My favourite way uses an old tennis racket. I take a bunch at a time and rub the bunch gently against the strings of the racket in a sideways motion. The ripe berries go through the strings without difficulty, with just a few of the less ripe berries remaining on the stalks; these I throw away.

I must emphasise that under-ripe berries, leaves and stalks must be removed since they contain substances that may bring about stomach upsets.

Elderberries are certainly the king of the red/black fruits for me. I use them as a substantial part of all the red wines I make that I want to match up to commercial styles. Contrary to popular belief, elderberries do contain a fair amount of acid. They are also rich in mineral salts, and because of this the taste is modified and seems less acid. Technically, the explanation is that the mineral salts adjust the pH of the juice, thus making the juice seem less acid and more full-bodied.

**Loganberry, raspberry etc.** Raspberries have a powerful aroma and flavour, so relatively small amounts of the fruit have a big effect on the aroma and taste of the wine. The berries are also rather acidic. For these reasons I recommend using raspberries in much the same way as blackcurrants, and adding only 100-200 grams (4 - 8 ounces) of berries to 4.5 litres of must. This can be increased for dessert wines, of course, where stronger flavours can be tolerated. Related fruits such as loganberries and Tayberries should be treated like raspberries.

**Mulberry.** If you are lucky enough to have access to a mulberry tree, do take advantage of the fruit. It is messy to pick, though, because the strongly coloured juice gets everywhere. And make sure that the fruit is really ripe. The recommended way of "picking" the fruit is to put a clean plastic cloth under the tree and then shake the tree vigorously. I believe that the fruit is best used in a blend of other fruits, since my experience with wines using just mulberries is that it takes a fairly long time for the wine to reach its best - at least two years in the bottle was needed, I found.

**Redcurrant.** It is perhaps unfortunate that the berries do not have more colour, since the lightness of the pigmentation leads some winemakers to think of this fruit as being most suitable for making rosé wines. I do not feel that redcurrants give of their best in rosé wines. They have a flavour that seems to fit in better with a red wine mix. Bear in mind that the fruit is fairly acidic. As with blackcurrants and whitecurrants, the berries should be removed from the stalks before use, because the stalks contain rather fierce astringent tannins.

**Sloe.** After blackberries and elderberries, sloes are probably the most promising ingredients available to us for making red wines. But great care must be taken to make sure that the fruit is really ripe, because unripe sloes are very astringent and contain a lot of acid. Ideally the fruit should not be picked until the colder weather has arrived and the berries just begin to wrinkle. At all events do make sure that the berries are no longer hard. My own experiments have shown that there is no point in picking the fruit while it is still rather unripe and then leaving it to ripen in the storeshed. The taste of this early picked fruit remains unpleasant and makes the berries unsuitable for winemaking. The tannins in sloes is quite different from that in elderberries, and much more of it will drop out of the wine after it has been stored for six months or so.

**Strawberries**. I find the strawberry wine has a rather sickly taste, and I do not use strawberries very often - I eat them instead! There is one wine that can benefit by the inclusion of a few strawberries in its make-up, though, and that is a heavy sweet, golden wine in the Sauternes style. It may seem strange to use a red fruit in this way, but much of the colour fades during the fermentation stage, and after a relatively short period of maturation it is an amber tint rather than a red one that remains. I use a small amount of strawberries in this way because analysis has shown that they contain some of the same chemicals that are found in the Sauternes style of wine. Do try it, but with not more than say 150 grams of strawberries in 4.5 litres of white must.

## Other fruits that might be used

**Wild berries**. Most home winemakers experiment from time to time, and are tempted by the plentiful display of wild berries that the countryside yields. The three fruits most commonly considered are rose hips, hawthornberries and rowan berries. **Hips** of the wild dog rose are easily gathered and can be used in winemaking. I use the ripe berries in my white dessert wines, where the colour they produce fades to a golden colour as the wines age. Dried rose hips are available from most home-brew shops and I use them as part of my make-up of Sherry musts. Recently I came across some almost black rose hips in our local park, and on investigation found that they were from the "Scotch Rose" or "Burnet Rose", (*Rosa pimpinellifolia*). Experiment showed that these hips were chock full of anthocyanins (the colouring found in the skin of black grapes) and I made good use of the hips by using them as part of the ingredients for one of my red table wines.

One plentiful fruit is the **Hawthornberry**. Because they are so readily available, the berries are tempting. On the other hand they seem to have a rather bland flavour. Extracts of the berries have been used by herbalists through the ages, although the effects they may have on our body would appear to be very mild, and prolonged treatment is evidently necessary. Basically the extract seems to be a gentle heart tonic, working by enlarging the coronary arteries. Both the sugar and acid contents of the berries are small, so at first sight the berries do not appear to be promising winemaking material. However some recent experiments of mine have shown that half a kilo of berries used together with a litre of supermarket white grape juice gave a wine that had a better bouquet and mouthfeel than a wine using just the grape juice. I include the recipe later on.

Mountain Ash berries (**Rowanberries**) tempt me much less since they contain very bitter principles. It is possible that really ripe berries may be useful in making aperitif styles of wine, but so far I have been unsuccessful in producing a worthwhile wine from these berries.

**Tropical fruits.** Our markets are now offering a surprising range of imported fruit, such as Paw Paw, Ugli Fruit, Star Fruit etc., but the prices are high and this makes the fruit unattractive to winemakers. But there are now various blends of tropical fruit juices to be found in supermarkets, and I recommend trying out some of them by adding small amounts (say half a litre to 4.5 litres of must) to simple apple and grape juice musts. In particular I suggest that you try Passion Fruit juice, but do go easy with it because the flavour is pronounced.

## Vegetables

Older winemaking books contain lots of recipes for wines to be made from all kinds of vegetables, ranging from root vegetables such as parsnips to leaf vegetables such as lettuce. And, of course, they invariably include stinging nettles. There is no doubt that interesting flavours can be added to wines by incorporating small quantities of herbs etc., but these wines are rather an acquired taste, and I do not propose to include them in this book.

### Root vegetables

Table 4.6 gives information about the composition of some of the vegetables winemakers may be tempted to use.

**Table 4.6 The composition of root vegetables**

| Vegetable | Acid (% as tartaric) | Sugar (%) | Starch (%) | Pectin (%) | Protein (%) |
|---|---|---|---|---|---|
| Artichoke (Jerusalem) | - | 10-15* | 0 | - | 1.8 |
| Beetroot | 0.19 | 6-8 | - | 0.3-0.4 | 1.3 |
| Carrot | 0.06 | 5-7 | 0 | 1.8 | 1-1.5 |
| Parsnip | 0.12 | 10-13 | 2 | 3.2 | 1.5 |
| Potato (old) | 0.1 | 0.5-1 | 16-20 | 2 | 1.5 |
| Swede/turnip | - | 4-6 | 0 | - | 1 |

* Present as inulin (a polymer of fructose)

The most promising root vegetables for the winemaker are parsnips, beet and carrots. Parsnips, for instance, contain a lot of sugar once they have been exposed to the frost or kept in a very cold store. Without such a treatment, the parsnips will contain mainly starch and very little sugar, and are not really worth bothering with; the starch level will be too high and produce a hazy wine that is difficult to clear. Parsnips do give the wine a distinctive taste that is somewhat off-putting when the wine is young but after a substantial storage period (say two years), it develops into a very acceptable aroma. I have had success in blending parsnips with bananas to give a heavy sweet wine in the Sauternes mould.

Carrots contain roughly the same amount of sugar as blackberries and this makes a contribution to the must that is worth considering. Again the taste is not ideal, and the colour can be a nuisance; I am not enthusiastic about carrots, but many home winemakers make drinkable wines based on recipes with a substantial carrot content. Beetroots also contain a decent level of sugar, but the wine made from this vegetable usually has a fairly earthy taste in the early stages. The deep red colour is not the same as that produced by red and black fruits, and it fades to a golden colour when the wine has been kept for a year or so. I believe that storage is essential if the wine is to be worth drinking.

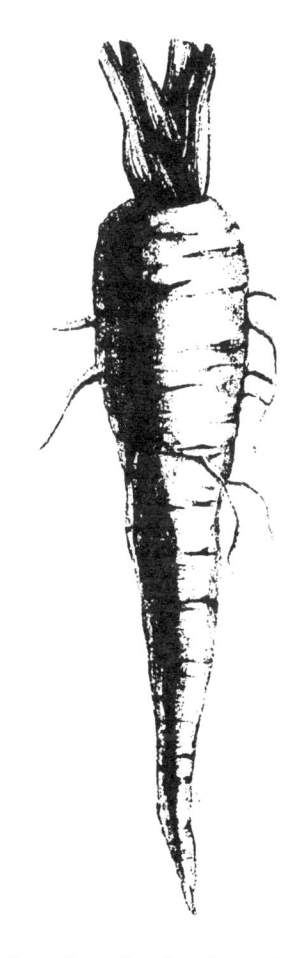

We can now turn to the other root vegetables listed in Table 4.6. The Jerusalem artichokes cannot be used beneficially, since the inulin is not fermented by the yeasts normally available to us. And now to potatoes. Almost no sugar, a lot of starch and little flavour. Frankly they just aren't worth bothering with, especially since the protein contains the amino acid leucine which is a potential source of unwanted higher alcohols. As for swedes and turnips, they do contain a small amount of sugar, but the flavour of wines made from them is earthy and I think they have too little to offer us.

One wine curiosity from the vegetable world is the infamous "marrow rum", the recipe for which calls for the marrow to be hollowed out and stuffed with brown sugar. This is then hung up in a warm place and allowed to ferment and drip into a container below. If you really believe that this can make a worthwhile wine then you must believe in fairies! There is no yeast, so you wait for nature to provide one, and there is no acid apart from the tiny amount in the remaining marrow flesh. Add to that the impossibility of any yeast fermenting out more than 25% or so of sugar, and you will see the stupidity of this recipe. Should any reader be unfortunate enough to have a book with this recipe in it I suggest that you burn it (or the author) as soon as possible, since I question whether any of the other recipes given in the book will have been logically thought out.

### "Leaf" vegetables

Leave brassica well alone unless you like sulphury wines. Bland vegetables like lettuce offer nothing but chlorophyll and cellulose, so leave them out. Some winemakers are very fond of adding parsley to their musts, since it contributes to the aroma; it is the leaves that are used, of course, rather than the roots, which are used in herbal medicine as a diuretic. I know that recipes exist for such oddities as pea pod wine, but really these are examples of products from the fertile imaginations of authors with little or no knowledge of what such ingredients contain. As I have already mentioned, there are many herbs that provide characteristic aromas and tastes, but I think it best to extract these by soaking the herbs in a fairly neutral wine rather than adding the herbs to the fermenting must. One reason for my caution is that the soaking will simply extract the substances that are in the herbs, whereas it is possible that the fermentation process will change these substances into other substances that could have unwanted side effects. It is better to be safe than sorry!

## Cereals

Table 4.7 lists the contents of the commoner cereals. It can be seen that none of the cereals contain significant amounts of sugar, although they abound with other carbohydrates (principally starch). The protein content is of the order of 10% in most cases, and it is this protein that may be the source of the higher alcohols that give cereal wines their reputation for strength. In fact the legendary hangover produced by wheat and raisin wines can be attributed to the fusel oil content of the wine. If you think about it, what does, say, polished rice have to offer the winemaker. It has virtually no flavour, an enormous amount of starch and a fair amount of protein. Now the usual wine yeasts will not ferment starch. For this purpose you need *Saccharomyces diastaticus* yeast and this is not available in dried form.

If you must try out cereals then make sure that you limit the likelihood of the formation of substantial quantities of higher alcohols being formed in your wine by adding plenty of yeast nutrient. Then the yeast will not need to extract the nitrogen from the protein and higher alcohols will not be formed from that source.

Be warned, though. You may get a cloudy wine at the same time as you get the extra "body".

**Table 4.7  Composition of cereals**

| Cereal | Sugar (%) | Other carbohydrates (%) | Protein (%) |
|---|---|---|---|
| Barley | 2.5-3 | 60-65 | 10-12 |
| Corn | 2-2.5 | 60 | 8.5 |
| Oats | 1-2 | 55-60 | 10-12 |
| Rice (polished) | 0 | 80 | 6-7 |
| Wheat | 2-3 | 65-70 | 10-13 |

# Flowers

The first point that must be emphasised is that flowers add smell but little else, apart from colour. Accordingly flowers are best regarded as additives to musts to provide aroma that would otherwise be lacking. All flowers should be picked well before they are past their best, and used the same day. Once flowers have been picked they deteriorate fairly quickly, and in cases such as elderflower introduce unpleasant "catty" notes. If the flowers are wild ones, make sure that the fields have not recently been sprayed with herbicide etc. And it goes without saying that many wild flowers are protected so that primroses and cowslips and the like cannot be used for winemaking.

As far as I know, no-one will object to you taking dandelions if you feel they are worth bothering with. I make this remark because dandelion wine is a traditional one. Ideally you should pick the flowers in the morning on St. Georges day, provided the sun is shining. Then all traces of the green sepals must be removed together with any remnants of stem. Only the yellow flowers should be used. The flowers have very little smell, but they contribute colour and flavour of a sort. Be warned though, the politer West Country name of "Wet-a-bed" for the dandelion indicates the reputation the flowers have as diuretics. People with weak bladders might give this ingredient a miss!

Several garden flowers are worth using, including roses and mock orange (philadelphus). Any garden flower with a delicate scent is worth trying, but go easy with it. Honeysuckle for instance is sometimes considered a suspect plant with harmful properties; it is the berry that should be avoided, though, and flowers used in small amounts will add smell to your must but nothing harmful. Roses are one of the most popular choices of winemakers, but care must be taken to ensure that the flowers have not recently been sprayed to kill aphids etc.

With all the flowers, I recommend shaking the petals in a flour sieve, this often lets the many tiny insects present drop through. This is especially so for elderflowers, and with these there is the added bonus that many pollen grains will drop through as well; such grains can be a source of hazes if not removed.

In the next chapter I will comment on the various ways which we can use to extract the desirable aroma from the flowers.

## Other ingredients

Under the heading of leaf vegetables I have already commented on the questionable value of "leaves", but I know that there are winemakers who swear by oak leaves etc. I will just have to beg to differ. Vine leaves are a different story, of course, since they do contain substances that will add flavour to a wine; but use such leaves together with a decent fruit base to get the best effect. Another type of potential ingredient is tree sap, normally taken from silver birch trees in the spring. Frankly I doubt whether the hassle of tapping the tree and collecting the sap is justified. The sap will contain some sugar and perhaps a little flavour, but it will lack acidity. If you want to experiment with such materials do adjust the must with extra acid, nutrients and sugar; and don't forget to plug the hole you made in the tree!

## Honey

Mead, which is made from honey, has a long and distinguished history in Britain, such that the various medieval banquets laid on in some ancestral homes (and hotels) make much of providing a sample of a sweet version. But if that is your first introduction to mead, don't despair. You can make vastly better meads than that. I have to say, though, that honey does give the mead a flavour that doesn't appeal to everyone.

The first safeguard is to select your honey so that it does not have an aroma you don't like. Thus some Australian honeys have more than their fair share of eucalyptus. If you can go for one of the more floral honeys. Both Argentinian and Canadian honeys are good for mead making, clover being the main sources of the nectar collected by the bees. I like the Mexican honeys, too. If you have access to British honey, then by all means take advantage of this, but make sure that it hasn't picked up undesirable aromas. We will look at how honey should be treated for mead making in the next chapter.

# Plants unsuitable for winemaking

Not all of nature's fruits and flowers are safe to use, unfortunately, so care must be taken. Generally speaking any poisons are likely to be concentrated in the seeds, roots or leaves with comparatively little in the flowers. The simple rule is not to use any plant unless you are sure that it is safe. In particular avoid the temptation to pick wild berries when you are not sure what the plant is. Just a few berries of plants such as the deadly nightshade and cherry laurel will "see you off" quite quickly, but there are many others that will make you unwell and cause you sleepless nights attending nature's call! A detailed discussion of poisonous plants would be out of place in this book, but some of the common ones that should be avoided are the berries of bryony, buckthorn, cherry laurel, cotoneaster, cuckoo pint, holly, nightshades, privet and yew; the kernels of stone fruit such as apricots and peaches; all bulbs; horsechestnut "conkers"; lily-of-the-valley flowers.

# Chapter 5
# Processing Ingredients

## Introduction

As we have seen already, there are two basic winemaking methods, namely fermenting the juice and fermenting "on the pulp". For quality white table wines there is much to be said for extracting juice from the ingredients as far as is possible, diluting it appropriately, adding when necessary extras such as acid, nutrients and sugar, and then starting the ferment. We will look at the various ways of extracting fruit from both hard and soft fruits, and consider how best to extract the juice from fruit such as gooseberries which at first sight may seem rather an unpromising source.

With red wines, pulp fermentation is nearly always required because the colouring substances (anthocyanins) are mainly in the skins; and fermentation on the pulp also extracts the tannins (phenolics) that we want. The exception is when the wine is based entirely on red grape concentrate plus other fruit juices. Pulp fermentation may also be worth considering when we want to make a heavy white dessert style of wine.

But the fruit etc. must be properly prepared whether it is to be used as pulp or persuaded to give up its juice. We will review the process in the next section.

Before we discuss this preparation, though, it is worth mentioning the possibility of letting fruit ripen in store. This particularly applies to hard fruit such as apples. Picked apples may improve if they are kept in a cool place for several weeks. The fruit should be spread out in a single layer and looked over every few days. If any apple starts to rot then it should be removed straight away before it affects other apples. Although the storage results in some loss of acid and an increase in sweetness, it will gradually lose its crispness as the pectin present changes its character. Unfortunately this means that the fruit is not quite so easy to juice by any pressure method since the fruit pulp tends to develop a somewhat slimy feel.

Another storage method that can be applied to virtually all fruit is that of freezing. After the fruit has been cleaned and prepared (next section), it is placed in sealed plastic bags or more rigid containers and put into the freezer until it is needed. I can offer one useful hint here. When fruit is frozen, the water in it turns into ice crystals, and these ice crystals will help to break down the texture of the fruit if they grow large. Now we will want fruit that is intended for fruit salads and the like to retain the original texture as far as possible, and this means making sure that the ice crystals are small. So for fruit subsequently intended for eating the freezing process should be carried out as rapidly as possible, which means putting the freezer on "fast freeze" and having the fruit in a single layer. By contrast, fruit destined for wine making should be frozen much more slowly so that the ice crystals grow larger and break up the texture. This means that the freezer is not put on fast freeze, and that the fruit is packed in more bulky lots.

# Preliminary preparation.

In Chapter 4 we discussed the varieties of the various fruits that seemed to be the best for wine making, and I will limit my remarks here to a reminder that fruit for winemaking should always be ripe, and never under-ripe. Only in the case of bananas should somewhat over-ripe fruit be used. Badly bruised fruit should be rejected, or at least have the bruised sections removed.

Fruit that has split open should be avoided since it may be a rich source of bacteria. This is especially so in the case of gooseberries, which can become infected with lactic acid bacteria when the over-ripe berries split.

**Cleaning.** The first stage of the preparation is the removal of all unwanted fragments of vegetation, such as leaves and twigs. "Strangers" such as earwigs and various grubs should be removed; this may be easiest at the washing stage.

Apples and pears and other hard fruit can be thoroughly washed with cold water to wash away the grime that is always likely to be present, especially in suburban areas. While cold water is the norm, it is worth using fairly hot water with fruit such as greengages and plums, since the fruit often has a waxy surface that can cause difficult hazes in the wine. One winemaker of my acquaintance goes to a lot of trouble to remove any plum wax and adds a little gentle detergent (e.g. Fairy Liquid) to his wash liquid. This may seem rather a drastic solution but it works well and all the detergent is easily removed with subsequent washing with cold water. I have used this approach and I can assure readers that it does not leave a detergent taste provided that the fruit is not damaged and that the final wash is a thorough one. A further point is that any plums oozing gum should be rejected because this plum gum will produce a pectin-like haze in the wine.

Greater care has to be taken with soft fruit, because drastic washing will remove a lot of juice. My approach is to put my de-twigged soft fruit into a bucket and cover it with cold water. Then I gently stir the mix with my hand, which encourages all the little bits of leaf etc. to float to the top. Unripe berries of fruit such as elderberries will also float and can be skimmed off. It is at this stage that blackberries infested with grubs will give up their tenants; if I find more than the odd grub I reject the batch of fruit since I prefer not to have the extra "body".

Dried fruit usually has a surface treatment of sulphite to reduce the chance of the fruit fermenting during storage, and a mineral or vegetable oil coating to keep it soft. Both sulphite and oil can be removed from the fruit by giving it a quick wash with cold water. It is surprising what floats to the top of the wash liquid even with dried fruit that is said to have been spin washed!

Cut off any leaves from root vegetables such as carrots and parsnips and wash the roots thoroughly and scrub them to remove every trace of earth. Wash grain with cold water to remove any contamination that may have taken place during storage. Flowers cannot be treated very much without losing their aroma, so it is really a matter of careful inspection to pull out defective blossoms, plus shaking in a sieve to remove some of the pollen grains.

**Peeling and skinning.** If apples are to be used in pulp fermentation then peel them, but there is no need to remove the peel if the fruit is going to be juiced or stored in the freezer as a temporary measure before the juice is pressed out. Although we usually think of apples and pears and the like as constituents of musts for white wines, they can be valuable as a part of the make-up of musts for red wines that are of the fruity (Beaujolais) style. In such circumstances do not peel the fruit for the pulp fermentation, but simply chop it up. The small amount of tannin in the skins of the fruit will help to give the red wine its "bite". If you are intending to make a white wine and ferment on the pulp, though, you may sometimes wish to store the sliced, peeled fruit in the freezer as a temporary measure. In this case do remember that apple slices or pulp turn brown very quickly, and treat your fruit slices with a little sulphite before freezing them.

The skins of fresh peaches should always be removed if you want to get the more delicate flavour coming through. Provided that the fruit is ripe then the skins can be removed very easily by plunging the peaches into near boiling water. If the skins cannot be peeled off without difficulty after this immersion then the fruit is not really ripe and it is best used for making pies etc. I also recommend removing the stones from the peaches. If the stones are left in the fermenting must the wine often develops quite a strong "stone" flavour which is a pity. I try to remove the stones from other fruit if I can, but while this is possible with ripe plums it is at best extremely tedious and at worst almost impossible with fruit such as bullaces and sloes. Then I content myself with slitting the fruit with a sharp knife to help flavour extraction, and limit the period of fermentation on the solid fruit to a maximum of four days.

While we are on the subject of stones I do urge readers not to crack these stones and so expose the kernels to the fermenting liquor. The kernels contain a substance called amygdalin, which is a source of hydrogen cyanide; this cyanide may be changed by the fermentation into other undesirable substances. The amounts of such substances that are likely to be left in the wine will be small, but common sense tells us to make sure that we reduce such contamination to a minimum by not having exposed fruit kernels in our fermenting musts.

Peaches, like apples, turn brown very easily, so treat the peeled peaches or peach pulp with a little sulphite to prevent this happening.

By contrast, rhubarb does not go brown when cut up. This is because it lacks the enzyme that brings about the browning. The sticks of rhubarb (the petioles) should have their ends cut off, especially the end that is attached to the broad leaf, to eliminate the possibility of adding poisonous oxalic acid to our must.

## Processing methods.

### Crushing

The fruit can be reduced to pulp or slices etc. by a variety of methods, depending upon the scale of the operation and the facilities available. If the amounts are quite small then soft fruit such as blackberries, elderberries and grapes can be easily squashed with a potato masher. I put about half a pound of the fruit into a flat-bottomed plastic bowl and crush it gently with the masher. This splits open the berries and releases the juice but does not damage the seeds and pips, and so avoids releasing the very bitter tannins. I then repeat the mashing process as many times as is necessary, putting the crushed berries into the fermentation vessel after each crush. When I want to use only the juice from the fruit, then I press the crush by one of the methods we shall discuss shortly.

Another small scale method is the use of one of the small choppers. These consist of a set of blades that are forced down on to the fruit by putting pressure on the attached handle. These choppers are convenient for dealing with small amounts of dried fruit and for macerating herbs.

It is possible to use some of today's kitchen power tools to cut out some of the hard work. Most soft fruit can be pureed in a blender, and the puree added to the fermentation vessel. Care has to be taken not break open the seeds, though, and it should be appreciated that while the pureed fruit readily releases its flavour it leaves a considerable volume of "sludge" at the bottom of the fermentation vessel. This means that racking after the first stage of the fermentation is either rather wasteful (as it leaves behind a lot of liquid in the sludge) or by no means complete. In practice I use the blender approach only when I want to extract the maximum amount of flavour, as with dessert wines. Otherwise I prefer the gentler approach.

The kitchen food processor can be very useful for slicing up hard fruit, but remember my cautionary words about damaging the pips and releasing their bitter principles. When I use a food processor I avoid this by first cutting open the fruit and removing the pips as much as possible.

Another kitchen appliance of some value to us is the old fashioned mincer. Used with care this will reduce seedless dried fruit to small particles and ensure an adequate release of flavour during the fermentation. But put the mincer on coarse cut to avoid reducing the fruit to a puree. Finally, do make sure that the mincer has not been used recently for onions!

Winemakers who are also Do-it-Yourself enthusiasts will almost certainly own a power drill, and this can be used to reduce apples and pears to a pulp. The drill needs a suitable attachment, namely a long rod plus a set of propeller-like blades at the end. The fruit is placed in a bucket with a lid that has a hole in it. The rod is pushed through the hole in the lid and attached to the power drill. Within a few seconds of the drill being switched on some 8-10 pounds of apples can be reduced to a pulp. You can omit the lid, of course, but this may result in some fruit pulp escaping and possibly hitting you!

For the dedicated winemaker who works on a larger scale I strongly recommend buying a grape crusher to break down the fruit. The standard grape crusher contains two metal or wooden rollers which are turned by means of a handle. The gap between the rollers can be adjusted to suit the degree of crushing that is required. Now such a crusher works well with grapes, of course, although the stems have to be removed from the crush, but it is much less satisfactory with hard fruit such as apples. I bought a grape crusher especially to deal with the several hundredweight of apples that I process each autumn, but I soon found that in order for it to work the fruit had first to be cut into quite small pieces that would go through the rollers without difficulty. It was quite impossible to use the crusher with whole apples or even apples cut in half. Accordingly I swopped my crusher for one fitted with a a set of cutters that chopped up the apples before they reached the rollers. Figure 5.1 shows the crusher that I use. In practice I put the washed apples in the hopper, sprinkle the fruit with a little sulphite to prevent undue browning and then crush the fruit with the rollers first set fairly wide apart. I then carry out a second crush with the rollers close together. The crush is then placed in the grape press for the extraction of the juice.

I have one on the larger models of crusher, but smaller ones are available, and they can be supplied complete with the press which nestles neatly below the crusher. Such luxuries are expensive, unfortunately, and there is much to be said for the equipment to be bought by a wine circle or a group of winemakers, so that the cost is shared. In some areas the local homebrew shop may have a crusher that can be hired.

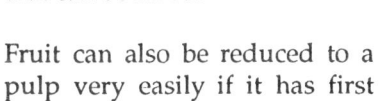

**Figure 5.1**

Fruit can also be reduced to a pulp very easily if it has first been frozen. A typical case is that of gooseberries. My approach is to take about four pounds of fruit from the freezer, put it into a plastic or Pyrex glass vessel and pour over it about three pints of boiling water. This results in the mixture coming to room temperature. I then put my hand into the suspension and crush each gooseberry. I can assure readers that the berries crush very easily indeed under these circumstances. Next I add a good pectolytic enzyme; for me this is one of the powerful Gervin tablets. I cover the vessel and leave the mixture for three to four hours to let the pectolytic enzyme do its job. The fruit is then well broken down and the fruit/water mixture is ready for pressing.

**Pressing the pulp.** This can be carried out in several ways. The simplest and least expensive method is to use a simple nylon straining bag (sterilised first of course), fill it two-thirds full with the gooseberry mixture and force through the gooseberry extract solution by means of simple hand pressure. The process is repeated with successive quantities of the gooseberry mix as many times as may be necessary.

While simple hand pressure is reasonably effective, the use of one of the less expensive commercial presses gives a more thorough separation of the gooseberry extract, and is less messy. I use a Walker-Desmond press which consists of a plastic coated metal cylinder which is placed inside a plastic tube. The straining bag is placed inside the metal cylinder and filled with the gooseberry mix. Initially the solution runs through the bag and out through the exit hole into the waiting container without the need for more than a gentle squeeze of the bag with the hand. But once the free-flow "juice" has run out of the press then the bag is folded over, a heavy metal pad placed on top and pressure applied by means of a metal screw arrangement. Figure 5.2 shows the press. Once again it must be emphasised that all parts of the press must be thoroughly washed and sterilised before use.

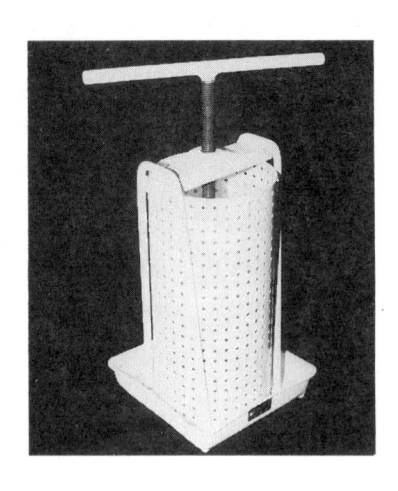

Figure 5.2

Irrespective of whether the separation is done by hand or with the press, the original four pounds of gooseberries will have been reduced to just a handful of pulp. I know that some economically minded winemakers will think about using this pulp in a second batch of lesser wine. Frankly I don't think there is enough goodness or flavour left in the pulp to bother with it. I throw it on to the compost heap!

Other fruit can be pressed by hand or with the press if it is first frozen and then allowed to thaw. Rhubarb is especially suitable for this treatment. In this case I simply put the bag of frozen rhubarb into a plastic bucket and wait for it to thaw. This takes up to 36 hours, but rhubarb does not contain the enzyme responsible for fruit browning so the thawing fruit will not develop unwanted colour. With rhubarb I do not add pectolytic enzyme since the juice comes out easily and I prefer not to make the "fruit" disintegrate completely.

I do add pectolytic enzyme to other fruits taken from the freezer once they have thawed; usually I find that the addition of boiling water is a sensible way of speeding up this thawing process. The only exception is with fruit such as apples and pears where I do not want the fruit juice to be diluted too much. But bear in mind that most fruit will turn brown as it thaws, so add a little sulphite to the mixture. Thus with apples I put a little sulphite solution into the original polythene bag with the whole, unpeeled apples. When the apples are taken from the freezer there will have been some darkening of the outside skins, but the inside of the apples will not have been affected, and the sulphite protects it during the pressing.

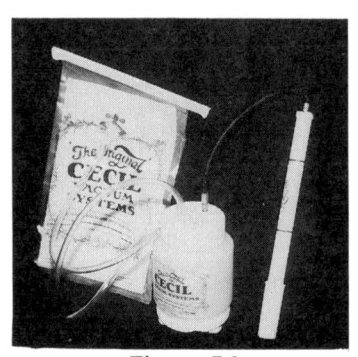

Figure 5.3

Another comparatively cheap piece of equipment that can be used to extract the juice from soft fruit, or fruit from the freezer, is the Cecil press. This is an extremely ingenious device which enables us to suck out the air in the system with a bicycle pump; the juice is then pulled over into the waiting container. Figure 5.3 gives a diagram of the system. It works quite well on suitable fruit but of course it only deals with a couple of pounds of fruit at a time. The juice that comes over has not been filtered in any way so it may be fairly cloudy. It should be treated with pectolytic enzyme.

For winemakers working on a much larger scale there is much to be said for using a grape press to extract the juice. I use this on the apples and pears that I have crushed in the modified grape crusher I discussed earlier. It is important to put a little sulphite solution into the bucket used for collecting the juice as it comes from the press to prevent it turning brown.

**The centrifuge type of extractor.** Juice can be extracted easily and in high yield from hard fruit such as apples, pears and quinces, by using either a special machine designed for the purpose or an attachment to the kitchen food mixer. Some years ago there were Swiss-made extractors, sold under the trade name of Nature's Bounty, but they were fairly expensive and appear to have disappeared from the market. They worked on the centrifuge principle. The apples were cut into pieces which were fed into the machine where they met a rapidly spinning plate with raised notches. The fruit was torn to threads and the pulp flung against the perforated cone that rotated with the plate. The juice passed through the holes in the cone and ran out into the waiting container; the pulp residue, now minus most of the juice, was carried out through a much larger exit into the waiting bowl, ready for disposal on the compost heap.

**Figure 5.4**

Smaller versions of this type of machine are available at the time this book is being written, although usually the "dry" waste pulp is not thrown out but collected on a nylon filter strip placed around the inside of the rotating drum. The problem here is that this pulp has to be removed at frequent intervals, such that the machine must be stopped after the treatment of just a couple of pounds of apples.

My current preference for this type of equipment is the attachment that fits on to the Kenwood Food Mixer. It works exactly like the Swiss machine but is much cheaper. If the fruit is a little sticky, as for instance if the apples have been kept in store for a while and gone rather soft, then the juice separation is not quite so efficient and the spent pulp is not ejected quite so well. This means that the machine has to be stopped at intervals and accumulated pulp removed. Even so this year I used this equipment (see Figure 5.4) to extract some 40 litres of apple juice in about three hours. It has made a splendid wine!

Although this centrifuge type of extractor works well with hard fruit it cannot be used with soft fruit.

**The steamer method.** Another method of extracting juice from fruit is by means of a steamer. Figure 5.5 shows this equipment in diagrammatic form. The fruit is placed inside a colander-like vessel (A), which is enclosed in a second vessel (B). B has a dome-shaped bottom with a hole in it and rests on a shallow boiler (C). When the water in the boiler is heated strongly, the steam generated rises through the perforations in A and penetrates the fruit, thus breaking it down and releasing the juice. This juice together with some condensed steam, falls to the bottom of the outer vessel (B), and at intervals can be run off through the tube (D) by releasing the spring clip.

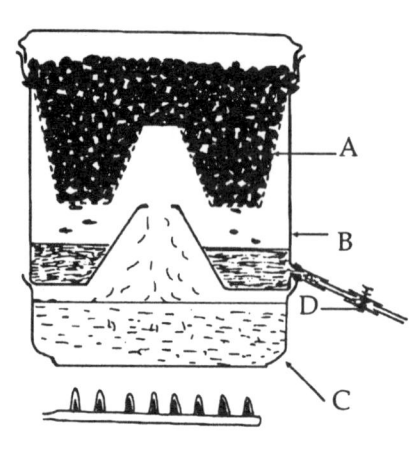

Figure 5.5

There are several points to note here. First of all the steamer can be made of either aluminium or stainless steel. I strongly recommend paying the extra and buying the stainless steel model, since the acid juice will attack the aluminium vessel and pit it in due course. The aluminium that dissolves goes into the juice, of course, and hence into the wine. Although much of this aluminium is likely to precipitate out with the lees I think it best to take no chances. In the first place aluminium can react with the colouring material (anthocyanins) and tannins in red and black fruits to produce blue colours and sometimes hazes. Secondly there may be a possible connection between aluminium and Alzheimer's disease. My memory is going quickly enough without helping it on its way!

The next point is that the extraction only works well if the heat source is a powerful one. I have found that putting the boiler vessel on an ordinary gas or electric stove is not good enough. The extraction then seems to take for ever and the quality of the juice suffers. I use a large gas ring attached to a Calor gas supply, and this means that I can extract the juice from six to eight pounds of fruit in 30-40 minutes. I should point out that the juice is diluted with some condensed steam, and is about 80% strength. It is said to be sterile as it comes from the steamer so there is no need to add sulphite if it is to be used the same day. But I would not recommend keeping the extract for long periods before putting it in the must.

Last, but by no means least, I have to comment on the suitability of the various fruits for the steamer treatment. I do not recommend it for "white" fruit such as apples, peaches etc. I found that the extract from such fruits had a gentle but distinctive cooked taste. Red and black fruits on the other hand responded well to the steamer method, and I could not detect any cooked note in the flavour or any browning of the colour. Table 5.1 shows the sort of results I obtained with four of the commoner fruits.

**Table 5.1 Juice extract using the Säftborn steamer.**

| Fruit type | Amount (kilos) | Time of steaming (mins) | Amount of juice (litres) |
|---|---|---|---|
| Blackberries | 2.0 | 40 | 1.6 |
| Blackcurrants | 2.4 | 40 | 1.5 |
| Elderberries | 2.25 | 40 | 2.0 |
| Redcurrants | 1.35 | 30 | 1.25 |

I also had success with fruit such as bullaces and sloes. I found that wines made just from such steamer extracts were rather "softer" in flavour, and I decided that the extracts were most suitable for use as part of the must make-up for dessert or social styles of wine.

**Boiling ingredients.** This is the old-fashioned method for the extraction of all kinds of ingredients. Some books still recommend boiling but it must be appreciated that if the boiling is lengthy then the flavour will be impaired, and many of the nutrients and vitamins destroyed. One good result of boiling, though, is that it kills any wild yeast or unwanted bacteria. But do remember my comments on aluminium steamers and avoid using the large aluminium preserving pans that are still around.

Boiling is probably the best way of extracting the goodness from root vegetables such as parsnips, but if used with fruit the extract should be for a short period only, and with simmering rather than vigorous boiling.

**Adding pectolytic enzyme.** During the discussion of juice extraction I have suggested adding pectolytic enzyme to the pulp of fruits such as apples and peaches before the pulp is pressed. This helps to break down the fruit and assists with the release of juice. It also destroys any residual pectin and prevents haze formation at a later stage. Accordingly I recommend adding the enzyme to all fruit extracts once the pressing has taken place, unless it has already been added. I must also emphasise that vegetables such as carrots and parsnips are very rich in pectin and pectolytic enzyme must be added if hazes are to be prevented.

The Gervin pectolytic enzyme is a very powerful one and it is produced in tablet form (rather like an Alka-Seltzer tablet), which fizzes as it dissolves and disperses the enzyme throughout the must. Because the enzyme is embedded in the tablet it is largely protected from the environment and has a long shelf life; I find that the tablets retain most of their strength for several years if they are stored in a cool dry place. The pectolytic enzyme commonly sold in the form of a white powder is much weaker and has a shorter shelf life, so it should be purchased from a home brew shop that has a good turn over.

Another enzyme that is on the market is sold under the name of Rohament P. This is excellent for breaking down the fruit and releasing the juice, and it is especially valuable for treating fruit intended for dessert wines, where maximum body is wanted. But this enzyme does not destroy pectin, so the normal pectolytic enzyme should be added to the juice or must in addition.

**Obtaining aroma from flowers.** There are several ways that flowers can be used to add aroma to a wine. If the flowers are available at the time the wine is being made, then the petals can be added to the must, but usually the flowers are ready in the spring or early summer, and this is not when ripe fruits become available. Accordingly I suggest that one of the following methods is used to extract the beautiful aroma from the flowers and keep it until it is needed:

> Extraction of the flowers with wine to give a "concentrate";
>
> Extraction of the flowers with water and freezing the extract in cubes;
>
> Making a wine with say grape or apple juice (supermarket) with a lot of flowers in the must;
>
> Extraction of the flowers with Vodka;
>
> Freezing or drying flowers.

**Extraction with wine.** The aroma of the flowers is extracted best with a sweet wine. I use an apple and grape wine with about a double handful of florets to a litre of wine. I leave the flowers to soak overnight and then strain to remove the florets. The wine is then treated with the usual level of sulphite to prevent possible refermentation, and bottled in 100 ml amounts. If I feel that my white wines would benefit from the extra floral note, then I add one such bottle of "essence" to five gallons of wine just after the fermentation is complete. Readers should experiment with the quantities to get the aroma they want, but I urge caution. Start with a little essence and add in small quantities. If you overdo things you will have to blend the wine with another which is low in bouquet.

**Extraction with water and freezing.** If possible I like to use distilled or demineralised (not from the domestic water softener which may be rich in sodium salts) to extract the aroma from the flowers. If this quality of water is not available I boil the tap water thoroughly, pour it into a suitable container and allow it to go cold. This boiling treatment will remove excessive levels of "chlorine" and help to get rid of temporary hardness. Add the florets to the water and leave the mixture overnight so that the aroma can be extracted. Now take the ordinary tray that you use for making ice cubes, fill it with the "flower water" and pop it into the freezer. When the cubes are fully frozen, take them out and pop them into a conventional freezer container. Do remember to label the container. I forgot on one occasion and I found that my year's supply of elderflower essence had been thrown out as unwanted ice cubes!

**Making strong flower wine.** For this purpose you will need a simple base such as apple and grape, fermented out to give a wine of 10 - 12% alcoholic strength. We will discuss how to make just such a wine later (page 84). Use the same recipe but add some three or four handfuls of flowers to the must, and remove them with a sieve after the fermentation has lasted four or five days. Now fine the wine, stabilise it with sulphite and bottle it in half bottles. I find that just one half bottle of elderflower wine made in this way gives just the aroma I want in five gallons of German style white wine.

**Extraction of flowers with Vodka.** Vodka is a neutral spirit and is suitable for the extraction of the aroma of flowers. I find that putting two handfuls of florets in a bottle of Vodka and letting them soak overnight gives me a very useful essence. I do caution readers though, since care must be taken to remove the flowers after 12 - 24 hours so as to avoid spoilage. The extract should be treated with a little sulphite solution (about 5 ml of 10% solution to a bottle of the essence) to prevent oxidation.

**Freezing or drying flowers.** This is not my personal choice of method for preserving the aroma of flowers, but many winemakers find it convenient. The florets should be removed from the stems, placed in a polythene bag with a little sulphite solution and frozen. The sensible way is to make up several such small bags and enclose them in a larger bag. Then one bag of flowers can be used without disturbing the rest. The frozen flowers are simply added to the must just as though they were fresh.

You can dry your own flowers, of course, by carefully removing the stems, spreading the florets out on to a tray and letting them dry in a warm, dry atmosphere, although many winemakers prefer to buy them from health food stores etc. If you do buy dried flowers for winemaking purposes, they should be chosen with care, because some are quite unsuitable; buy them always in small sealed packs and never loose.

**Honey.** The problem with preparing honey is that there has to be a compromise between heating the solution of honey very strongly in order to kill off any micro-organisms present, and retaining the highly desirable aroma. My approach is to heat the honey solution to around 60°C for around 15 minutes. I skim off any scum or wax etc. that rises to the surface and then let the solution cool to room temperature.

## Summarising ingredient preparation.

In this chapter we have looked at the various ways of handling the natural ingredients that we will use in our winemaking, and various examples have been given. For the convenience of busy winemakers who will not want to read the text in detail every time they prepare a must I now summarise the procedures I have found most suitable for each of the more commonly used ingredients.

**Hard fruits.**

These include apples, pears and quinces. If I am making table wines then I always juice the fruit by crushing and pressing it, or by using the centrifuge type of device. The juice is then treated with pectic enzyme, allowed to stand overnight and racked before use.

**Stone fruits.**

Plums, and related fruits such as damsons and greengages I destone as much as possible, crush and ferment on the pulp. The stones should also be removed from apricots and peaches, and in the latter case the skins should be removed. I squash the flesh, add water, a little sulphite solution and pectolytic enzyme, and then press out the water/juice mixture a few hours later. It is much more difficult to remove the stones completely from cherries and sloes, especially sloes, so I simply remove all stalks, remove such stones as come out easily, then cut a deep grove in the other drupes and ferment on the pulp for just three to four days; the stones are then removed with a sieve.

**Citrus fruit.**

With oranges, I use the juice only, apart from adding a small amount of the zest, obtained by rubbing the whole fruit against a domestic grater. Other related citrus fruits such as clementines and tangerines are used for their juice only. I rarely use lemons or limes but if I do I restrict myself to using the juice; this juice is used primarily as a source of citric acid, although the flavour can contribute to a must intended to produce a citrus-style aperitif wine. Grapefruit juice is especially useful for aperitif wines. The pith of all citrus fruits is quite bitter and should be excluded from the must; the only exception I make here is when I use whole oranges of the marmalade type to make an aperitif.

**Soft fruit.**

This category includes all the following fruits:- bilberry, blackberry, blackcurrant, elderberry, loganberry, redcurrant, strawberry and whitecurrant.

All of these fruits should be destalked and washed gently in cold water before they are processed further. I recommend freezing all the fruit since when it is subsequently thawed it will release its juice more easily. The thawed fruit can then be crushed carefully and used in a pulp fermentation. Whitecurrant is something of an odd man out because of its colour, but because it contains quite a lot of tannin I think it is best used as part of a recipe for a red wine. If whitecurrants are going to be used to make a white wine then crush them, add water and pectolytic enzyme and press out the "juice" a few hours later.

The steamer method can be used on any or all of these fruits but I suggest that the extract is used as part of the must together with some crushed fruit for making a heavy dessert style of wine.

**Other fruits.**

These include the various fruits that do not obviously fall into the other categories listed above. **Bananas** we have seen should be slightly over-ripe and must be peeled and only the flesh used. I believe that the best flavour results when the flesh is pulped with a potato masher and added as such to the must. Some winemakers prefer to place the banana flesh in a nylon straining bag and suspend it in boiling water for 15 minutes or so. This produces the so-called "banana gravy", which is then added to the must.

**Gooseberries** should be taken from the freezer, boiling water poured over them, the berries crushed between finger and thumb (when cool!), pectolytic enzyme added and the mix pressed several hours later. This was described on page 51.

**Grapes** should be destalked and crushed. If a white wine is being made then press the grapes to obtain just the juice and add this juice to the must; some winemakers like to leave a proportion of the skins of suitable grapes in the must since the skins are a source of flavour ingredients and add to the complexity of the wine. This is most likely to be successful when the somewhat heavier style of table wine is being made.

**Hawthornberry.** This is not one of the most promising winemaking fruits, since it contains very little sugar, and not much flavour. I have used it with some success in conjunction with grape and apples juices, though, and I made a careful choice of berry, avoiding busy roadsides, and then removed all stalks before washing and then crushing the berries gently. The pulp was added to the must.

**Melons** are not used a great deal in winemaking, although I find that the juice of the cantaloupe variety adds a pleasant note to the flavour of my medium-sweet wines. The juice of other types of melon, including the watermelon, rather lack flavour but again provide a useful, if fairly neutral, background to the other ingredients, and I use it when the fruit is cheap. I peel the fruit, pulp it and press out the juice.

**Pineapples** should be used primarily for their juice, and then rather sparingly. I find it more convenient to buy the juice rather than extract it from the fresh fruit, but with care the juice can be pressed from the crushed fruit. When a dessert style of wine is required then I recommend adding the pulp (but not the skins) to the must.

**Rowanberry**. These berries are very bitter because of the presence of a substance called parasorbicide. Russian enthusiasts use the berries to make various herbal liquors, and the best process seems to be to pick the fruit when it is really ripe, wash and freeze it, and then heat it for a period to 60-70°C. Now treat with pectolytic enzyme and later press out the juice. The juice must be well diluted to reduce both the acid level and the effect of the yeast-destroying sorbic acid which is present.

**Rhubarb**. As we saw earlier, the sticks of rhubarb should be cut up and the juice extracted either by means of the centrifuge style of juicer, or after freezing (see page 52).

**Dried fruit.**

All dried fruit should be washed and then chopped or minced up. Of course all seeds or stones should be removed first; this will not be possible in the case of dried figs, so limit your treatment to a basic chop. The fruit is then used for a pulp fermentation.

**Canned fruit.**

In the case of canned stone fruit buy fruit without stones when this is possible. In any case take out any stones and then reduce the flesh and juice to a pulp by giving it a quick whirl in a blender.

**Fruit juices (commercially prepared).**

These can sometimes be purchased as fresh juice without stabilisers, especially in the case of apple juice. Both cartons and bottles of juice can be obtained. I strongly recommend that you read the label and avoid juices with any additives likely to cause problems; this means stabilisers primarily, although I will not buy juices that have been doctored with flavouring, colouring etc. Use the juices straight from the pack without further preparation.

**Cereals.**

In general cereals just need a good wash, followed by a treatment to break down the grains; a mincer normally does the trick. If you wish you can heat up the washed grain with water to really soften it before adding it to the must. Since all grain contains a lot of starch be prepared for problems with starch hazes. You will find information about this problem on page 207.

**Root vegetables.**

There are two possible approaches here. You can either extract the juice from vegetables such as carrots and parsnips with a centrifuge type of extractor, or simmer the cleaned roots in water before sieving them off. In case any reader should get too carried away with the juice extractor, I must relate a cautionary tale. When I first got an extractor I used it on a range of vegetables including turnips and swedes and put the juice into my must. The sulphur content of these vegetables produced a wine with more than a hint of "rotten eggs". As a keepsake I still have a couple of bottles of this 1967 vintage; the third one I opened last year and found to be as unpleasant as ever!

Beetroot is used by some winemakers and at least it contains some 6-7% of sugar. I recommend cleaning the roots thoroughly, cutting off the leaves, and then chopping the roots up before simmering them in water. Wines based on beetroot tend to have an earthy taste although this usually disappears if the wine is stored for a couple of years. At the same time the distinctive red colour fades to an amber. This fading is because the source of the red colour is not the same as in fruits but produced by a substance called betanin, which is less stable.

**Other vegetables.**

Generally speaking I avoid giving recipes using such dubious ingredients as nettles, pea pods and oak leaves, although I know that some country winemakers use them. Parsley is one herb that does give a wine a distinctive taste, and this is simply washed well and chopped up before being added to the must; other leaf vegetables should be treated in the same way. But do leave out the brassica!. Herbs that are intended to give the wine a herbal note are best chopped up and added to the finished wine rather than added to the fermenting must. This is just a precaution since herbs contain many substances and the yeast may well bring about changes in these substances, and this is not necessarily desirable.

# Chapter 6
# The Must

## Introduction

We saw in Chapter 3 (page 16) that if the yeast is to work well the must (the solution of sugar and fruit juices etc.) has to meet a number of criteria. We mentioned some of these in the brief summary, but we will now look at these in more detail. In turn we will consider flavour, aroma (bouquet), sugar, acid, nutrients, pectolytic enzyme, water, yeast, all of which are necessary, with comments about possible extras such as bentonite and oak chips.

## Must composition

### Flavour

In many ways this is one of the most important factors in making successful wines, but the question of which flavour is best for a particular style of wine is a knotty one, since all our palates vary and quite naturally we have our own preferences. Before we draw up a few ground rules on which ingredients are most suitable for specific wine types, let us generalise about how much flavour we want in our wines. To start with, I have listed in Table 6.1 the more common styles of wine that we are likely to want, and I have given in general terms suggestions for the most suitable levels of flavour, alcohol and acid, plus a few other relevant tips.

Table 6.1     Commoner styles of wine

| Wine style | Alcohol level (%) | Flavour intensity | Comments |
| --- | --- | --- | --- |
| Light white table | 9-10 | low-medium | e.g. Soave |
| Heavier white table | 11-13 | medium | e.g. White Burgundy; hint of oak |
| White social | 13-14 | medium-full | e.g. Barsac; medium sweet |
| White dessert | 15 | full | Hint of oak |
| Light red table | 9-11 | medium | e.g. Beaujolais; fruity |
| Heavier red table | 11-13 | medium-full | e.g. Rhone; hint of oak; medium tannin |
| Red dessert | 15 | full | Hint of oak; medium tannin |
| Sparkling | 10-13 | low | Acid on high side |
| Aperitif (Vermouth) | 14 | low | Added herbs; low acid |
| Sherry | 15 | varies | Essence may be needed |
| Port | 15 | full | Oak needed; low acid |

We will return to these guidelines later on and expand on them when we come to develop suitable recipes. For the moment we should note that if the alcohol level is on the low side, and the wine dry, then we shall not want a wine with massive amounts of flavour. Similarly sparkling wines are best made using as a base a wine with a fairly neutral flavour; the secondary fermentation and the flavour that comes from storage on the spent yeast cells gives us the flavour we look for in such a wine.

As the alcohol level builds up so the wine tolerates more flavour, which means incorporating more fruit into the recipe. The degree of sweetness also influences the flavour, and generally speaking a sweeter wine needs more flavour; otherwise it tends to taste like a non-descript sugar-water plonk.

But what about the suitability of a given ingredient for a given wine? Personal opinion comes into this, and the suggestions I now make are just that; at the end of the day you must use what you like best.

Perhaps I can recap some of the points I made in the last chapter and pull them together a little.

**White wines.** Many people find this style of wine the hardest to make. This is because even minor defects show up badly in a dry wine, but may be masked if the wine is a sweeter one. We shall look at the best way of making a light-bodied dry white table wine from readily available juices in the next chapter. But for the moment note that the lighter wines in particular should be made from juices (diluted) only. I find that apple and grape combinations work the best, although pear juice is a useful extra and the addition of a small amount of gooseberry "juice" adds a modicum of sophistication. A flower essence adds any required aroma.

When more weighty whites are wanted then I find that the gooseberry content should be increased, and that small amounts of quince juice and whitecurrants work wonders. Another hint for the more full bodied whites is the addition of just a tiny amount of oak granules.

Moving to the sweeter white wines then I suggest that you introduce either peaches or apricots, together with a little pineapple juice, but go easy with the latter. These fruits mix well with the basic apple and grape combination. More fruit is needed, which lifts up the acid level, but this can be balanced by the sweetness. Some bananas and orange juice also come in handy when the requirement is a medium-sweet social wine, ideal for slurping when you are having a pleasant evening with friends or simply relaxing in front of the TV!

White dessert wines need much more fruit, so a problem may arise with the acid level. In order to keep this down you must make sure that you use really ripe fruit or fruits which are not naturally too acidic. This is where bananas, peaches and some apples are useful. Dried fruit can be brought into the dessert wine recipes too, since although this means an increase in the golden-brown colour this will be acceptable in this type of wine. Oak granules will add that little touch of oak "vanilla" that makes all the difference.

**Red wines.**

For the lighter luncheon style of red wines, perhaps in the style of a Valpolicella, care must be taken to keep down the tannin level. This means rather less fruit and avoiding the excessive use of fruits that are rich in phenolic compounds. Bilberries and blackberries fit the bill here, and elderberries can be included if they are really ripe. The other tip is to add white grape juice or apple juice to keep up the fruitiness without adding tannin. Redcurrants are often used by winemakers to make rosé wines, largely on account of their light colour. I find that the lovely fruitiness goes even better in a red wine mix.

There are occasions when a youthful, fruity red wine goes down well. The Nouveau Beaujolais style of wine is what I have in mind. Again the tannin level has to be kept down, and again adding apple juice to the must helps to produce the desired fruitiness. Later on (page 77) I discuss the home winemaker's "carbonic maceration" method, and I recommend this if you really want young fruity wines.

Heavier dry red table wines need more fruit, and if the wine is to have elegance it needs to be made from a mixture of fruits, and have more tannin. Chapter 10 gives several such recipes. It will be seen that these wines need blackcurrants, and possibly raspberries, in small amounts, to add both depth of flavour and the characteristics of Burgundies and Clarets. Once again a touch of oak smoothes out the wines.

In the commercial world there are very few red wines that are medium or sweet, but amateur winemakers fill such a gap by making a wine with plenty of fruit flavour, but with low tannin. These are our social wines, and I like to use blackberries and cherries plus grapes as my base. A good red grape concentrate can help to flesh out this type of wine.

When it comes to red dessert wines then we need fruit, fruit and more fruit, but we must keep the acid level within bounds, so that the fruits must be ripe. Excessive amounts of high acid fruits such as blackcurrants must be avoided. Oak is essential in my view. For most of us this means adding oak chips although real enthusiasts will use barrels. Remember though that barrels soon become exhausted as far as flavour extraction goes, so that after three or four batches of wine have been held in them they will no longer give the wine the oakiness you may want. Then use oak chips to get the flavour but store in barrels for the other benefits they give.

**Sparkling wines.**

Rhubarb is an excellent base for your sparkling wines.

**Aperitif wines.**

These fall into several categories, namely citrus, sherry and Vermouth. We shall look at various recipes in Chapter 10. For the citrus style of aperitif, various combinations of grapefruit, lemon and orange can be used, but go gently and avoid overdoing the flavour. In addition keep out bitter forming pith. Sherry-style wines are difficult to make. It is almost impossible to produce the flor that develops, although at the moment you can at least use a true sherry yeast. The base is either apple or a mixture of various dried fruits. I prefer the dried fruits since we want a fairly low acid wine and this is more difficult with an apple base.

Frankly I make a good sound base wine with a rather neutral flavour and add a special sherry essence.

Last but by no means least we come to Vermouth-style wines. The flavour comes from mixed herbs. You should make a low acid neutral wine and then either soak the mixed herbs in the wine or use the excellent herb extract essence that is available to us. I do not recommend adding the herbs at the start of the ferment since this can result in the extraction of too much bitterness.

**Port.**

As we shall see later, true port is made by a method that is not really economical for us. We imitate the commercial product by taking a mixture of red/black fruits with a must and yeast capable of giving us an alcohol level of 18% or more. The acid level has to be lowish, which restricts our choice of fruits. Oak is necessarily followed by a lengthy period of maturation.

# Aroma and bouquet

Many people use the terms aroma and bouquet without distinction. But basically the aroma is the smell that comes from the ingredients, while bouquet is the extra (and modified) smells that come from the fermentation and maturation. Commonly we use bouquet to describe the overall smell, although this is frequently said to be the "nose" by wine writers. We shall talk about the role of fermentation and maturation later on, but as far as aroma goes once again we have to decide on both how much and which.

Table 6.2 gives an indication of the intensity of aroma that is likely to be produced by most of the more commonly used ingredients. It is over-simplified of course because the variety of a given fruit for instance will be a significant factor, so it should be taken only as a guideline. I have listed the ingredients under five categories, with a 0 to 4 rating, 4 being the highest.

The choice of which aroma is most appropriate is often dictated by the choice of a particular ingredient for its flavour. But apple aroma goes well with the German style of white wine, especially if it is supplemented with a little elderflower. Most other flower aromas go well with the lighter white wines, but don't overdo things - you are not making toilet water! The aroma of culinary gooseberries is suitable for wines aimed at imitating a Chablis or Burgundy, and such up-market wines also benefit from a touch of the oak vanilla.

For the sweeter white wines the apricot and peach aromas are very suitable. I find that rhubarb adds an interesting touch to such wines when trying to approach the Sauternes style. And strangely enough a few strawberries fit well in such a wine, and give it the aroma we are searching for if used in moderation; the colour fades during fermentation and maturation and just a gentle golden hint remains.

Table 6.2    Aroma intensity of ingredients.

| Intensity rating | Ingredient |
| --- | --- |
| 0 | cereals, most vegetables, dandelion |
| 1 | melon, parsnip, pear, plum |
| 2 | apple (culinary), bilberry, blackberry, cherry, damson, elderberry, gooseberry, grape, orange, redcurrant, whitecurrant |
| 3 | apple (dessert), apricot, banana, blackcurrant, honey, peach, pineapple, strawberry quince, rose petal |
| 4 | elderflower, loganberry, raspberry |

While blackcurrants and raspberries have very distinctive and powerful aromas, in small amounts they are essential components of musts for the classic French red wines (Bordeaux and Burgundy styles). The other major red fruits such as bilberry, blackberry elderberry and sloe, can be used in any type of red wine provided no one fruit is used at such a level that its aroma becomes too evident.

A last point about aroma is that some recipes may give a wine that is rather bland; indeed the lack of aroma/bouquet is often said to be one of the main shortcomings of amateur wines. As we have seen, this can be put right by adding a suitable aroma-strong ingredient to the must. An alternative is to add one of the better natural essences that are available. One that has been developed especially for home winemakers facing this aroma problem, is the Gervin White Wine Improver. This essence is a mixture of the substances that are produced naturally in the fermentation or maturation, or found in the Riesling grape. Used in moderation this essence can bring about a significant improvement in the nose of the wine.

# Sugar

Most of our ingredients will contain fermentable sugars as we saw with the data listed in table 4.1. Some fruits contain sucrose, others a mixture of glucose and fructose, and some all three. In practice this doesn't matter because the yeast will break down any sucrose into a mixture of glucose and fructose, and it is these two sugars that the yeast cell takes in and converts into alcohol.

What I want to emphasise is that the yeast does break down sucrose very easily so that there should be no temptation to buy invert sugar (sugar that has been broken down for us already). I mention this since some older books advise buying invert sugar, reasoning that this saves yeast the job and makes the fermentation faster. I can assure readers that our experiments have shown that the improvement in fermentation rate is trivial at best, so don't bother looking for this relatively expensive and elusive commodity.

Ordinary granulated sugar is all the extra that you need. And in my view it doesn't matter whether the sugar is from the cane or the beet. My own carefully monitored experiments with parallel wines made from the two varieties of sucrose have shown that they ferment in identical fashion, and that no-one can tell the difference between the wines. Sugars sold as icing and caster sugars are chemically identical with granulated and although they dissolve in water quicker than granulated they have no other advantage; and they are much costlier. If you should have a cheap source of glucose (sold commercially as dextrose monohydrate), by all means use it, but don't go to any additional expense.

There are various "brown" sugars on the domestic market, some of which are simply granulated sugar with a covering of caramel. The flavour of such sugars makes them unsuitable for inclusion in wine musts, although they have a place in liqueur making (see my book *Straightforward Liqueurmaking*).

Syrups such as Golden Syrup and treacle should not be used in view of their distinctive flavour. There are commercial syrups made from corn starch; these are referred to as glucose syrups and are available in various grades. One grade is high in glucose, but the others have fair amounts of other sugars that are either unfermentable or which only ferment slowly. We shall discuss these in Chapter 13. The average winemaker is unlikely to be able to buy these glucose syrups but they are used by many manufacturers of "kits" because they are relatively cheap and have no colour. Since some sugar remains unfermented and leaves both a residual sweet taste and some "body", it is understandable that many kits incorporate them.

Returning to fermentable sugars, namely those found in our fruits and our granulated sugars, we must now ask how much we should put in our musts. In Chapter 3 I drew readers' attention to the simple rule of thumb that the complete fermentation of 10% of sugar will produce 6% of alcohol. I strongly recommend the use of this guideline. Thus if we want to make a table wine containing 12% of alcohol then we will want a must containing 20% of fermentable sugar. But before we start adding our bags of sugar we must first make an allowance for the sugar present in the other ingredients.

In Table 4.1 (page 25) I gave details of the likely levels of sugars that we find in most of our ingredients. As a simple example, let us consider elderberries. I have suggested that they contain between 10 and 13% of sugar when they are ripe. If we then take a kilogram of elderberries we shall be adding between 100 and 130 grams of sugar; many readers will prefer to think in the good old British units of pounds and ounces; then a pound (16 ounces) of elderberries will give us just under two ounces of sugar. The arithmetic is 0.1 x 16 = 1.6 for the 10% rating, and 0.13 x 16 = 2.08 for the 13% rating. In round figures we can assume that a pound of ripe elderberries will provide two ounces of sugar for the fermentation.

If we then make a gallon of wine using 3 pounds of elderberries, we will have 6 ounces of sugar from the fruit and will need a further one pound ten ounces of granulated sugar in our gallon of must. (A gallon of water weighs ten pounds so that two pounds of sugar in a gallon of must gives us a 20% solution). As a metric example let us stick with elderberries and add two kilos of fruit to 4.5 litres. The fruit will give us between 200 and 260 grams of sugar, say 230, and we need a total of 900 to give us a 20% solution (i.e. 900/4500 x 100 = 20%). Hence we must add 900 - 230 = 670 grams of sugar to our must.

There is no need for us to make our calculations any more accurate since the difference of an ounce of sugar (or say 25 grams) will only modify the alcohol level by about 0.3%. The variations in our fermentation procedure (temperature, choice of yeast, availability of nutrients etc.) are likely to produce larger variations than this. The main point is to get the alcohol level reasonably close to the value you want. Then you can add more sugar when the fermentation is over and if you want a sweet wine. We will examine this approach further when we look at particular recipes in the next chapter. To help readers, I have grouped the ingredients into four categories of sugar providers; the simplified data is given in Table 6.3.

Table 6.3. Sugar provided by various ingredients.

| Class | % sugar in fruit | Sugar provided by fruit g/kg | oz/lb | Examples |
|---|---|---|---|---|
| 1 | 0 - 2 (mean 1) | 0-30 (mean 15) | 0-0.2 (mean 0.1) | cereals, leaf vegetables, lemon juice, potato, rhubarb |
| 2 | 5-7 (mean 6) | 50-70 (mean 60) | 0.8-1.0 (mean 0.9) | apricot bilberry, blackcurrant, gooseberry (culinary),loganberry, melon, raspberry, redcurrant, strawberry, whitecurrant, beetroot, carrot, turnip. |
| 3 | 8-12 (mean 10) | 80-120 Mean 100) | 1.2-1.9 (mean 1.55) | cherry, damson, elderberry, gooseberry (dessert), orange, peach, pear, pineapple, parsnip |
| 4 | 18-22 (mean 20) | 180-220 (mean 200) | 2.9-3.5 (mean 3.3) | banana, grape |

All you have to do now is to look up the ingredient in this table, check the number of grams per kilo, or ounces per pound, and determine how much sugar the ingredient will be providing.

**Acid.**

Once again our questions are how much acid and which acid. Acids will be discussed in much more detail in Chapter 12, but for the moment it is only necessary to realise that there are only three acids likely to be found in winemaking ingredients to any significant extent. These acids are citric, malic and tartaric. Any one of these acids is satisfactory in the must, but if there is a choice then I come down strongly in favour of tartaric acid.

My reasons are firstly that the taste of tartaric acid is usually preferred to the taste of either of the other two acids. While taste is a personal matter, it should be said that malic acid is usually thought of as having a rather sour taste and citric acid a rather sharp taste. In tests I have carried out with solutions of each of the three acids dissolved in 10% alcohol, I have found again and again that the majority of winemakers give their taste preference as

$$\text{tartaric} > \text{malic} > \text{citric}.$$

A second reason for preferring tartaric acid is that it is much less likely to be attacked by bacteria than either of the other two, and last, but by no means least, excess of tartaric acid can often be removed from a wine simply by chilling the wine. This is not the case with either citric or malic acid, since these acids and their salts are much more soluble than the relevant salt of tartaric acid.

Table 4.2 gave the likely acid levels in our winemaking fruits, and it can be seen that except for grapes, tartaric acid is unlikely to be present. In fact citrus and soft fruits are dominated by citric acid and "tree" fruits by malic acid. Don't let this worry you. I simply recommend that if it is necessary to add more acid to the must it is probably best to add tartaric.

Now to the level of acid that is needed in the must. We shall go into this matter in greater detail in Chapter 12, but for the moment we can talk in terms of the acid present as its tartaric acid equivalent. In round figures, 75 grams of tartaric acid are equivalent to 64 grams of citric acid and 68 grams of malic acid. For most purposes we can take all three acids as roughly equivalent.

During the fermentation some changes in the acid levels will take place, and normally there will be some increase, of the order of 0.1-0.15% (or 1.0-1.5 grams/litre). For this reason I always set the level of acidity in my must just that little bit lower than I want the acidity to be in the finished wine. For most purposes, having the acidity of the must between 0.4 and 0.5% (4 to 5 grams/litre) results in the production of a satisfactory wine.

I try to avoid having too high a starting acidity since this causes the fermentation to be slow, and inevitably produces a wine that is still too acid and needs treatment to drop the acid level. At the other end of the scale I keep the starting acidity at least as high as 0.35% since a lower level can result in some yeasts producing undesirable substances.

We will look at the acid levels in typical wines when we consider the recipes in Chapters 9 and 10; more details about acidity are given in Chapter 12.

Nutrients.

The big four minerals needed by the yeast are magnesium, nitrogen, phosphorus and potassium, but much smaller quantities of other minerals such as copper, iron, molybdenum and zinc are needed too. A successful fermentation will also demand the presence of certain growth factors, including various vitamins. All of these nutrient requirements are present in a quality grape juice, but may not be present in other ingredients in the necessary amounts.

Thus flowers contain virtually no nutrients, while the nitrogen present in cereals and vegetables is mainly in the form of the aminoacids that make up the proteins. When the yeast needs nutrients it takes them from wherever it can, so if necessary it will extract its nitrogen from the amino acids of cereals and vegetables, and when it does that it may leave behind higher alcohols. These higher alcohols (commonly grouped together under the term fusel oil), will give the wine a hot, burning taste, and in excessive amounts will cause a substantial hangover because the body has difficulty in metabolising them. For this reason I always recommend adding nutrient salts to a must, especially to those likely to be short of what is needed; one nutrient mix that contains all the necessary minerals and growth factors is sold under the name Minavit. This is suitable for all musts, and especially for musts that contain no fruit.

Generally speaking, fruits contain most of the necessary nutrients, although the addition of a little extra nutrient mix will ensure a good fermentation. But try to avoid adding really large amounts of nutrient because a lot of it will remain behind after the fermentation is over. This may affect the taste of the wine, but even more important it will act as a good medium for the growth of unwanted bacteria.

Pectolytic enzyme.

As we saw in the last chapter (page 55), pectic substances are found in all fruits and many vegetables where they make up the necessary structural backbone, and when the fruit or vegetables are processed this pectin is released into the must and is likely to cause a haze in the wine later on. For this reason we should always add a good pectolytic enzyme to the must where it will break down the pectic substance into non haze-forming substances. More information about these pectic substances and the enzymes that break them down is given in Chapter 15.

**Water.**

Unless you have the luxury of working with pure grape juice, then in almost every case you will need to add water to dilute the ingredient extract. How important is the quality of this water? Well to start with it is essential to use a water that is free from any flavour taint, such as the occasional phenolic taste that subsequently bedevils our beer-making friends, and water that has been over chlorinated. In the case of chlorinated water, a good boiling will normally remove the excess.

But some of us live in hard water areas and others where the water is remarkably soft. Both sorts of water can be used in winemaking without undue difficulty, but it should be appreciated that soft water may be short of essential minerals, and this will need supplementing if the ingredients do not supply what is needed. The colour of some water from peaty soils can be rather brown in colour and this spoils the look of the wine if not the taste.

What about hard water? It can be used without the wine suffering too much, although it can result in some haze developing because of the formation of tiny crystals of calcium tartrate. My experiments have shown that I get a marginally better wine, with less likelihood of problems if I first boil the water. I take a large 6-pint kettle, fill it with water, bring the water to the boil and let it boil for several minutes. Then I pour the boiling water into a Pyrex or plastic vessel and allow it to cool. If the hardness of the water was caused by calcium bicarbonate (i.e. temporary hardness) then calcium carbonate will form and precipitate out (this is the scale that forms in kettles). The softened water is then poured from its chalk deposit and used to make up the must. But remember that the boiling removes all the air from the water, and this will be missed by the yeast. So give the boiled water, or the must made with it, a really good shake to replace this air.

Some readers may have a source of either demineralised or distilled water. As the names imply, such water is free from virtually all dissolved matter; I have found it makes extremely good wine provided that I give it the necessary nutrient supplement.

I am often asked about the desirability of using water that has been softened by a domestic softener. It should be appreciated that this type of softener does not remove all the minerals but merely replaces the calcium (which causes hardness) with sodium. Personally I prefer to keep my sodium level to a minimum and prefer not to use this type of water, but at worst it is only a marginal effect; however I prefer to boil hard water to soften it for winemaking.

Finally there are several brands of water purifiers that aim to remove contaminants rather than minerals. Apart from the expense involved I can see no objection to using such water, and in fact I would expect it to be a worthwhile improvement on untreated tap water in many cases.

**Yeast.**

Despite the suggestions that once appeared in old winemaking books, there really is no such thing as a no-yeast method of making wine. Many old fashioned books relied on the so-called natural yeasts that is found on the surface of vegetation. These yeasts are most unlikely to be of the type suitable for winemaking, and will almost certainly be grossly contaminated with bacteria. The usual result will be a sweet, sickly, low-alcohol wine, formed as a result of a stuck ferment; and it may well be laced with acetic acid (vinegar) because of the action of the bacteria. So if you do become tempted to try out a really old recipe make sure that you add a decent yeast.

Pre-1945, many home winemakers used fresh bakers' yeast, and even now this is still the favourite with some writers of books on making country wines. It is possible to make a reasonable wine with such a yeast, of course, provided you take the wine off the yeast as soon as the ferment is over. If you leave it for even a short time on the lees an overwhelming yeastiness will pervade the wine, as a consequence of the breakdown (autolysis) of the yeast cells.

Furthermore, such bakers' yeast has not been bred for producing wine but to produce a lot of carbon dioxide gas. This means a loss of volatile compounds (bouquet) and alcohol; and the ferment will stop if the temperature drops a little. These days fresh bakers' yeast is not so easily come by, so dried bakers' yeast is often used in its place. It is equally likely to produce a yeasty-tasting wine and to stick if the temperature falls.

The truth is that to be sure of making a decent wine you should use a respectable true wine yeast. These are available in all homebrew shops. Look at the label to make sure that it is said to be a wine yeast, since some brands on the market have bakers' yeast in the sachets!

My second piece of advice is to buy a brand that contains just yeast, and not dried yeast mixed with nutrient or sugar or both. In the first place such mixtures are likely to have a relatively short shelf life, and secondly it is foolish to pay yeast prices for nutrient salts or sugar. The yeast/nutrient mixes do not contain enough yeast for a successful ferment but have to go through a process of yeast growth first, and this is a needless time-wasting procedure.

My final piece of advice is to see if the label gives you information about the origin of the yeast. This may take the form of giving the strain number, or alternatively the yeast type. But beware again. Many sachets are labelled as suggesting that they are Sauternes yeast or Port yeast. Such active dried wine yeasts are not available, I'm afraid. The yeast inside a so-called Sauternes pack is most likely to be a strain of *Saccharomyces bayanus* (a Champagne yeast). This may be alright for making the style of wine that you want but in my view it is misleading the homewinemaker.

What we are looking for is a yeast that will suit the particular style of fermentation we want. It may be for fermenting at a relatively cool temperature, in order to get a fruity bouquet, or perhaps to be tolerant to high levels of alcohol, as when we wish to make a dessert wine, or restart a stuck ferment. Ideally we want a yeast that doesn't froth too much, will give a decent bouquet and will settle firmly and quickly without breaking down too soon.

Avoid yeasts that are labelled as giving specific wines, because the style of the amateur wine will depend more on the mix of ingredients than the yeast type. Thus even if you could get a sample of yeast from one of the top port producing wineries it wouldn't give you a port style wine if the must was made from just blackberries. Indeed port is made by stopping the ferment by adding brandy when the alcohol level is only 8 or 9%; we need a yeast capable of producing the alcohol level we want and we must choose a must whose flavour roughly matches that of port.

Buy your active dried yeast in long-life (triple-layer) sachets and never buy pots of yeast - nutrient mix. Once opened, such mixtures pick up moisture and deteriorate rapidly. Winemaking takes time and money so don't waste either by using an inferior yeast, or by buying a large pack of yeast/sugar/nutrient mix.

A typical sachet of active dried wine yeast will contain around 5 grams of yeast, and this is sufficient for the fermentation of 5 gallons or so of must if it is rehydrated properly. No harm will come if all the yeast in a sachet is added to just a gallon of must, but economically minded winemakers will be inclined to stretch the yeast if they can. I suggest that if you want to make just a gallon of wine you should open the sachet and use about a third of the yeast and then seal the sachet up again with a little sellotape. It will start to deteriorate once the sachet has been opened but should be quite satisfactory provided it is used within three or four months. As with sealed sachets of yeast, keep the resealed sachet in a cool place until required.

Good makes of yeast should retain their active life for at least two years if kept in a cool place. Thus Gervin yeasts come with a guaranteed minimum shelf life of two years provided they have been stored properly. Tests show that at 5°C the dried yeast loses between 5 and 10% of its activity each year. I can say that I have found many of these yeasts still in fine fettle after even five years!

To get the best results the rehydration should be carried out carefully. First of all make up a 5% solution in water of ordinary granulated sugar (5 grams/100 ml, or a half teaspoonful in two fluid ounces), with the temperature about blood heat; if in doubt have the water just off the chill, but around 35°C if possible, and not above 40°C. Add the yeast from the sachet and stir gently. If the yeast is in good condition it will start to froth in 10-15 minutes. Then stir vigorously, and leave the yeast for a further 5 minutes before adding it to the must. The reasoning behind this procedure will be discussed in Chapter 11.

**Optional extras.**

These include bentonite and oak granules. Bentonite is widely used in commercial winemaking to remove unwanted protein that can produce hazes. If it is added to the must at the start of the fermentation it will provide a surface on which the carbon dioxide gas bubbles will form, and this will ensure a smooth fermentation with less frothing and less chance of a sudden surge and an overflowing ferment. If possible buy one of the granular bentonites prepared for the commercial winemakers. This is much easier to get into suspension.

Oak granules can be added to the must if you want to add the lovely vanilla note that is found in many of the top wines, both red and white. In my view this treatment improves all the red wines, and used at a low level brings a roundness to the heavier whites. Granules (i.e. large "sawdust") from the American oak, Quercus alba, is available in this country under the Gervin label. It is best added at the start of the fermentation, but can be used at the end if necessary.

English oak is not really suited for winemaking since it contains a high level of phenolic compounds. I have had some success with it by taking a piece of oak or the branch of a tree that has "matured" for a couple of years, and taking thin (1 mm) slices or chippings from the wood with a plane or chisel. I then soak the chips in hot water for 15 minutes or so. This removes the more astringent phenolic compounds and some of the colour. I then let the chippings drain and toast them to a golden colour under the grill. The secret is not to overdo the toasting. I use such chippings in my red wines.

# Chapter 7
# Special Techniques

## Thermal Vinification

In Chapter 5 we looked at various ways of getting the best out of our ingredients when we processed them. We considered using heat in two ways, namely the steamer method, whereby steam was passed into the fruit and extracted the juice, and a simple boiling approach. Both methods had the advantage of essentially sterilising the fruit, but had the disadvantages of destroying some of the ingredients that act as growth factors for the yeast, and of altering the flavour. In addition, hazes may develop later.

At a professional level the heating process is referred to as thermal vinification. Basically it consists of heating the fruit (grapes) in a variety of ways so that the skin cells are broken down and release colouring matter, tannin, acids, sugars and nutrients. The process may be a batch one, or it may be continuous. Either way the grapes may be treated whole, or after they have been crushed.

With whole grapes, the bunches may be dipped into boiling water for a short period, or steam may be passed over them. The skin temperatures probably reach 75 to $80^{\circ}C$, but it is said that the pulp rarely goes above $30^{\circ}C$. The heated grapes are allowed to cool and then crushed. If crushed grapes are used they will be destemmed, to avoid subsequent extraction of bitter principles. Heating is then done in bulk with hot water circulating in double-walled vessels.

It is clear that a considerable amount of extra colour is extracted if the grapes are heated before fermentation. It is known that the temperature should be taken up to $80^{\circ}C$ in order to destroy oxidase enzymes. If this is not done then the enzymes may attack the colouring substances, thus reducing the red colour and possibly introducing some yellowing. There is some doubt about whether the increase in colour lasts more than a few years. There may be other disadvantages in that the wines tend to be more reluctant to clear, and may contain somewhat higher levels of fusel oil (higher alcohols).

While thermal vinification may be a mixed blessing, some enthusiastic readers may like to try it out. There is little evidence on how fruits other than grapes will behave, though. I suggest putting the fruit into an inner vessel which is itself surrounded by a second vessel full of water kept at 80°C or thereabouts for up to 30 minutes. A second possibility is to take just part of the fruit and drop it into hot water, and allowing the mix to cool. The remainder of the fruit is then added and fermentation initiated.

## Carbonic Maceration (macération carbonique)

### The commercial aspect

The carbonic maceration technique, which has been practised in some areas of France for a long time, is one in which the whole grapes are placed in a tank under an atmosphere of carbon dioxide. The tank is then sealed. A so-called intracellular fermentation takes place within the whole grape, which results in the production within the grape berry of 1-2% alcohol. The cause of this fermentation is not immediately obvious, particularly since accounts of the process do not mention the addition of any yeast. If the fermentation is a conventional one then presumably there must be some penetration of the skin by yeast cells indigenous to the winery. The process is complicated by the attack on malic acid in the berry, apparently by lactic acid bacteria (see Chapter 11), which destroys a considerable amount of the malic acid present. Once this partial fermentation is over, the grapes are crushed.

There are pros and cons for this carbonic maceration approach. The disadvantages are that it produces less juice, and that with black grapes the wine produced has less colour than that produced by the conventional pulp fermentation method. Moreover, if the process is not monitored carefully, there is the increased chance of contamination by unwanted bacteria and an increase of volatile acidity.

The advantages of the process are the considerable reduction in the level of malic acid present, and an accompanying enhanced aroma and increased fruitiness. The process seems to be favoured when grapes of the "lesser" varieties are being made into wine, because any varietal character becomes less noticeable in the carbonic maceration approach. The main use of the method is in the production of wines in the Nouveau Beaujolais style, where youthfulness, fruitiness and early easy drinking is essential.

There is still a lot of mystery about just what goes on, and there seems to be a real need for an extensive microbiological study of the changes that go on in the process. Thus is it a fermentation within the berry that is important, and which ceases after the formation of a small amount of alcohol, or is it that when grapes are stored under carbon dioxide the skin cells die and release their contents more readily? And yet again is it that because the fermentation is slower and less heat is generated there is a greater yield of fruity esters?

Enthusiasm for carbonic maceration is not universal, since although a number of French winemakers adopt the method with enthusiasm, American oenologists seem rather sceptical.

**The amateur approach**

As amateurs we cannot hope to imitate the carbonic maceration technique very closely. For one thing we do not have the necessary equipment, but more importantly many of our winemaking fruits do not have such well defined skins as the grape. But it is possible for us to go part of the way by conducting the early stages of fermentation under an atmosphere of carbon dioxide, and under slight pressure.

The simplest way of all is to put all the fruit into a stout plastic bag, itself being inside a second bag as a safeguard in case the inner one should split, add the rehydrated yeast and then "seal" the neck of the bags with rubber bands. The bags are put into a supporting rigid container, such as a bucket, and the fermentation allowed to proceed for a week. The bag is then opened, and the fermenting mass pressed to extract the liquid, to which is added the sugar and nutrients. The fermentation is then allowed to go to completion in the usual way.

Figure 7.1

An alternative method makes use of a simple plastic jar normally used for holding 5-7 lbs of sweets (see Figure 7.1). These jars are non-returnable so you should have no problems obtaining one from your local sweet shop. Wash the jar out thoroughly and then add to it the fruit that you intend to make your wine from. In one recent experiment I took two pounds of blackberries and one of blueberries from the freezer, thawed them out in the microwave oven and put them in the jar. I then added my yeast starter, together with about half a pint of boiled water and screwed down the lid.

I have never had a jar split yet, because the lid is not a perfect seal, but we may come across an exceptional one so I placed the jar inside a bucket just in case the pressure that built up too much in the jar. And to give my wife some peace of mind I also covered the jar with a clean cloth. Because I wanted the atmosphere in the jar to be that of carbon dioxide, I undid the lid of the jar once or twice to release the pressure and hopefully force out some of the air. Of course I could have added a little sodium bicarbonate to the fruit in the first instance, before adding the yeast, so that carbon dioxide would be released by the action of the fruit acid, and thus displace the air.

I then let the fermentation proceed for a week before opening the jar, sieving off the fruit pulp, and adding the remainder of the ingredients. The fermentation went to completion in the normal way, and gave me a nice fruity wine in the required style.

Knowledgeable readers will note that the fruits I used contain mainly citric acid, so that there was little reduction of acidity in this case. Enthusiasts may like to try the approach with say gooseberries that have been first softened by freezing and then thawed by the addition of boiling water.

# Sparkling wines

### The commercial process

Champagne set the standard that all other producers of sparkling wines try to attain. It is the name Dom Perignon that is the famous one in Champagne, because he was the distinguished cellarman of the Benedictine Abbey of Hautvillers, and pioneered the art of blending. It is said that he introduced the use of Spanish cork for bottle closures. Although he is often described as the father of Champagne production, he lived almost two centuries before Francois published the necessary sugar tables in the early nineteenth century. It may be that his fame is rather overstated but it still lives on, at least on the label of a well known brand of Champagne.

Champagne has always been a symbol of the "good life", and it was the popular drink amongst the courtiers of France; during the time of Louis XV the notorious Madame de Pompadour exclaimed "It is the only drink that lets a woman stay beautiful after she has drunk it". More recently, readers may recall "Champagne Charlie", who was certainly full of the joys of life!

But to turn to how Champagne is made. To start with the grapes are chosen with care and pressed very gently, with minimum contact time between juice and broken skins. This reduces the amount of colour and tannin that gets into the juice. The subsequent fermentation is usually carried out in stainless steel tanks, these days, rather than wooden vats, and the intention is to obtain a sound basic wine without noticeable varietal aroma. As soon as the fermentation is over, the base wine is racked and clarified.

The base wine is then put into stout, clean bottles capable of withstanding pressures of six atmospheres, and sugar syrup and yeast are added. The bottles are corked and placed in a relatively cool (15°C) place so that a slow second fermentation can take place. During this stage the carbon dioxide gas will be formed slowly and will subsequently generate the classical tiny, long-lasting bubbles when the wine is poured into the glass. The bottles are then stored horizontally for a year or more, while the yeast autolyses and gives the champagne the characteristic note.

The process of riddling comes next, when the yeast is shaken in stages down to the neck of the bottle. The traditional method involves inverting the bottles and placing them into a sloping rack. Each day the "riddler" gives every bottle 1/8th of a turn, so persuading the yeast to slip gradually down to the neck. The angle of the rack is increased from time to time until all the yeast is in the neck. This riddling can take up to three months of daily dedicated twirling. Understandably, science has now played a part in the production of mechanical riddlers, in which a mounted set of racked bottles is rotated regularly, the whole process being computer controlled.

Then it is the "crunch" time, when the yeast has to be removed, and there is no time for the faint hearted. The bottles are cooled and their necks plunged into a freezing mixture of ice and salt. The cork is then removed and the plug of frozen wine plus yeast forces its way out. Surprisingly, when this is done carefully there is no massive gushing, and there is time for the bottle to be topped up with either base wine or sugared wine, and given its final corking and wiring.

This classic method of fermenting the second stage in the bottle is called the **méthode champenoise.**

Other, cheaper methods are used to produce sparkling wines. Quite good wines are produced by the closed tank method, in which the secondary fermentation is carried out in closed tanks under pressure at a temperature of around 13°C. The wine is filtered, but in such a way that the gas is not lost, and then bottled. These sparkling wines do not have the long period on the yeast, so they do not develop the taste I referred to earlier. And the gas bubbles will be larger and have a shorter life in the glass. Nevertheless these wines are excellent value for money.

The other method in use, is the carbonation method, in which the base wine is injected with the gas, rather in the way soda water is made. These wines are much inferior to those made by the methode champenoise, and they go flat quite quickly once poured into the glass.

## The amateur approach

We produce the base wine according to the basic requirements of it being sound, without too much characteristic aroma, and with its acidity at the higher end of our scale of acceptability. Then we have to follow through the méthode champenoise approach, bearing in mind our limited facilities.

First of all get the bottles ready, choosing them carefully, and rejecting any with obvious scratches. Such scratches are weak spots and can cause a failure of the bottle, with a consequent mess! Now clean them thoroughly and sterilise them. Now choose your stoppers. These will be plastic rather than cork, but there are various styles available, ranging from simple open-ended ones to spring-loaded reusable ones. Take your choice but do select them so that they fit the bottles properly. I say this because there are various sorts of sparkling wine bottles in use and not all the stoppers fit all of the bottles. The stoppers you will have chosen for this initial stage of the secondary fermentation will not be ones with closed ends of course, these being reserved for the final bottling after the yeast has been removed. But while you are selecting stoppers that fit, select the closed ended ones as well and attach the "final stopper" to each bottle with a rubber band. Then you will be sure that you will get a good fit.

Now dissolve 50 grams (2 oz) of granulated sugar in the 4.5 litres of base wine and fill the bottles to within an half inch of the place where the stopper will go down to in the bottle. Do not add more sugar than the amount mentioned, since too much pressure will then develop and the bottles will burst. In round figures, a sugar addition of 4 grams per litre, or 18 grams per 4.5 litres, will generate enough carbon dioxide gas to produce a pressure of one atmosphere in the bottle. Thus our addition will give just under three atmospheres; this is about half of what we find in the highest quality Champagne, but we need a safety margin since we are using second-hand bottles. A little more rehydrated yeast should be added to each bottle, after which the bottles should be closed with an open-ended stopper and the wire cage fitted. Following the commercial Champagne producers the bottles should be laid on their sides and stored for several months at a temperature around 15°C.

The riddling, or remuage, then follows. The simplest technique is to put the bottles into an empty wine carton, neck end downwards, and put a few books etc. under one end of the carton so that the bottles are on a slope. Each day or so give the bottles a gentle twist, and periodically increase the slope of the carton. Then leave the bottles upside down but vertical for three to six months.

Once again the testing time has arrived. First of all prepare a freezing mixture using the recipe given at the end of this section, and then immerse the neck end of the bottles into this mixture until the plug of yeast and associated wine is frozen. This usually takes about five minutes.

Now stand the bottles in an upright position and remove the cage and stopper very gently. I recommend that you wear a glove and use a cloth as well to hold the bottle. If you are careful the yeast will come out cleanly, and you will be able to fit a clean, closed-end stopper and wire cage before there is any significant loss of wine.

All this needs is practice, and you have the consolation that if you are clumsy the first time you will still have most of a bottle of sparkling wine; so have a jug ready to pour it into just in case.

A final point is that for those of us who are "cowards", or feel we are too clumsy to carry out the disgorging, there is always the beermakers' approach. Simply riddle the wine so that the yeast goes to the bottom of the bottle rather than the neck. Then chill it well, open the bottle carefully and pour out the wine into a jug, leaving behind the yeast deposit and just a little wine. It is an easy way to do things and many of us use this approach for our everyday sparkling wines.

Readers especially interested in making sparkling wines should see if they can lay their hands on "How to make wines with a sparkle", by John Restall and Don Hebbs. It is published by Argus Books Ltd., and though it is now out of print, copies can still be found in some homebrew shops.

**Freezing solution.** Mix together one part of common salt (sodium chloride) and three parts of crushed ice. This will give you a temperature of $-21.3^{\circ}C$.

# Chapter 8
# The First Gallons

## Introduction

In the previous chapters we have looked at the background to commercial winemaking and noted how the procedures have to be changed when we work on a smaller scale and use fruits other than the grape, as well as cereal, flower and vegetable ingredients. In the last chapter we saw how we have to adjust the must to allow for the shortcomings of our ingredients.

It is now time to run through the way of making one or two styles of wine from ingredients that have been processed for the food industry and which are quite suitable for inclusion in the simpler recipes. Typically we shall use the fruit juices found in supermarkets and food stores, and use them to make the lighter style of table wine; initially we will make a dry wine and then talk about the best way of changing this into a sweeter one. I will also add a short section on making wines from bought concentrates.

In Chapters 9 and 10 respectively I will extend the discussion to making other, more complex wines. Chapter 9 will be dedicated to wines more in the "country style", where the wines are based on comparatively simple recipes, in which one ingredient dominates. Typically we will consider making blackberry wine in two different styles. Chapter 10 will include more complex recipes which incorporate a mixture of different ingredients, where the aim is to make really top quality wines in particular commercial styles. In this way I hope to provide recipes for Winemakers of all philosophies.

We will start with an apple and grape juice recipe suitable for making a dry white table wine and run through the various steps from juice to wine.

With this and every other recipe I list the quantities of ingredients required to make 4.5 litres (one gallon) of wine. Should any reader want to make larger amounts he should simply multiply the amounts accordingly. With each recipe I give the quantities first in metric units (grams, millilitres, kilograms and litres) and then put the equivalent Imperial units (ounces, fluid ounces, pounds and gallons) in brackets. The metric units don't always convert into Imperial units to give whole numbers, of course, so I give the nearest whole number. This approximation makes a negligible difference to the final wine.

**Recipe for dry white table wine**

| Apple juice | 2 litres | (70 fl.oz) |
| White grape juice | 1 litre | (35 fl.oz) |
| Granulated sugar | 425 grams | (15 oz.) |
| Nutrient salts | sufficient | |
| Pectolytic enzyme | sufficient | |
| Water | to 4.5 litres | (to one gallon) |

For this wine I suggest that you visit the nearest supermarket and buy the cartons of apple and grape juices; the supermarket's own brands are normally the cheapest on the shelves and they are quite satisfactory. I have used juices from Asda, Marks and Spencer, Sainsbury and Waitrose and obtained excellent results, but fellow winemakers in other parts of the UK have found equal satisfaction with juices from their local store. In addition there are brands that have national circulation, and can often be found in Health Food shops; again these will do well.

As I mentioned in the last chapter, the only sugar you need consider using is granulated, and it doesn't matter whether it is beet or cane.

I have given a vague idea of the amounts of nutrient salts and pectolytic enzyme that are needed, and this is because it depends on the source of these materials. Thus with nutrient salts, I suggest that you use half a teaspoonful of the mixtures commonly sold in home brew shops, but if you can buy Gervin Minavit locally then you need a lot less. A quarter of a teaspoonful is plenty! Similarly if you have access to Gervin pectolytic enzyme tablets then use just half of a tablet for 4.5 litres. The type of enzyme sold as a white powder is very much weaker and you will need much more. Use it as instructed on the packet; my guideline is a teaspoonful of powder if no information is provided.

Your choice of yeast clearly depends on what is available to you, but do insist on a proper wine yeast that is packed in a sachet without nutrient or sugar diluent. Most good home brew shops now stock Gervin yeasts, all of which are professional wine yeasts. For this recipe I suggest Gervin No. 1 yeast (Green Label). This is a Bordeaux yeast that ferments out the must quite quickly and settles well afterwards, and gives no trace of yeastiness.

The water should be boiled first if it is particularly hard or has a hint of chlorination.

When the must is made up it has the potential to produce a wine with around 11% of alcohol, and an acid level of 5-6 grams per litre. I will explain how I arrive at these figures. First of all the must is likely to contain about 820-830 grams of sugar, some 400 grams coming from the juices and the rest from the granulated sugar. This gives us a concentration of say 825/4.5 grams per litre, or close to 18.3%, when the must is made up to 4.5 litres. On the basis of my rule of thumb of 10% giving 6% of alcohol, we can see that our must should produce around the 11% of alcohol quoted.

In calculating the likely acid level, I have taken the typical acid levels found in the juices (6-7 grams/litre), and allowed for the dilution of the 3 litres of juice to 4.5 litres. This gives a calculated acid level of between 4 and 4.7 grams per litre in the must. As we have seen, some extra acid is usually produced during the fermentation, so that the finished wine is likely to have an acid level of between 5 and 6 grams per litre. This is about right for the sort of wine we are trying to make, so the recipe does not call for more acid.

**Making up the must.** First of all clean the gallon jar (demijohn) thoroughly and sterilise it with some sodium metabisulphite solution. You should make up a 10% solution of this chemical in water and store it in a plastic bottle with a screw cap. Pour about 20 to 30 ml (say a fluid ounce) of the solution into the jar and then add a few crystals of citric acid. This will release sulphur dioxide gas (don't take great gulps of it) which is the active sterilising agent. Swill the solution around the jar, let it stay in the jar for a few minutes and then pour the solution away. Wash the jar out with cold water.

Now dissolve the sugar and nutrient salts in about a litre of the cold, previously boiled water, contained in the jar, and shake vigorously to get some air into the solution. Now add the juices and adjust the level of the solution in the jar to the shoulder of the jar by the addition of a little more water if necessary. But don't fill the jar to the brim because we must leave a little room to take care of any frothing.

Now add the pectolytic enzyme and the rehydrated yeast (see page 74 for details of the rehydration procedure). Plug the neck of the jar with clean cotton wool and cover it with a layer of cling film. This cotton wool/cling film combination allows gas bubbles to escape but prevents the inquisitive flies etc. from getting into the must. Alternatively you can use a fermentation trap (see page 20) rather than the cotton wool/cling film. The trap should be partly filled with water to act as a one-way seal. I prefer to use a trap straight away, but some Winemakers prefer to use the cotton wool/cling film closure because should the fermentation be a little too vigorous than the trap will get filled with fermenting must and be difficult to clear; the cotton wool plug can be thrown away and replaced with less trouble.

**The fermentation.** This will start within a few hours of the yeast being added to the must and will take anything from a week to two weeks to go to completion. The time depends on the temperature especially, and in my view this should be kept relatively cool (15 - 20°C) if possible, when the fermentation should take about ten days or so. If you have used the cotton wool plug as a closure, I suggest that you replace it with a fermentation trap after the first two or three days, since you can then follow the extent of the fermentation more easily. Thus the bubbles of carbon dioxide formed in the fermentation pass out through the water in the trap, and the rate at which the bubbles pass through the trap is an indication of the rate of fermentation. The fermentation can be judged complete when the flow of gas bubbles stops.

But let us return for the moment to the temperature of the ferment. Some winemakers are tempted to speed things up by standing the gallon jar on the surface of the central heating boiler or on a special hot plate. This is not recommended, since the yeast is largely at the bottom of the fermenting must and in direct contact with the hot glass surface. Not surprisingly it is not too happy at the prospect and frequently gives up and often breaks down giving the wine a very yeasty flavour. The ferment then stops and you will have a sweet sickly brew that will not be worth drinking! Generally speaking, white table wines should be made at lowish temperatures, so much so that I never make my white wines when the weather is very hot.

**Racking.** When the fermentation stops, the yeast cells settle to the bottom of the fermentation vessel. Once most of the yeast has settled, the wine should be syphoned off (racked) into a second clean sterile jar, and one teaspoonful of 10% sodium metabisulphite solution added to it. The liquid level is then taken right to the neck of the jar by the addition of a little boiled water, and a fermentation trap fitted. The sodium metabisulphite solution I refer to is really a solution of Campden tablets, so if you wish you can crush one of these tablets, dissolve it in a little water and add the solution to the wine. This chemical helps to persuade any yeast cells remaining in the wine to settle firmly on the bottom of the jar, so that the wine may then drop completely clear in another week or so. A second racking then gives us a clear wine ready for bottling.

It must be emphasised that the syphon tube must be clean and sterile before it is used. The gallon jar is tilted a little on its side and kept this way by placing a book or piece of wood under the raised edge. The syphon tube is then lowered gently into the wine, care being taken not to disturb the sediment (lees), and the end of the plastic tubing is sucked gently so as to fill the whole tubing with the wine. This is not a difficult thing to do, although occasionally you may suck a little too hard and get some wine in your mouth; not really a hazard! When the wine has almost filled the tubing, stop sucking and place your finger over the end to stop the wine running back into the jar. Now put the end of the tubing into the clean jar, which should be a foot or so lower, removing your finger just as the tubing enters the jar.

The wine from the first jar will run down into the clean jar. As the racking gets near the end lower the U-tube of the syphon as far as you can without disturbing the sediment. Done carefully the racking will remove virtually all of the wine from the sediment and there will be almost no wine lost.

**Clearing the wine.** There is a good chance that the wine will clear naturally after the first racking, but this does depend on the juices that you have used, and some yeasts may drop out very quickly. If the wine remains hazy then I recommend that you clear it by fining it. This means adding a substance that will combine with the haze particles and carry them to the bottom of the wine. We will talk about fining, and filtering, in Chapter 16, and see how fining works, and which fining agents are most suitable for specific wines. For the light white table wines I like to use a fining agent that is both gentle and quick.

Accordingly I use two-part finings. This is sold as two separate bottles of solution, one being silicic acid and the other gelatine. Half a spoonful of the silicic acid solution is added to the cloudy wine which must then be shaken very thoroughly. The same quantity of the gelatine solution is added next and the wine again shaken well. An immediate precipitate forms which settles overnight, leaving a sparklingly clear wine. The name silicic acid sounds faintly sinister, but it is really only pure silica (sand) changed into a hydrated form in suspension, and it is completely harmless. One tip, though. Do make sure that the wine is not full of gas bubbles because this will make the settling of the precipitate much slower. There are other fining agents that can be used and we will review their use in Chapter 16.

**Bottling.** Some winemakers, especially those with a much greater capacity than I, keep their wines in gallon jars and then use the wine as required. This is a little like having your own wine box, but without the opportunity of having it collapse as the wine is withdrawn. The bulk storage is quite alright if the whole gallon is going to be drunk within a day or so, such as at a party, but otherwise I believe it is better to put it into bottles. Another benefit of putting your wine into bottles is that this keeps the wine safe from attack, especially with respect to oxidation. Furthermore you can then put some of your wine on one side and let it mature for a few months before drinking it.

Prepare for bottling by cleaning and sterilising the bottles properly. Give the bottles a thorough brushing with the brush with a little detergent in the water. Then wash out the detergent solution and sterilise the bottles with sulphite solution (use a few fluid ounces of solution and pour it from bottle to bottle). Pour out the sterilising solution and rinse the bottles with water from the hot tap. Let the bottles drain.

Now rack the wine for the last time, add a teaspoonful of sulphite solution (or the solution of one crushed Campden tablet), and fill the bottles carefully. I find it best to fill the bottles to just above the shoulder by pouring the wine from the jar into

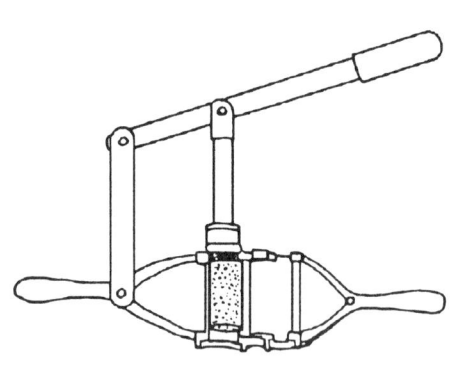

Figure 8.1

the bottles by means of a small funnel. I then do a final topping up by pouring in wine from a small jug.

**Corking.** While the bottles are being sterilised, get the corks ready. Soak them in warm water for 15 to 30 minutes. If you have any glycerol (glycerine), then put a teaspoonful into the soak water to help soften the corks. You may find it difficult to carry out the soaking because the corks float. I put the water in a small jug, add the corks and then put on top a bottle filled with sufficient water to weigh down the corks and keep them immersed. There is some merit in adding about half a teaspoonful of sulphite solution to say half a pint of water, so that the outside of the corks will have been sterilised.

When the bottles have been filled, remove the corks from their soaking, rinse them to wash away odd bits of cork dust etc. and remove the excess of water from the outside of the corks with a little clean kitchen paper.

The principle of corking is to compress the cork so that it is slightly smaller than the neck of the bottle and then push the cork into the bottle until the end of the cork is flush with the open end of the neck of the bottle. There are several hand corking guns that can be used to squeeze the cork and then plunge them into the neck of the bottle before they can spring back to their original diameter. I strongly recommend that you spend a few pounds on such a corker if you plan to make wine regularly (see Figure 8.1). They make corking an easy and quick process. But a warning. Place the bottle firmly on the floor between your feet before you force in the cork. If you try to do this on the bench top without holding it firmly it can slip away from you and you may spill some wine or even have a broken bottle.

There is a "poor man's" corking method that works quite well (see Figure 8.2). What you do is to put the end of the soaked cork into the neck of the bottle, and slide down the side of the cork a length of plastic coated copper wire. This wire creates a tiny channel down the side of the cork which lets out the air as the cork is forced in. All you have to do then is to thump the cork home by means of a wooden mallet, taking care not to whack the neck of the bottle of course. The last part of the cork insertion can be carried out with the aid of pressure from the handle of a plastic spoon if you are uncertain of your skills. As the cork is forced into the bottle so the air in the neck of the bottle escapes up the channel created by the wire. The wire is then pulled out and the corking is complete.

As an alternative to the wire you can use a piece of strong twine, putting it inside the neck of the bottle before you force home the cork.

**Storage and the maturation process.** The bottles should be allowed to stand upright for a couple of days to allow the corks to expand back to their normal size. They should then be stored by laying them down such that the wine remains in contact with the cork and keeps it moist. If you keep the bottles upright for too long the corks become dry and air can get into the wine and oxidise it, giving you an accidental "sherry" flavour.

This particular wine is a relatively light one and can be drunk quite quickly. Accordingly I suggest that you broach a bottle or two after it has been in bottle for five or six weeks. Leave the remaining bottles for the

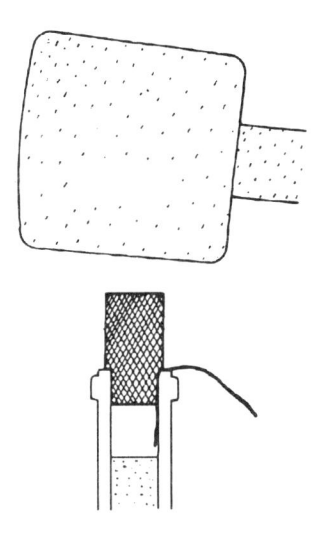

**Figure 8.2**

time being and test at monthly intervals. I have found that the wine is usually pretty good after four to six months, but begins to lose its character after a year or eighteen months. In other words it is a wine for fairly quick drinking.

# Modifying the recipe

**Sweetening.** Many wine drinkers prefer a wine that is sweeter. The most obvious way of satisfying this demand is to add the necessary amount of sugar to the wine. Although this can be done just before the wine is bottled, this is an uncertain practice because even the clearest wine is likely to have some yeast cells still. Then refermentation can take place and you will get an unintentional sparkling wine. Unfortunately this can result in blown corks, a mess and lost wine, or much worse the bottle might explode. The exploding bottle is really quite dangerous and it is best avoided by adding the sugar to the dry wine an hour or so before you want to drink it. You won't get quite the harmonious effect that you would by sweetening the wine and storing it as such but it is much safer. The alternative is to stabilise the wine chemically or pasteurise it. The chemical approach is easier and is carried out by adding both sulphite (or a Campden tablet) and a small amount of potassium sorbate. The latter chemical, which is a permitted food additive, kills the remaining yeast and so prevents further fermentation. You can buy potassium sorbate in little packs or tablets, one being sufficient for the treatment of a gallon of wine. If the additions are done at the recommended level, the taste of the wine will not be affected.

In my view you will get a much nicer wine if you use fruit juice rather than sugar to sweeten the wine. My practice is to make my base apple and grape wine just a little bit stronger, by adding 500 grams of sugar (18 ounces). The alcohol level then goes up to 12% or a little bit more. Then to each gallon of the dry wine I add half a litre (say a pint) of apple juice. This dilutes the wine, of course, and lowers the alcohol level to about 10.5%, and sweetens it nicely. The extra aroma of the apple juice also improves the wine. The result then takes on the style of a German table wine in the Liebfraumilch style, so much so that a neighbour of mine swears that he can't tell the difference between my five-week old sweetened wine and a very well known brand of German wine.

**Changing the flavour.** You can ring the changes on the basic recipe and get a little variety in your white table wines. One approach is to use two litres of grape juice and one of apple juice, then cutting down the sugar that you add by 100 grams (4 ounces) to allow for the extra sugar content of the grape juice. You can also get somewhat different wines by using different brands of juice. One example is the use of Muscat grape juice that is to be found in a number of supermarkets, including Asda.

Rather larger flavour changes can be brought about by putting in up to half a litre of either pineapple or orange juice and dropping the amount of grape to the same extent. Really adventurous winemakers should try adding comparatively small amounts of some of the tropical fruit juices in place of some of the grape; do try juice containing passion fruit, but don't use more than 250 ml (9 fluid ounces) in a gallon of must. If you look around the shelves of good food stores and health food shops you will come across all sorts of nectars and syrups that can be added to your basic must. I suggest that you try the apricot nectar if you plan to make a rather sweeter wine; another one to try is peach nectar.

A final change you can make is to add both extra flavour and extra body by adding the contents of a small can of peaches. Get a 15 ounce tin of good quality peaches and puree the contents in a blender; then add this puree to the must before you start the fermentation, allowing for the extra volume of the puree by reducing the amount of water that you use. This addition will give you a more full-bodied wine with about 12% alcohol. It will give you a wine that goes down well at summer parties, especially if it has been chilled.

Many winemakers like to make a wine based on oranges or similar fruits. We shall consider a recipe using fresh oranges in the next chapter (page 109) but to start with let us again take advantage of the products prepared for the food industry, namely orange juice and frozen orange juice.

One thing that must be appreciated is that producers of orange juice go to a fair amount of trouble to retain the cloudiness of fresh juice, which means that they try to stabilise the cloud formed by pectic substances. We can counteract this by adding plenty of pectolytic enzyme. The other point I should make is that cartons and bottles of orange juice are really intended for our breakfast tables, and some brands may have added flavour and acid. Such drinks may be fine for drinking but will be less suitable if we want to make a decent wine. The moral is to look closely at the label and buy only juices that have not had flavourings etc. added to them.

Most of the juices in one-litre cartons will have been made from concentrated orange juice. While satisfactory wines can be made from such juices they do lack something of the quality of freshly-pressed juice, and I suggest that you look around the shelves of your local supermarket to find bottles of fresh juice.

The recipe that follows is for a simple "social" style of wine, intended for drinking at parties or at gatherings of friends as at wine circle meetings.

**Recipe for 4.5 litres (one gallon) of orange wine**

| | | |
|---|---|---|
| Orange juice | 1 litre | (35 fl.oz.) |
| Apple juice | 500 ml | (18 fl.oz.) |
| Granulated sugar | 860 grams | (30 oz.) |
| Tartaric acid | 5 grams | (1 tsp.) |
| Nutrient salts (Gervin Minavit) | 1 gram | (1/4 tsp.) |
| Pectolytic enzyme (Gervin) | 1 tablet | |
| Gervin No.1 yeast | 1 sachet | |
| Boiled water | to 4.5 litres | (to 1 gallon) |
| Sugar for sweetening | 225 grams | (8 oz) |

In this recipe, and in subsequent ones too, I have specified Gervin Minavit (nutrient salts), pectolytic enzyme and yeast, because I know that these are the most reliable. If these products are not available locally then replace the 1/4 teaspoonful of Minavit with one teaspoonful of standard nutrient salts, and the pectolytic enzyme tablet with a heavy dose of whatever pectolytic enzyme product you can find. For yeast buy a sachet of dried wine yeast that does not contain nutrient salts or sugar, and ask the advice of the proprietor of your home brew shop about the best brand to use.

The recipe is designed to produce a wine containing just over 13% of alcohol and an acid level of about 5 grams per litre. I have put in some apple juice since it improves the fruitiness necessary for this kind of social wine, but you can replace it with grape juice if you prefer; the small amount of extra sugar this gives the must will produce a little more alcohol in the finished wine, but this will not come amiss.

Make up the must as for the apple and grape wine and ferment to dryness, but keep back the 225 grams of sugar that I have listed separately. This is to be added to the wine after it has finished working and has dropped completely clear. If you want to play safe and avoid the risk of refermentation, then bottle the wine dry and add about 35 grams of sugar to each bottle of wine about an hour before you intend drinking the wine. I suggest that with this wine you do sweeten it in bulk, but stabilise it by adding 5 ml (one teaspoonful) of 10% sodium metabisulphite solution (or one crushed Campden tablet), together with one gram of potassium sorbate. I mentioned earlier that this can be bought in sachets containing a gram, which is just enough for one gallon of wine. I recommend that you dissolve this sorbate in a small amount of water, and add the solution to the wine, rather than adding the powder directly to the wine. But you must use both potassium sorbate and sodium metabisulphite together, because if you leave out the sulphite the wine can oxidise rather easily, and there is the possibility that bacteria may infect the wine and attack the sorbate. This attack is not common, but it can occur unless sulphite is there to kill the bacteria, and if an attack does take place the wine develops the distinctive taste and smell of "geraniums".

This combined sorbate/sulphite treatment normally prevents any further fermentation of sugar, and it is quite unusual for the yeast to recover. My approach is to keep the treated wine in the gallon jar for a further three or four weeks as an extra precaution, and just in case there is any sediment formation. I haven't had problems with sediment forming in this apple and orange wine, but it can sometimes take place with stabilised wines and it is infuriating to find that the beautifully clear wine that you have bottled throws a haze or deposit in a week or so's time.

I then bottle my stabilised wine in the usual way, but I take care not to let it splash too much as it runs into the bottle. The point of this is to stop the wine collecting too much air, which might encourage the odd surviving yeast cell (or yeast cells that inevitably pervade all wine making areas) from multiplying and causing problems. If you are the "belt and braces" type then treat the wine with a further half teaspoonful of 10% sulphite solution before the final bottling.

An alternative to using cartons or bottles of orange juice is to use frozen orange juice. I have had good results with all the brands that I have tried. I take two 174 ml (6.25 fl.oz.) packs of frozen orange juice and make it up into roughly a litre with boiled water. It can then be used in the recipe I have given for orange wine.

If you prefer to have a dry orange wine, then cut down the sugar to 700 grams (25 oz.), ferment out completely and bottle without sweetening up the wine. This gives a wine with rather less alcohol, and is more suitable as a table wine. I strongly recommend that you use either the freshly pressed juice or the frozen juice if you are making the dry version of the wine, since wines made from cartons of reconstituted concentrated juice can have a hint of bitterness.

# Making a rosé wine

Various red fruit juices or syrups are available in food stores and health food shops, blackcurrant being a favourite. If you search hard you may be able to find syrups of fruits such as blackberry; I found the French Monin brand of blackberry (Sirop de Mûre) especially good. Be a little careful in your choice of syrup, though, because some may be stabilised against fermentation and contain the inhibitor sodium benzoate. This will make the task of the yeast more difficult, even when the syrup is well diluted, and the fermentation may stop when there is still some sugar left unconverted.

The recipe that follows is for a simple, refreshing rosé wine that is medium dry, and makes use of easily available blackcurrant drinks. One of the brand leaders is Ribena, and my recipe is based on that, but other brands may be equally satisfactory.

**Recipe for 4.5 litres of medium-dry rosé wine**

| | | |
|---|---|---|
| Blackcurrant cordial (e.g. Ribena) | 340 ml | (12 fl.oz.) |
| Apple juice | 500 ml | (18 fl.oz.) |
| Granulated sugar | 600 grams | (21 oz.) |
| Nutrient (Minavit) | 1 gram | (1/4 tsp.) |
| Pectolytic enzyme (Gervin) | 1/2 tablet | |
| Yeast (Gervin No.1) | 1 sachet | |
| Boiled water | to 4.5 litres | (to 1 gallon) |

The must is made up as before, by dissolving the sugar and nutrient salts in about 2 litres of water, and then adding the fruit juices. Dilute with more water such that the must comes to the shoulder of the jar, then add the pectolytic enzyme and the yeast. When the fermentation is complete and the wine racked and subsequently completely clear, add sufficient sugar to sweeten up the wine to a medium dry one. For my palate this means adding about 100 grams (4 ounces) of sugar to the gallon of wine, and then stabilising with sorbate and sulphite. Some readers may prefer their wine to be rather sweeter, and will wish to increase the amount of sugar added.

If you want the wine to have rather more fruit character then add 500 ml of apple juice rather than the sugar. Either way I suggest that you serve this wine well chilled. It goes down splendidly at summer barbecues!

# Making wine from grape concentrates

As we saw earlier, the quality of grape concentrates is rather variable, and on occasion it may be diluted with glucose syrup. Some of these modified concentrates make perfectly acceptable wines, but I do suggest that you replace the yeast that is provided with a known brand of true wine yeast. Thus while some manufacturers supply a true wine yeast, this is not always the case.

I assume that any reader of this book will be genuinely interested in making wines from chosen ingredients rather than producing a "kit" wine, and with this in mind I suggest that you look for a straight grape concentrate with a label that states the country of origin. I find it more convenient to use white grape juice than white grape concentrate, particularly since the latter may be rather darker than I like.

But I do not buy red grape juice from the supermarkets because all the ones I have looked at are rather an apology for a red juice, the colour tending to an orange. Good red grape concentrate is a much better bet for making red table wines in my view. Decent concentrates are imported from Italy and Spain in particular, and more recently concentrates have been coming from Eastern European countries such as Hungary. I particularly like some of the concentrates said to be made from the juice of named grape varieties.

As with all fruit concentrates, the manufacturing process strips out much of the aroma; some manufacturers collect these aroma chemicals and return them to the concentrate, but this is not always done. As a consequence the reconstituted juice tends to lack aroma and this is reflected in the lack of nose of the wine they produce. There are two ways of improving the aroma of the wines made from such concentrates, one being to add a little fresh fruit juice to the must, and the second is to use a yeast that is notable for its ability to produce a fine fruity nose.

To make a gallon of dry red table wine I suggest that you take a standard kilo can of concentrate, dilute the contents with water, and add 225 grams (8 ounces) of granulated sugar to bring the juice up to strength. You can add a little blackcurrant juice if you want the wine to have a commercial note, and you should add the usual amounts of nutrient salts and pectolytic enzyme. I recommend that you use Gervin Varietal D yeast, since this produces a real bonus in respect of the bouquet. It will also metabolise some of the malic acid present (see Chapter 11, page 162) though, which may leave the wine just a little flat on the palate. If this seems to be the case then add 5 grams (one teaspoonful) of tartaric acid to the gallon of finished wine.

If you like a hint of oak vanilla in your wine add the recommended amount of Gervin Oak Granules, or your own prepared oak chips (see page 75) to the must at the start of the fermentation. I "improve" the flavour and nose of some of my red table wines by adding a small amount of Gervin Superior Port Essence, and I recommend this for all wines that are just a little below par on depth of taste.

In Chapter 10 we will be looking at how to make our wines approach the standard set by good commercial grape wines, and I shall then have more to say about the best way of getting the right flavour mix.

# Chapter 9
# Country Wines

## Introduction

Many winemakers have a touch of nostalgia and feel that we are missing out in some way if we make all our wines so as to imitate particular styles of commercial wine. While much of my own winemaking is unashamedly designed to produce wines of commercial quality, with flavours to match, there is a lot to be said for making wines that reflect the beautiful flavours that characterise many of our country fruits. If we let one fruit dominate the must, then the wine will obviously reflect this. But why not? We happily buy fruit liqueurs and drink apricot and peach brandies with gusto, and never run them down as being "non-commercial", so why not cash in on the special qualities of our native fruits etc.

The problem with the so-called country wines in the past has been that many of the recipes have been ill thought out, and include massive amounts of sugar that no yeast could hope to ferment. The result is often a sickly sweet beverage, of relatively low alcohol content, frequently with glaring defects. Recipes have been handed down without a thought of whether the wines they produce can give any kind of balance of flavour, sweetness and bouquet. Even now we find authors offering recipes with four or more pounds to the gallon, or made from ingredients with little or no acid content. If you add to this the recommendation to use bakers' yeast, it is hardly surprising that home produced wines get a bad press.

In this chapter I want to give much better recipes for country wines in which one particular ingredient dominates. This may be for blackberry or gooseberry wines, for instance, in which the lovely flavours of these fruits show through. More than that I want to give recipes that will show these ingredients at their best. Thus with blackberry, a splendid flavour, I will give two recipes, one for a dry wine of moderate alcohol levels that will be suitable for drinking with a meal, and the other a stronger, sweeter wine in the social style that will give us a lift in the cold winter's evenings when we entertain our friends. In each case I will give a straightforward recipe but at the same time I will suggest ways in which we might add a touch of sophistication that will take the wine "up market".

# The recipes

First of all I have provided a table listing most of the more likely winemaking ingredients, with a suggestion of the type of wine the ingredient is best for, and a recommendation of which yeast to use. The table reflects my personal preferences, of course, and some readers may wish to make a somewhat different style. With banana, for instance, I find the flavour rather intense and I suggest making a heavy sweet wine. If any reader wants to make this wine dry, all that has to be done is to leave out the sweetening stage; and the alcohol level can be reduced by dropping the sugar level to an appropriate extent.

Table 9.1 Ingredients and Wine Types

| Ingredient | Recipe number | Type of wine | Yeast variety |
|---|---|---|---|
| Apple | 9.1 | Dry-medium | B or E |
| Apple | 9.2 | Medium-sweet social | C |
| Apricot | 9.3 | Medium-sweet social | 3 |
| Banana | 9.4 | Sweet | 3 or C |
| Blackberry | 9.5 | Dry table | 2 or A |
| Blackberry | 9.6 | Medium-sweet social | 3 |
| Blackcurrant | 9.7 | Medium-dry rosé | 1 |
| Cherry | 9.8 | Medium-sweet social | 3 |
| Damson | 9.9 | Medium sweet social | D |
| Elderberry | 9.10 | Dry table | 2 or A |
| Gooseberry | 9.11 | Dry table | 3 or 5 |
| Gooseberry | 9.12 | Sweet social | 3 or C |
| Greengage | 9.13 | Sweet social | 3 |
| Grapefruit | 9.14 | Aperitif | 1 |
| Lemon | 9.15 | Aperitif | 1 |

**Table 9.1 (contd.)**

| Ingredient | Recipe number | Type of wine | Yeast variety |
|---|---|---|---|
| Loganberry | 9.16 | Sweet social | 3 |
| Mulberry | 9.17 | Dry table | 2 |
| Orange | 9.18 | Sweet social | 3 |
| Peach | 9.19 | Medium-sweet social | 5 |
| Pear | 9.20 | Dry table | 5 |
| Pineapple | 9.21 | Medium-sweet social | 3 |
| Plum | 9.22 | Dessert | 3 or C |
| Raspberry | 9.23 | Sweet social | 3 |
| Redcurrant | 9.24 | Dry-medium rosé | B |
| Rhubarb | 9.25 | Sparkling | C |
| Rhubarb | 9.26 | Sweet social | D |
| Sloe | 9.27 | Dry table | 2, D |
| Strawberry | 9.28 | Medium-sweet social | 1 |
| Whitecurrant | 9.29 | Dry table | 5 or B |
| Cereals | 9.30 | Sweet social | D |
| Carrot | 9.31 | Sweet social | D |
| Parsnip | 9.32 | Sweet table | D |
| Elderflower | 9.33 | Medium-sweet social | 1 |
| Rose petal | 9.34 | Medium-sweet social | 1 |
| Dandelion | 9.35 | Medium-sweet social | 1 |
| Honey | 9.36 | Medium-sweet mead | E |
| Folly | 9.37 | Dry table | 1 |
| Ginger | 9.38 | Sweet social | 1 |

I have listed the variety of Gervin brand yeast that is likely to work best with each ingredient. If your local supplier does not stock this brand, first suggest that he should, and if that doesn't work then ask him for the nearest equivalent that he keeps in stock.

**Recipe 9.1 Apple Wine (Dry-medium Table)**

| | | |
|---|---|---|
| Fresh apple juice | 2.5 litres | (4.5 pints) |
| Granulated sugar | 650 grams | (1lb 7oz) |
| Tartaric acid | 2.5 grams | (1/2 tsp.) |
| Pectolytic enzyme | 1/2 tablet | |
| Minavit nutrient | 2.5 grams | (1/2 tsp.) |
| Bentonite | 5 grams | (1 tsp.) |
| Gervin Varietal B or E yeast | 1 sachet | |
| Boiled water | to 4.5 litres | (to 1 gallon) |

The wine should have an alcohol content of around 12%, making it very suitable for drinking with a meal. It can be sweetened up to the dry-medium style by adding about 100 grams of sugar to the bulk wine and stabilising with sorbate and sulphite before bottling. Alternatively you can sweeten up the wine to suit your palate an hour or so before you intend drinking it.

The amount specified for the nutrient should be doubled if any nutrient other than Minavit is used; with all future recipes Minavit is specified, but the simpler and cheaper mixes of nutrient will usually be satisfactory if used in the larger amounts. Use Gervin pectolytic enzyme tablets if you can get them, but otherwise use adequate quantities of the less powerful powdered variety. If you can get granular bentonite then use it in preference to the powdered variety, since it has been especially prepared for the wine industry and is easy to hydrate. If you have to use the bentonite powder, which is easier to purchase, then make sure that you get this into a slurry before you add it to the must; the simplest way is to use a kitchen whisk.

If you can, use a mixture of cooking and eating apples (see page 29), and go easy on the Bramley Seedlings variety; always use a mix of varieties if possible. Juice the apples by one of the methods described in Chapter 5, add the pectolytic enzyme and allow the juice to settle overnight. Rack off the clear juice from the deposit and place it in your fermentation jar.

Dissolve the sugar and acid in about a litre of the water and add to the apple juice, add enough extra water to bring the level of the must up to the shoulder of the jar, and then shake well to mix the juice and sugar solution. Add the minavit, bentonite slurry and rehydrated yeast, and plug the neck of the bottle with clean cotton wool and cover with clingfilm. If you wish, the fermentation lock can be inserted even at this early stage.

Carry out the fermentation as described in Chapter 8 (page 86), and bottle and stabilise the wine when the fermentation is complete and the wine is clear. This wine will benefit from two or three months in the bottle before it is drunk.

## Recipe 9.2 Apple Wine (Medium-sweet Social)

This recipe is included for the benefit of those readers who have limited facilities for juicing their apples and would like to make their wines by "fermenting on the pulp". This recipe is designed to produce a wine containing between 13 and 14% alcohol, and to be medium sweet.

| | | |
|---|---|---|
| Mixed apples | 2 kg | (4.5 lbs) |
| Sultanas | 450 grams | (1 lb) |
| Granulated sugar | 500 grams | (1lb 2 oz) |
| Minavit nutrient | 2-3 grams | (1/2 tsp.) |
| Pectolytic enzyme | 1 tablet | |
| Gervin Varietal C yeast | 1 sachet | |
| Boiled water | to 4.5 litres | (to 1 gallon) |
| Sugar for sweetening | 300-350 grams | 11-12 oz |

Because the apple pulp is to be used, the apples should be peeled before they are either pulped or chopped up into little pieces. Remember that the chopped or pulped apples will oxidise readily so add 5 ml (1 tsp.) of 10% sulphite solution together with about two litres of water to cover the apple. Wash and chop the sultanas and place them and the apples in the fermentation vessel; this will have to be big enough to hold the bulk, and can be either one of the special brewing vessels or a plastic bucket. Add the sugar (but leaving out that reserved for later sweetening), the nutrient and the pectolytic enzyme. Stir well to dissolve the sugar; this will also get rid of most of the sulphite which is no longer needed. Now add the rehydrated yeast, cover the fermenter and let the yeast do its work for the next four or five days. Each night and morning give the mixture a gentle stir to make sure that the apples and sultanas get a regular immersion.

After this initial period of fermentation remove the solids by means of a sieve and put the liquid into a normal fermentation jar. If you pulped the apples, a lot of the pulp will have come through the sieve, but this can be removed at the first racking stage. When the fermenting must is placed in the demijohn the level of liquid should be just above the shoulder; water should be added at this stage if it is needed. Exact quantities of water cannot be given here because it depends on just how much juice came out of the fruit and how much pulp comes through into the jar.

The fermentation is then allowed to go to completion under a fermentation trap, racked again, the liquid level then taken to the neck of the demijohn, and the jar put on one side to allow it to drop clear. Fine if necessary and then bottle. The sweetening sugar can be added before bottling if the wine is stabilised or it can be added in appropriate amounts as each bottle of dry wine is prepared for drinking. The amount of sugar suggested for sweetening may be increased or decreased to suit the taste buds, but it should not be increased too much since the wine does not have enough body to permit a massive dose of sugar.

### Recipe 9.3 Apricot Wine (Medium-sweet Social)

As we saw in Chapter 5, dried apricots may often be preferred to fresh ones, since the fresh fruit we get in this country does not always reach the proper level of ripeness. Because of this I have given two possible recipes, one for fresh fruit and the other for dried fruit. Even if fresh apricots do come up to our requirements, they will not be available all the year round, so dried fruit will then come into its own.

| | | |
|---|---|---|
| Fresh apricots | 2 kg | (4.5 lbs) |
| Granulated sugar | 900 grams | (2 lbs) |
| Pectolytic enzyme | 1/2 tablet | |
| Minavit nutrient | 2-3 grams | (1/2 tsp) |
| Gervin No.3 yeast | 1 sachet | |
| Boiled water | to 4.5 litres | to 1 gallon |
| Sugar for sweetening | 300-350 grams | 11-12 oz |

Dissolve the sugar (except that required for subsequent sweetening), nutrient, and pectolytic enzyme in about three litres of the water. Now de-stone the fruit, chop it into small pieces and add it to the solution. Rehydrate the yeast and add it to the must which should be in the fermentation bin. Cover the bin and ferment on the pulp. Now continue as in recipe 8.2 (apple and sultana).

If you prefer to use dried apricots use the following recipe:

| | | |
|---|---|---|
| Dried apricots | 500 grams | (18 oz) |
| Sultanas | 250 grams | (9 oz) |
| Granulated sugar | 680 grams | (1 lb 8 oz) |
| Pectolytic enzyme | 1 tablet | |
| Minavit nutrient | 2-3 grams | (1/2 tsp.) |
| Gervin No.3 yeast | 1 sachet | |
| Boiled water | to 4.5 litres | (to 1 gallon) |
| Sugar for sweetening | 300-350 grams | (11-12 oz) |

Dissolve the sugar, pectolytic enzyme and nutrient in about three litres of water. Wash, then chop up the dried fruit and add it to the solution. Add the yeast and ferment as before, with the standard racking, stabilising and bottling procedures.

With both these recipes, as with Recipe 9.2, and indeed for all the others that follow which use solid ingredients, the aim should be to use sufficient water in the first stage, but not too much. Then after the removal of the solids, the fermenting must should be put into a clean demijohn and the level brought up to just above the shoulder of the jar. After the next racking the jar is topped right up to the neck.

### Recipe 9.4  Banana Wine (Sweet and Full-bodied)

| | | |
|---|---|---|
| Bananas (flesh) | 3 kg | (6-7 lbs) |
| Muscat raisins | 250 grams | (9 oz) |
| Granulated sugar | 350 grams | (12.5 oz) |
| Pectolytic enzyme | 1/2 tablet | |
| Minavit nutrient | 2-3 grams | (1/2 tsp) |
| Tartaric acid | 5 grams | (1 tsp) |
| Gervin No.3 yeast | 1 sachet | |
| Boiled water | to 4.5 litres | to 1 gallon |
| Sugar for sweetening | 350-400 grams | (12-14 oz) |

Select the bananas when they are over-ripe and peel them. Pulp the flesh and place in the fermentation bin, covering it with about two litres of water containing the sugar, nutrient, pectolytic enzyme and tartaric acid. Wash and chop the raisins and add them to the bin. Add the rehydrated yeast, ferment on the pulp for three to four days, then remove the pulp and complete the fermentation, racking, sweetening, stabilising and bottles in the way described earlier.

The wine should contain about 14% of alcohol and have a fairly strong and distinctive flavour.

### Recipe 9.5  Blackberry Wine (Dry Table)

The aim with this wine is to make a blackberry wine that retains its distinctive flavour but which is suitable for drinking with a meal. It should contain around 12% of alcohol and have an acidity of about 5 grams per litre.

| | | |
|---|---|---|
| Ripe blackberries | 1350 grams | (3 lbs) |
| Granulated sugar | 900 grams | (2 lbs) |
| Tartaric acid | 5 grams | (1 tsp) |
| Pectolytic enzyme | 1/2 tablet | |
| Minavit nutrient | 1-2 grams | (1/4 tsp) |
| Gervin No.2 or | | |
| Varietal A yeast | 1 sachet | |
| Boiled water | to 4.5 litres | (to 1 gallon) |

This wine is made by the standard pulp fermentation method. The fruit should be selected and prepared as described in Chapters 4 and 5.

Some readers may like to try a little variation on this recipe by incorporating some red grape concentrate into the must, since this will give roundness without distorting the blackberry flavour. I suggest using some 170 ml (6 fl oz) of concentrate, and allowing for its sugar content by reducing the granulated sugar in the recipe to 800 grams (1 lb 12 oz). Further sophistication can be achieved if a couple of teaspoonsful of oak granules are added to the must, while an extra smoothness is evident if 5 ml of Gervin maturing solution are added to the wine at the first racking.

This wine needs about six months of bottle age to reach its peak, but if the oak granules and maturing solution have been added the effect is to reduce the waiting time by a couple of months.

**Recipe 9.6  Blackberry Wine (Medium-sweet Social)**

If we want a wine for slurping, then it is difficult to beat one based on blackberries. The recipe that follows is essentially the same as the previous one, except for the addition of some sultanas, which increases the sugar content of the must such that the alcohol level rises to around 14%. Again I have suggested a medium-sweet finish, but the wine has sufficient body for a higher level of sweetness if that is what your palate prefers.

| | | |
|---|---|---|
| Blackberries | 1350 grams | (3 lbs) |
| Sultanas | 225 grams | (8 oz) |
| Granulated sugar | 850 grams | (1 lb 14 oz) |
| Pectolytic enzyme | 1/2 tablet | |
| Minavit nutrient | 1-2 grams | (1/4 tsp) |
| Gervin No.3 yeast | 1 sachet | |
| Boiled water | to 4.5 litres | (to one gallon) |
| Sugar for sweetening | 300-350 grams | (11-12 oz) |

Apart from the sultanas, which should be prepared in the usual way, this wine is made just like the dry version, but sweetened up with the extra sugar.

**Recipe 9.7  Blackcurrant Wine (Medium-dry Rosé)**

This gives a lovely fruity wine of just under 11% alcohol, and when sweetened slightly is just what we need for summer parties. Although the flavour is that of the blackcurrants, I have included some white grape juice to round it out. The result in many ways is rather like the famous Cassis, which is made by adding a little blackcurrant liqueur to a white grape wine, and it is equally suitable as an aperitif if served well chilled.

| | | |
|---|---|---|
| Blackcurrants | 340 grams | (12 oz) |
| White grape juice | 500 ml | (18 fl oz) |
| Granulated sugar | 700 grams | (1 lb |
| Pectolytic enzyme | 1/2 tablet | |
| Minavit nutrient | 2-3 grams | (1/2 tsp) |
| Gervin No.1 yeast | 1 sachet | |
| Boiled water | to 4.5 litres | (to 1 gallon) |
| Sugar for sweetening | 100 grams | (4 oz) |

As the amount of solid fruit is so small this fermentation can be carried out in the demijohn, but the fruit should be removed after just three days so that the amount of tannin that will be extracted from the blackcurrants is kept fairly low. Otherwise the fermentation through to bottling follows the standard method.

**Recipe 9.8 Cherry Wine (Medium-sweet Social)**

Unless you have a cherry tree this is a fairly expensive wine to make, so go for it and use really ripe juicy black cherries; they make much better wines than the whitehearts.

| Black cherries | 1.5 kg | (4 lbs) |
| --- | --- | --- |
| Sultanas | 250 grams | (9 oz) |
| Granulated sugar | 680 grams | (1 lb 8 oz) |
| Tartaric acid | 5 grams | (1 tsp) |
| Pectolytic enzyme | 1/2 tablet | |
| Minavit nutrient | 2-3 grams | (1/2 tsp) |
| Gervin yeast No.3 | 1 sachet | |
| Boiled water | to 4.5 litres | (to 1 gallon) |
| Sugar for sweetening | 300-350 grams | (11-12 oz) |

Make this wine as for any wine made by fermenting on the pulp; remove the stones from the cherries if you can.

**Recipe 9.9 Damson Wine (Medium-sweet Social)**

Damsons make a lovely medium-sweet social wine provided the fruit is ripe. If this is so the stones can be removed without difficulty. As with the other medium-sweet social wines, we are aiming for around 14% of alcohol in the finished wine with a fair level of sweetness.

| Ripe damsons | 1 kg | (2 lbs 3 oz) |
| --- | --- | --- |
| Sultanas | 250 grams | (9 oz) |
| Granulated sugar | 860 grams | (1 lb 14 oz) |
| Pectolytic enzyme | 1/2 tablet | |
| Minavit nutrient | 2-3 grams | (1/2 tsp) |
| Gervin Varietal D yeast | 1 sachet | |
| Boiled water | to 4.5 litres | (to 1 gallon) |
| Sugar for sweetening | 300-350 grams | (11-12 oz) |

There are one or two points worth mentioning. First of all make sure that you get true damsons, and not "damson plums". Secondly, I recommend Varietal D yeast because this breaks down about 20-30% of the malic acid coming from the damsons, and in so doing produces a little extra alcohol. This yeast also gives the wine a particularly good bouquet. If you cannot get this particular yeast then use Gervin No.3 yeast.

I always "improve" my damson wine by adding a little oakiness with oak granules and by smoothing out the initially rough edges by adding 5 ml of Gervin maturing solution. Neither addition is vital but both improve the wine.

**Recipe 9.10  Elderberry Wine (Dry Table)**

This is the classic red wine made by amateurs. But success depends on the careful selection and processing the fruit (see page 36). The following recipe will give a wine of 12% alcohol. Ideally the wine should be kept in bottle for a year or so to reach its peak. If drunk earlier than this it will still show a little too much astringency because of the tannin that has been extracted from the skins of the berries. There are two ways of making the wine ready for drinking rather quicker than this. The first method is to reduce the time of fermentation on the pulp to a maximum of three days; this results in less tannin being extracted, and the formation of a lighter style of wine. In commercial terms it will be a Valpolicella rather than a Claret! The second method of smoothing out the wine and making it ready for earlier drinking is to add some oak granules to the initial must and Gervin maturing solution to the wine.

| Ripe elderberries | 1.5 kg | (4 lbs) |
| --- | --- | --- |
| White grape juice | 500 ml | (18 fl oz) |
| Granulated sugar | 680 grams | (1 lb 8 oz) |
| Pectolytic enzyme | 1/2 tablet | |
| Minavit nutrient | 2-3 grams | (1/2 tsp) |
| Gervin No.2 or Varietal A yeast | 1 sachet | |
| Boiled water | to 4.5 litres | (to 1 gallon) |

If you do make the additions to get a wine for earlier drinking, keep a bottle back and taste it after a year. It will be superb.

**Recipe 9.11  Gooseberry Wine (Dry Table)**

Again we are making a 12% alcohol wine, and one that this time will grace any fish dish. It is one of my favourites, and made well has a hint of Sancerre about it. The secret is to use culinary gooseberries that are really ripe, and to extract the juice from them by the freezing method I described on page 51.

| Ripe culinary gooseberries | 1 kg | (2 lbs 3 oz) |
| --- | --- | --- |
| White grape juice | 500 ml | (18 fl oz) |
| Granulated sugar | 750 grams | (1 lb 10 oz) |
| Pectolytic enzyme | 1/2 tablet | |
| Minavit nutrient | 2-3 grams | (1/2 tsp) |
| Oak granules or chips | 7-8 grams | (1/4 oz) |
| Gervin No.5 yeast | 1 sachet | |
| Boiled water | to 4.5 litres | (to 1 gallon) |

This is an all-juice recipe, so the initial fermentation can be carried out in the demijohn.

### Recipe 9.12  Gooseberry Wine (Sweet Social)

The wine will have a fairly full flavour and if you wish you can increase the mouthfeel by including as an extra about half a pound (225 grams) of ripe banana flesh. For this wine you must use dessert gooseberries that are absolutely ripe but not splitting open. I think that you get the best results if you again extract the juice from the gooseberries first, but a reasonable wine will be produced if you ferment on the pulp but for not more than three days. The wine will contain about 14% alcohol. If you really want the maximum of flavour then increase the gooseberry content by a further 500 grams (18 oz) but use Varietal D yeast to help reduce the level of malic acid to some extent.

| | | |
|---|---|---|
| Dessert gooseberries | 1.5 kg | (4 lbs) |
| Sultanas | 250 grams | (9 oz) |
| Granulated sugar | 750 grams | (1 lb 10 oz) |
| Pectolytic enzyme | 1 tablet | |
| Minavit nutrient | 2-3 grams | (1/2 tsp) |
| Gervin No.3 or | | |
| Varietal C yeast | 1 sachet | |
| Boiled water | to 4.5 litres | (to 1 gallon) |
| Sugar for sweetening | 350-400 grams | (12-14 oz) |

This wine will have a slightly higher acid level than most of those we have considered so far, but this will match perfectly the flavour, alcohol level and sugar content.

### Recipe 9.13  Greengage Wine (Sweet Social)

If this wine is to be worth drinking it must be made from true greengages, otherwise the flavour is likely to be a disappointment. Use ripe fruit and remove the stones. Ferment on the pulp for four days and the result will be a wine of fair body and 14% alcohol.

| | | |
|---|---|---|
| Greengages | 1.5 kg | (4 lbs) |
| Banana (flesh) | 250 grams | (9 oz) |
| Muscat raisins | 250 grams | (9 oz) |
| Granulated sugar | 680 grams | (1 lb 8 oz) |
| Pectolytic enzyme | 1/2 tablet | |
| Minavit nutrient | 1-2 grams | (1/4 tsp) |
| Gervin yeast No.3 | 1 sachet | |
| Boiled water | to 4.5 litres | (to 1 gallon) |
| Sugar for sweetening | 350 grams | (12 oz) |

This wine should be kept for the best part of a year if it is to realise its potential. If you can't obtain really good greengages, then you can substitute ripe yellow plums.

**Recipe 9.14   Grapefruit Wine (Dry Aperitif)**

I'm putting this recipe forward for a dry aperitif, but it can be sweetened to a dry-medium level by adding 100 grams (4 oz) of sugar, and this will not drown the grapefruit flavour. While I assume readers will be using the normal grapefruit, they may like to experiment with some of the newer varieties coming on to the market. Some of these are rather less astringent and have a higher degree of sweetness. I offer one further suggestion, which is the inclusion of 450 grams of chopped Conference pears. This adds a wonderful roundness to this wine of 13% alcoholic strength I find.

| Grapefruit juice | 1 litre | (35 fl oz) |
|---|---|---|
| Granulated sugar | 900 grams | (2 lbs) |
| Pectolytic enzyme | 1/2 tablet | |
| Minavit nutrient | 2-3 grams | (1/2 tsp) |
| Gervin No.1 yeast | 1 sachet | |
| Boiled water | to 4.5 litres | (to 1 gallon) |

Do remember that this recipe requires freshly-pressed juice from ripe fruit, and that care should be taken to keep out the pith. You may find the wine a little bit "rough", and if this is so I suggest that you add 5 ml of Gervin maturing solution to the gallon of wine to smooth it out.

**Recipe 9.15   Lemon Wine (Dry Aperitif)**

This is another aperitif wine in the citrus mode, and with a similar level of alcohol (13%). If you use just lemon juice without any other ingredient that adds flavour, then you may feel that the wine is rather on the thin side. For this reason I suggest that you include the juice of the watermelon. You may also like to give the wine a somewhat unusual hint by adding a couple of sprigs of parsley to the fermenting must.

| Lemon juice | 250 ml | (9 fl oz) |
|---|---|---|
| Watermelon | 250 grams | (9 oz) |
| Granulated sugar | 950 grams | (2 lbs 2 oz) |
| Pectolytic enzyme | 1/2 tablet | |
| Minavit nutrient | 5 grams | (1 tsp) |
| Gervin No.1 yeast | 1 sachet | |
| Boiled water | to 4.5 litres | (to 1 gallon) |

A typical average lemon contains about 25 ml of juice, so you will need 8 lemons to make a gallon of this wine. Again make sure that you keep out the pith.

### Recipe 9.16  Loganberry Wine (Sweet Social)

Loganberries, like raspberries, have a very strong flavour and aroma, and are quite acid. Both of these fruits are highly desirable in small amounts, as we shall see with some of the more advanced recipes in the next chapter, but on their own their characteristics are almost overwhelming. I believe that when loganberry is the principal fruit it shows up best in a sweet wine, and the addition of a few pears improves the wine by giving it a welcome backbone.

| | | |
|---|---|---|
| Loganberries | 1 kg | (2 lb 3 oz) |
| Pears | 450 grams | (1 lb) |
| Granulated sugar | 900 grams | (2 lbs) |
| Pectolytic enzyme | 1/2 tablet | |
| Minavit nutrient | 2-3 grams | (1/2 tsp) |
| Gervin No.3 yeast | 1 sachet | |
| Glycerine | 5 ml | (1 tsp) |
| Boiled water | to 4.5 litres | (to 1 gallon) |
| Sugar for sweetening | 350 grams | (14 oz) |

Once again the pears should be Conference rather than Williams, and chopped up small; alternatively the juice can be extracted from the pears. The only new feature is the inclusion of a small amount of glycerine (glycerol). This gives a little extra mouthfeel and smoothness when added to a sweet wine; but do add it when the fermentation is complete, because the yeast will also produce some glycerol during the fermentation and this production could be restricted if glycerine has been added already.

The standard method for a pulp fermentation should be followed and the final wine kept for a few months before being sampled. The wine is likely to have an alcoholic strength of around 13%.

### Recipe 9.17  Mulberry Wine (Dry Table)

| | | |
|---|---|---|
| Ripe mulberries | 1.5 kg | (4 lbs) |
| Red grape concentrate | 170 ml | (6 fl oz) |
| Granulated sugar | 700 grams | (1 lb 9 oz) |
| Tartaric acid | 5 grams | (1 tsp) |
| Pectolytic enzyme | 1/2 tablet | |
| Minavit nutrient | 2-3 grams | (1/2 tsp) |
| Gervin No.2 yeast | 1 sachet | |
| Boiled water | to 4.5 litres | (to 1 gallon) |

Mulberries are not easily come by, I'm sorry to say, and for that reason my experience with them has been rather limited. I found that while they were excellent in any mixed fresh fruit wine, they gave of their best in a dry wine with the alcoholic level around 12%. I also found that the wine needed at least a year in bottle before it was drunk. Possibly this time could be reduced if the recipe included oak granules and maturing solution. Perhaps a reader with access to mulberries could try this out and let me know. In the simple recipe I have included only a little red grape concentrate to back up the mulberries. Follow the usual method for a pulp fermentation, simply squashing the fruit without damaging the seeds.

### Recipe 9.18  Orange Wine (Sweet Social)

The recipe will give a sweet wine containing 14% of alcohol. This seems to bring out the best flavour balance. Select really ripe juicy oranges and squeeze out the juice as you would if you were preparing juice for the breakfast table, avoiding the inclusion of pith as far as is possible. The wine is given a boost if a little zest is added. This is obtained by taking the fine gratings from the skin of just one orange, again taking care not to go too deeply and include some pith. The juice, zest, and chopped sultanas are then placed in the fermentation bin, the remaining ingredients added and the fermentation allowed to follow the usual pattern of four days on the pulp followed by completion of the fermentation in the demijohn.

| | | |
|---|---|---|
| Orange juice | 1 litre | (35 fl oz) |
| Orange zest | from one orange | |
| Sultanas | 250 grams | (9 oz) |
| Granulated sugar | 770 grams | (1 lb 11 oz) |
| Pectolytic enzyme | 1/2 tablet | |
| Minavit nutrient | 2-3 grams | (1/2 tsp) |
| Gervin No.3 yeast | 1 sachet | |
| Boiled water | to 4.5 litres | (to 1 gallon) |
| Sugar for sweetening | 350 grams | (12 oz) |

There are other fruits similar to oranges, such as clementines, satsumas and tangerines that can replace all or part of the oranges in the recipe. Each fruit has its own characteristic flavour, and all three mentioned do best in a sweeter wine.

If you want a drier wine then replace the sultanas by 500 ml of white grape juice and reduce the level of sugar for sweetening. The wine will contain between 12 and 13% alcohol.

### Recipe 9.19  Peach Wine (Medium-sweet Table)

This peach wine will have a lovely mellow taste with quite an elegant bouquet. But the peeled peaches should be processed as described for gooseberries (page 51), and just the extract used. I have suggested using Muscat raisins because they add a delightful aroma, but if you would prefer to keep the wine a little less flamboyant then replace the raisins with half a litre of white grape juice.

| | | |
|---|---|---|
| Peaches | 1 kg | (2 lb 3 oz) |
| Muscat raisins | 250 grams | (9 oz) |
| Granulated sugar | 650 grams | (1 lb 7 oz) |
| Tartaric acid | 10 grams | (2 tsp) |
| Pectolytic enzyme | 1/2 tablet | |
| Minavit nutrient | 2-3 grams | (1/2 tsp) |
| Gervin No.5 yeast | 1 sachet | |
| Boiled water | to 4.5 litres | (to 1 gallon) |
| Sugar for sweetening | 250-300 grams | (9-11 oz) |

To get the best results keep the temperature of the fermentation below 20°C; yeast No.5 has been recommended since it will ferment readily even if the temperature falls to as low as 12°C. Peaches will do well in heavier, sweet wines too, and readers may like to experiment by increasing the peach content by 50%, and the sugar (for fermentation) by 100 grams (4 oz). The stronger wine will then be really appreciated on social occasions.

**Recipe 9.20 Pear Wine (Dry Table)**

If you use Conference or Comice pears and extract the juice, then you will be able to make a reasonable dry table wine. You might find a wine using only pear juice as the flavour source a little bit bland, so I suggest that you round it out by including some juice from melons and rhubarb. If the must is all juice and no fruit solids, then carry out the fermentation in the demijohn. If you prefer to use the flesh of the pears and melon then do peel the pears before chopping them up. In any case use rhubarb juice, not pulp, extracting the juice by the simple freezing, thawing and pressing process I described on page 52. The wine will be of table wine strength (around 12%).

| | | |
|---|---|---|
| Pears | 2 kg | (4.5 lbs) |
| Melon | 250 grams | (9 oz) |
| Rhubarb juice | 250 ml | (9 fl oz) |
| Tartaric acid | 5 grams | (1 tsp) |
| Pectolytic enzyme | 1/2 tablet | |
| Minavit nutrient | 2-3 grams | (1/2 tsp) |
| Gervin No.5 yeast | 1 sachet | |
| Boiled water | to 4.5 litres | (to 1 gallon) |

**Recipe 9.21 Pineapple Wine (Medium-sweet Social)**

Pineapple juice has a strong and distinctive flavour, which tends to take over any wine. On its own I think the flavour shows up best when the wine is a sweetish one, and so I have designed this recipe to produce a medium-sweet wine, the only extra being a contribution from watermelon. I believe that the watermelon rounds out the flavour a little, but you can leave it out if you prefer to have a straightforward pineapple wine of 13-14% alcoholic strength.

| | | |
|---|---|---|
| Pineapple (flesh) | 1 kg | (2 lb 3 oz) |
| Watermelon | 250 grams | (9 oz) |
| Granulated sugar | 850 grams | (1 lb 14 oz) |
| Tartaric acid | 10 grams | (2 tsp) |
| Pectolytic enzyme | 1/2 tablet | |
| Minavit nutrient | 2-3 grams | (1/2 tsp) |
| Gervin No.3 yeast | 1 sachet | |
| Boiled water | to 4.5 litres | (to 1 gallon) |
| Sugar for sweetening | 300 grams | (11 oz) |

Try to get the pineapples before they are past their best and remove the skin before crushing the flesh. I find it best to cut the pineapple into slices first, since it is then easier to cut off the irregular skin.

**Recipe 9.22  Plum Wine (Dessert Style)**

I have to confess that I have rather less success with plums than most other fruit, and that some of my wines made from undistinguished plums have had a hint of alcoholic rubber bungs. To be successful I think that we really need black plums with a fairly strong flavour, and the wine will be improved if damsons are used to replace about a quarter of the plums given in the following recipe.

| | | |
|---|---|---|
| Black plums | 2 kg | (4.5 lbs) |
| Bananas (flesh) | 250 grams | (9 oz) |
| Muscat raisins | 250 grams | (9 oz) |
| Granulated sugar | 950 grams | (2 lbs 2 oz) |
| Pectolytic enzyme | 1 tablet | |
| Minavit nutrient | 5 grams | (1 tsp) |
| Gervin No.3 or Varietal C yeast | 1 sachet | |
| Boiled water | to 4.5 litres | (to 1 gallon) |
| Sugar for sweetening | 450 grams | (1 lb) |

Astute readers will have noticed that this recipe has a lot in common with Recipe 8.13 (Greengage), which is hardly surprising in view of the close relationship of the greengage to the plum. What I have done is to increase the amount of fruit by 500 grams and increase the amount of sugar; the result should be a wine with between 15 and 16% alcohol, which when sweetened up will be in the dessert mould. Choose and process the plums as suggested in Chapters 4 and 5. This wine should be kept for the best part of two years to give it a chance to mellow.

**Recipe 9.23  Raspberry Wine (Sweet social)**

Use the loganberry recipe (9.16) but substitute raspberries for the loganberries in the same amount.

**Recipe 9.24   Redcurrant wine (Dry-medium Rosé)**

| | | |
|---|---|---|
| Redcurrants | 1 kg | (2 lb 3 oz) |
| White grape juice | 500 ml | (18 fl oz) |
| Granulated sugar | 750 grams | (1 lb 10 oz) |
| Pectolytic enzyme | 1/2 tablet | |
| Minavit nutrient | 2-3 grams | (1/2 tsp) |
| Gervin Varietal B yeast | 1 sachet | |
| Boiled water | to 4.5 litres | (to 1 gallon) |
| For sweetening, apple juice | 500 ml | (18 fl oz) |

The aim is to make a "youthful" fruity wine that will serve us well on that rare occasion of a warm summer's evening in the garden. The wine will be quite light in body. I suggest that the juice should be extracted by the freezing technique. When the fermentation is complete and the wine clear, then the apple juice can be added to provide the necessary level of sweetness.

Some readers may prefer to use a pulp fermentation on the crushed fruit. If this is so then I suggest that the white grape juice be replaced by 150 grams (6 oz) of sultanas; but to avoid extracting too much tannin from the berry skins limit the pulp stage to just three days.

**Recipe 9.25   Rhubarb Wine (Dry Sparkling)**

The recipe that follows will give us the base dry wine which is then turned into a dry sparkler by the technique described in Chapter 7, page 79. The recipe has to produce a base wine that is fairly acidic and without a dominating flavour. The wine normally comes out with a titratable acidity of 7 grams per litre, and with 12% of alcohol.

| | | |
|---|---|---|
| Rhubarb juice | 1.5 litres | (53 fl oz) |
| White grape juice | 500 ml | (9 fl oz) |
| Granulated sugar | 800 grams | (1 lb 12 oz) |
| Pectolytic enzyme | 1/2 tablet | |
| Minavit nutrient | 5 grams | (1 tsp) |
| Gervin Varietal C yeast | 1 sachet | |
| Boiled water | to 4.5 litres | (to 1 gallon) |

The rhubarb juice is readily obtained by thawing the frozen fruit (see page 52), so start by freezing around two kilos of rhubarb. The fermentation should be carried out in the usual way in the demijohn under a trap. When the wine has been racked it should drop clear pretty quickly, but should there still be a little haze of yeast in suspension don't worry, because this will settle out in the secondary fermentation.

Use the secondary fermentation procedure described in Chapter 7, adding the extra sugar and some fresh yeast before bottling the wine. The secondary stage is a difficult one for the yeast because the wine contains 12% alcohol and it has a fairly high acid level, both factors likely to inhibit the refermentation. To help the process I have suggested that you add twice as much minavit nutrient as usual so that the yeast will have as receptive an environment as possible.

**Recipe 9.26   Rhubarb Wine (Sweet Social)**

| | | |
|---|---|---|
| Rhubarb juice | 1 litre | (35 fl oz) |
| Peaches | 450 grams | (1 lb) |
| Granulated sugar | 950 grams | (2 lb 2 oz) |
| Pectolytic enzyme | 1/2 tablet | |
| Minavit nutrient | 2-3 grams | (1/2 tsp) |
| Gervin Varietal D yeast | 1 sachet | |
| Boiled water | to 4.5 litres | (to 1 gallon) |
| Sugar for sweetening | 350-400 grams | (12-14 oz) |

Extract the juice from both the rhubarb and peaches and carry out the fermentation in the demijohn under lock. I have recommended the use of Gervin Varietal D yeast since this will reduce the malic acid level a little and give a superior bouquet.

Some readers may like to use a variation of the recipe in which the pound of fresh peaches is replaced by a 15 oz can of peaches. In this case puree the peaches and juice and add it all to the must. This will give slightly less peach flavour and a slightly higher level of alcohol in the wine. Keep it for a few months and then enjoy it.

**Recipe 9.27   Sloe Wine (Dry Table)**

Sloes are excellent for winemaking provided that they are really ripe. Otherwise they are very acidic and quite astringent. If the fruit is ripe then it will produce a reasonable level of colour when used at a kilo of fruit to 4.5 litres of must, but the colour and flavour is much improved if a small amount of red grape concentrate is added. Should this not be available, use 450 grams of ripe elderberries in its place plus an extra 100 grams of sugar.

| | | |
|---|---|---|
| Ripe sloes | 1 kg | (2 lbs 3 oz) |
| Red grape concentrate | 170 ml | (6 fl oz) |
| Granulated sugar | 730 grams | (1 lb 10 oz) |
| Pectolytic enzyme | 1/2 tablet | |
| Minavit nutrient | 2-3 grams | (1/2 tsp) |
| Gervin No.2 or Varietal D yeast | 1 sachet | |
| Boiled water | to 4.5 litres | (to 1 gallon) |

I strongly recommend adding about 10 grams (just over a quarter of an ounce) of Gervin oak granules, or the equivalent amount of your own prepared oak chips (see page 75), since this will help to round out the wine. I suggest that you leave this wine in bulk , but do make sure that the water in the fermentation trap does not evaporate; if it does, air will get at the wine and oxidise it. To make quite sure you can add a little glycerine to the water in the trap, since this will not evaporate. During this bulk storage period, unstable colouring matters will precipitate out, and later you can bottle the clear stable wine.

### Recipe 9.28   Strawberry Wine (Medium-sweet Social)

I find that strawberries give a rather sickly wine unless it is tarted up with an acid ingredient such as rhubarb juice. I suggest that you try it both ways and see which you prefer.

| | | |
|---|---|---|
| Strawberries | 1 kg | (2 lb 3 oz) |
| Rhubarb juice | 500 ml | (18 fl oz) |
| Sultanas | 500 grams | (1 lb 2 oz) |
| Granulated sugar | 650 grams | (1 lb 7 oz) |
| Pectolytic enzyme | 1/2 tablet | |
| Minavit nutrient | 2-3 grams | (1/2 tsp) |
| Gervin No.1 yeast | 1 sachet | |
| Boiled water | to 4.5 litres | (to 1 gallon) |
| Sugar for sweetening | 300 grams | (10-11 oz) |

The wine will contain between 13 and 14% alcohol and makes a pleasant summer drink. If you freeze it in the appropriate way it makes an excellent sorbet.

### Recipe 9.29   Whitecurrant Wine (Dry Table)

| | | |
|---|---|---|
| Whitecurrants | 1 kg | (2 lbs 3 oz) |
| White grape juice | 500 ml | (18 fl oz) |
| Granulated sugar | 750 grams | (1 lb 10 oz) |
| Pectolytic enzyme | 1/2 tablet | |
| Minavit nutrient | 2-3 grams | (1/2 tsp) |
| Gervin No.5 or | | |
| Varietal B yeast | 1 sachet | |
| Boiled water | to 4.5 litres | (to 1 gallon) |

The problem with white currants is that they contain a fair amount of tannin, and if this is fully extracted then the wine may have too much bite for it to be a suitable accompaniment to a meal needing a dry white wine to do it justice. There are three ways around this problem. The juice can be extracted from the whitecurrants by the freezing method, the fermentation on the pulp can be limited to a maximum of three days, or we can remove the tannin by fining if it is too obtrusive. We will look at fining in some detail in Chapter 16, but for the moment I will simply say that fining with gelatine solution will normally take out some of the more aggressive tannins. This wine tends to be one of the more austere types, but will go well with shell fish. You can smooth it out a little by adding 5 ml (1 tsp) of Gervin maturing solution.

**Recipe 9.30   Cereal Wine (Sweet Social)**

Many of the older recipes use cereals as part of their make up, but it must be appreciated that these ingredients do not add a lot of flavour, and virtually no acid or sugar. The following recipe is for Barley Wine, but either wheat or rice can be added if you wish.

I believe that it is essential to have some dried fruit in the must, and in my experience the addition of some pears works wonders. I recommend adding a full 5 grams of the nutrient, since the ingredients may not provide enough readily available nitrogen for the yeast otherwise. It is this shortage that leads the yeast to extract its requirements from the protein, leaving as its "thank you" some unwanted higher alcohols.

| | | |
|---|---|---|
| Barley | 450 grams | (1 lb) |
| Sultanas | 450 grams | (1 lb) |
| Pears | 1 kg | (2 lbs 3 oz) |
| Tartaric acid | 10 grams | (2 tsp) |
| Pectolytic enzyme | 1/2 tablet | |
| Minavit nutrient | 5 grams | (1 tsp) |
| Gervin Varietal D yeast | 1 sachet | |
| Boiled water | to 4.5 litres | (to 1 gallon) |
| Sugar for sweetening | 400 grams | (14 oz) |

Once upon a time there was a so-called cereal yeast available in dried form, but this is no longer the case. I assume that it was a strain of *Saccharomyces diastaticus*, which can metabolise starch. I have recommended the Gervin D yeast, not because it will use the starch, but because it will produce a really good bouquet. Do lay down this wine for a couple of years, because all wines with a substantial amount of cereals in them will improve a lot over this period.

**Recipe 9.31   Carrot Wine (Sweet Social)**

If you have the facility, do juice the carrots, because this gives a wine that will mature more quickly, and the all-juice must can be fermented in the demijohn. The wine will be quite a strong sweet one, the alcohol level being around 14%. Store it in bottle for the best part of a year to make the most of it.

| | | |
|---|---|---|
| Carrots | 1350 grams | (3 lbs) |
| White grape concentrate | 280 ml | (10 fl oz) |
| Granulated sugar | 800 grams | (1 lb 12 oz) |
| Tartaric acid | 20 grams | (4 tsp) |
| Pectolytic enzyme | 1/2 tablet | |
| Minavit nutrient | 5 grams | (1 tsp) |
| Gervin Varietal D yeast | 1 sachet | |
| Boiled water | to 4.5 litres | (to 1 gallon) |
| Sugar for sweetening | 350 grams | (12-13 oz) |

### Recipe 9.32  Parsnip Wine (Sweet Table)

If you follow this recipe and are patient, then after a period of at least two years in the bottle, the distinctive parsnip flavour will fade away to leave a most pleasant wine in the style of a light Sauternes or Barsac. But you must make sure that the parsnips have been exposed to cold weather, since then you will know that the sugar level is high and the starch level low.

| | | |
|---|---|---|
| Parsnips | 1350 grams | (3 lbs) |
| Bananas (flesh) | 450 grams | (1 lb) |
| White grape concentrate | 280 ml | (10 fl oz) |
| Granulated sugar | 600 grams | (1 lb 5 oz) |
| Tartaric acid | 15 grams | (3 tsp) |
| Pectolytic enzyme | 1/2 tablet | |
| Minavit nutrient | 5 grams | (1 tsp) |
| Gervin Varietal D yeast | 1 sachet | |
| Boiled water | to 4.5 litres | (to 1 gallon) |
| Sugar for sweetening | 340 grams | (12 oz) |

Once again I recommend extracting the juice with a juicing machine if you have access to one. Otherwise you will have to cut the parsnips into small pieces and cook them gently so that the sugar and flavour can be extracted; but simmer rather than boil in order to keep the extraction of any starch to a minimum. This 13% alcohol wine is one worth making providing that you are patient and let it mature.

### Recipe 9.33  Elderflower Wine (Medium-sweet Social)

Readers should refer back to page 43 to find the best way of selecting the flowers and processing them. My advice is to use the flowers sparingly in a light wine with a grape juice base. Since all these flowers, and any others for that matter, provide, is aroma, a little colour and possibly some flavour, it is clear that some ingredients must be included to provide the required body, sugar, acid and nutrients. And one last word. Do not pick the flowers today and use them tomorrow; that increases the chance of your getting the infamous "catty" wine.

| | | |
|---|---|---|
| Elderflowers | 250 ml | (9 fl oz) |
| White grape juice | 1 litre | (35 fl oz) |
| Granulated sugar | 800 grams | (1 lb 12 oz) |
| Tartaric acid | 15 grams | (3 tsp) |
| Pectolytic enzyme | 1/2 tablet | |
| Minavit nutrient | 2-3 grams | (1/2 tsp) |
| Gervin No.1 yeast | 1 sachet | |
| Boiled water | to 4.5 litres | (to 1 gallon) |
| Sugar for sweetening | 300 grams | (11 oz) |

I have suggested using 250 ml of flowers lightly packed, but the amount does depend on which flowers you have picked; some varieties have more aroma than others. I judge the smell of any elderflowers I have picked and use them accordingly. Often I use just a double handful of flowers. It is better to use too few rather than too many, unless you are prepared to blend a wine with too much aroma with another one that lacks it.

**Recipe 9.34 Rose Petal Wine (Medium-sweet Social)**

Use the same basic recipe as the previous one for elderflower wine, simply replacing the elderflowers with rose petals. But pick the petals before the roses start to go over, despite any objections from the keen gardener in the family, and make sure that the roses have not been sprayed with some toxic greenfly killer in the previous week.

You can try other flowers too in this type of recipe if you wish, using just enough of fragrant blossoms to produce the aroma that you want. I do not recommend using hawthorn blossom in case it is rather past its best, when it will produce a wine with a smell of the fishmonger's slab!

**Recipe 9.35 Dandelion Wine (Medium-sweet Social)**

This is an old country favourite, and produces a pleasant social wine when it has been allowed to mature for a year or so. It should be mentioned that the dandelion has known diuretic properties, as recognised by its many local names. One of the politest is the Somerset name of Wet-a-Bed. Just in case these properties should go through to the finished wine I suggest that readers with weak bladders should avoid it!

Because dandelions do not have much of a smell, they are used in fair quantity, and the fermentation is the pulp process. Traditionally the dandelion heads are picked in the morning on St George's Day; they must be in full bloom. To avoid a bitterness creeping into the wine remove every trace of stem and remove all the green sepals that enclose the yellow petals. The simplest way is to cut off the base of each head with the kitchen scissors and separate the petals from the sepals.

| | | |
|---|---|---|
| Dandelions | 2250 ml | (4 pints) |
| Sultanas | 450 grams | (1 lb) |
| Granulated sugar | 700 grams | (1 lb 9 oz) |
| Tartaric acid | 15 grams | (3 tsp) |
| Pectolytic enzyme | 1/2 tablet | |
| Minavit nutrient | 5 grams | (1 tsp) |
| Gervin No.1 yeast | 1 sachet | |
| Boiled water | to 4.5 litres | (to 1 gallon) |
| Sugar for sweetening | 350 grams | (12 oz) |

**Recipe 9.36   Honey Wine (Medium-sweet Mead)**

This was the Englishman's drink long before wine became popular, but it is not to everyone's liking. I prefer to use relatively small amounts of honey in other recipes where it adds body and roundness, although used in excess it takes over the flavour.

Apart from taking care over the selection of the honey, the main point we have to watch is the necessity for adding sufficient acid and nutrients, both of which are in short supply in honey. In addition the honey must be prepared along the lines discussed in Chapter 5 (page 58) so that unwanted wax etc. can be removed and micro-organisms destroyed without the loss of the honey aroma.

The following recipe is for a very simple medium-sweet mead containing 13% alcohol.

| | | |
|---|---|---|
| Honey | 1300 grams | (2 lbs 14 oz) |
| Tartaric acid | 20 grams | (4 tsp) |
| Pectolytic enzyme | 1/2 tablet | |
| Minavit nutrient | 5 grams | (1 tsp) |
| Gervin Varietal E yeast | 1 sachet | |
| Boiled water | to 4.5 litres | (to 1 gallon) |
| Honey for sweetening | 350 grams | (12 oz) |

Gervin Varietal E yeast is recommended because it will work well even if the nutrient levels in the must are not ideal. And to play safe I have suggested using twice as much as usual of the Minavit nutrient.

Readers with an adventurous outlook may like to try making spiced meads, often referred to as Metheglin (from the Welsh Meddyglyn), which are typically meads laced with mace, cinnamon, cloves and pimento. I am not making suggestions of the amounts to add because some readers may like their meads well spiced and others may prefer just a hint of spice. But since these spices can be added at the end of the fermentation we can add a little at a time until we get to the level we like best. I suggest that you take just half of the mead that you intend to add spices to, so that if you should accidentally overdo things you can always blend with the unspiced part.

In his book "Wassail! in Mazers of Mead", published in 1948, G R Gayre gives a fascinating account of "Mead, Metheglin, Sack and other Ancient Liquors", and I was especially interested in the one for the old recipe for making metheglin. This says:

*"Mix the whites of six eggs with twelve gallons of the best virgin honey and the peeling of three lemons; boil it an hour, and then put into it some rosemary, cloves, mace, and ginger; when quite cold add a spoonful or two of yeast, tun it, and when it has done working stop it up close. In a few months bottle it off, and deposit in a cool cellar"*

There are also the so-called fruit meads, in which up to 30% of the water is replaced with a fruit juice. Readers who also make liqueurs are reminded that honey is an essential part of such commercial products as Drambuie and Irish Mist.

## Other ingredients

Although I have given recipes for most of the ingredients that are likely to be of interest, it is inevitable that I have left out some. One such example of a missing fruit is the bullace, which was once a cultivated plum, and has characteristics roughly midway between those of the damson and the sloe. Use them in the recipes for either damson or sloe. I have also left out rose hips, although these can be used in either their fresh or dried form; I will refer to them again when we come to wines for aperitifs in the next chapter.

Other berries that are worth a mention, possibly, are the hawthorn and rowan (Mountain Ash). I don't use either regularly, but I have found that with hawthorn-berries I obtained quite a pleasant light wine with a distinctive orange colour. I made my 4.5 litres of wine with 500 grams of the well-washed berries, a litre of Sainsbury white grape juice, 650 grams of granulated sugar and 5 grams of citric acid. I used Gervin Varietal E yeast. After a pulp fermentation for two weeks at an ambient temperature of around 15°C, about two-thirds of the sugar had been used up, and the fermenting must was then removed from the pulp and placed under a trap in the standard demijohn. The fermentation was complete after four weeks from the time the yeast was added, and it cleared quickly. The wine tasted quite well two months later, being well rounded, with no trace of bitterness, but just a hint of plumminess. This wine certainly exceeded my expectations and I can recommend the recipe.

Although rowanberries are said to lose much of their astringency when they are really ripe, I have not yet made a rowan wine that I find attractive.

My deliberate omission has been that of producing recipes for making wine based on leaf vegetables such as pea pod, oak leaves and nettles, and the sap of birch trees. If you wish to investigate the mysteries of such ingredients, bear in mind that leaves of any source provide little other than a slight flavour, so that the must has to provide the body by including dried fruit, and all the necessary acid and nutrients. Use the recipe for flower wines (9.32) replacing the flowers with the "leaves" etc. of your choice.

**Recipe 9.37 "Folly"**

Readers who have any grape vines in their gardens may like to experiment with the young prunings of the vines. These leaves and stems do contain interestingly flavoured substances which are extracted during a fermentation. The product is commonly called "folly", and has its enthusiasts. If you want to try this, take a couple of handfuls of very young prunings and make them into a wine using about 900 grams (2 lb) of sugar, 20 grams (4 tsp) of tartaric acid, 5 grams of Minavit nutrient, half a tablet of pectolytic enzyme, and Gervin No.1 yeast. Chop the vine cuttings up small, and add to them the sugar etc. dissolved in water, and ferment on the clippings for three to four days. Then strain off into the gallon jar and let the fermentation go to completion. I have made this sort of "wine" very few times, and I have rather mixed feelings about it. The quality of the product depends a lot on which type of vine is involved as far as I can tell. If you have an inquisitive nature give it a try!

Birch sap can be used as a background liquid for the must, but on its own it will give a somewhat insipid wine, which owes more to the added acid and nutrient and the influence of the yeast than to the contents of the birch sap.

**Recipe 9.38 Sweet Ginger Wine**

If you like the flavour of ginger, and want a wine that will warm you nicely on a cold winter's evening, then try out the following very simple recipe. As I have given it, the recipe will produce a sweet wine containing just over 13% of alcohol, and with quite a strong ginger flavour. I must emphasise that this is a very simple recipe that just involves fermenting an acidified solution of sugar plus the ginger flavouring. Because there are no natural nutrients you must use much more nutrient mixture than usual. I have included caramel primarily for its colour, plus a little flavour, but if you wish you can leave it out, or possibly replace it with a vegetable dyestuff of your choice. I have suggested adding just 340 grams of sugar for the sweetening, but readers may like to know that one well known brand of ginger wine uses much more than this.

It is difficult to give a very firm suggestion about the amount of ginger flavouring to add. The Gervin essence is a powerful one, and 5 ml may be too much for some readers; so if you have a delicate palate cut the ginger down by half and add more to the finished wine if you need it.

| | | |
|---|---|---|
| Granulated sugar | 1 kg | (2 lb 3 oz) |
| Citric acid | 20 grams | (4 tsp) |
| Pectolytic enzyme | 1/2 tablet | |
| Minavit nutrient | 10 grams | (2 tsp) |
| Gervin ginger essence | 5 ml | (1 tsp) |
| Caramel | sufficient to colour | |
| Gervin No.1 yeast | 1 sachet | |
| Boiled water | to 4.5 litres | (to 1 gallon) |
| Sugar for sweetening | 340 grams | (12 oz) |

Real enthusiasts for ginger wine may prefer to use root ginger rather than the ready prepared essence. If this is so then I suggest replacing the essence with 50 grams (2 oz) of root ginger. Put the ginger between two layers of clean cloth, put it on a hard surface and thump it well with a hammer. This will break open the root ginger and help the extraction of the flavour.

Put the bruised ginger into two litres or so of water and simmer the mixture for 20 - 30 minutes. Now strain off the ginger and use the ginger extract to dissolve the sugar etc. Dilute with more water, place in the demijohn and ferment out the wine to dryness.

# A Final Recap

Throughout this chapter I have introduced topics as they became necessary, but I feel that it might be worthwhile summarising the main points briefly.

### Ingredients

Although I have briefly mentioned the best way of handling the ingredients in each recipe, readers should refer to Chapter 5 for the full details. When ingredients have been frozen, and then treated with boiling water, it is reasonable to assume that they will not be significantly contaminated with micro-organisms. When fresh fruit is used, wash with water containing a little sodium metabisulphite solution (1 tsp of 10% solution) added to a gallon of water.

**Acid.** Use tartaric when you have to add more. If tartaric is not available then citric will do. If the ingredients are likely to be very acidic neutralise some acid by adding sodium (or potassium) bicarbonate to the prepared ingredients before the fermentation.

**Sugar.** Ordinary granulated sugar is fine. Remember that 20% sugar solutions give 12% alcohol (to a first approximation).

**Nutrient, pectolytic enzyme** and **yeast** are all listed on the basis of the Gervin product that seems most suitable; if the Gervin brand is not available, consult your local homebrew specialist for alternatives.

**Special additives** are referred to from time to time. These include oak granules and maturing solution which round out a wine, glycerine (glycerol) that smoothes and slightly sweetens (to be added only to sweet wines), and various essences that add either aroma or flavour, or both. Those mentioned have been chosen to suit particular styles of wine.

**Fermentation.**

**Pulp or not?** The short answer is that with the more delicate white and rosé wines, you should use juice or extracts as much as possible. In almost every case of a red wine, the colour is largely in the skin of the fruit and pulp fermentation is necessary; but the time of fermentation on the pulp should be limited to not more than four days to avoid the extraction of excessive amounts of harsh tannin.

**Bentonite** is used to ensure a smooth fermentation and to remove protein that could cause later hazes. It can be used with beneficial effects in all white or rosé musts, but if used when a pulp fermentation method is adopted, the bentonite should be added after the pulp has been removed.

The **temperature** of the fermentation should be below 20°C for all the more delicate white and rosé wines. With red wines 20 to 25°C is best.

The **level of liquid** in the demijohn should be at the shoulder for the first stage of the fermentation - to allow for any frothing. Then the level should be topped up to the neck and a fermentation trap fitted. When the initial fermentation is in a fermentation bin (for pulp fermentation), use only part of the water calculated as necessary to make up the 4.5 litres, and top up when the fermenting must is transferred to the demijohn.

**Finished wine.**

**Sweetening.** This is done either by adding sugar to the clear wine (and then stabilising the wine) or the wine can be bottled dry and the sugar added when the bottle is opened. As an alternative to sugar, fruit juice can be used for sweetening; this will dilute the alcoholic strength according to how much juice you add.

**Stabilising.** All wines, but particularly white ones, need to be protected against oxidation. This is achieved by adding either 5 ml of 10% sulphite solution to 4.5 litres of the wine just before it is bottled, or adding a crushed Campden tablet. If the wine has been sweetened before bottling, then it has to be protected against a further fermentation. Potassium sorbate helps to prevent such fermentation but when it is used sulphite must be added at the same time.

# Chapter 10
# Wines with Style

## Introduction

Table 6.1 (page 63) gave an outline of the main characteristics of different styles of wine, and to a limited extent we have already followed these guidelines when producing recipes for country-style wines. While the recipes for these country wines were intended to produce wines suitable for drinking with meals or for "social slurping", they were particularly designed to bring out the best from individual ingredients. We will now consider going a step further and use different mixtures of fruits etc. to produce wines in which the blend of ingredients gives more complex flavours. The intention is to make wines that not only fall within the general categories of table wines, social wines, aperitif wines and dessert wines, but to try to imitate the style of specific types of wine within these categories.

Our attempts to make wines that are indistinguishable from named commercial styles will not be perfect, of course, but at least they will have the correct levels of acid, flavour, sweetness and tannin. As an example I have given recipes for various types of dry red table wine, and I hope that each wine will at least be in the style of the named type of wine. Thus I have given a recipe for a Beaujolais style of wine, which is youthful and fruity, and while it cannot produce the unique flavour of the Gamay grape it will have the right style. In contrast, the recipe I have given for a Rhone-style wine will produce a heavier wine that needs a longer period of maturation before it is ready for drinking.

Many of the recipes given are those I set out in the Gervin Recipe Book; this was produced as an interim measure pending the publication of this much more substantial book. In many instances the recipes have been modified somewhat to improve them further. Other recipes relate to those I produced for my quarterly magazine Wine for All Seasons, now sadly no longer published.

I will give the recipes under the broad headings of red wines, white wines, rosé wines, aperitif wines and dessert wines, and I will say what the intention is in respect of the likely levels of acidity, alcohol, sweetness and tannin (phenolics). I shall not give details of the calculations leading to these figures, but enthusiastic readers will be able to deduce the arguments for themselves, using the data given in the tables for acid and sugar content of ingredients (Chapter 4). I have used the 20% sugar producing 12% alcohol rule to predict the likely alcohol content, and assumed that in most fermentations there will be in increase in the acidity of around 1.0 to 1.5 grams per litre; where the ingredients contain malic acid and I have recommended using Gervin Varietal D yeast, the overall increase will be less than this because of the partial metabolism of the malic acid. I have given the likely specific gravity of the finished wine for the benefit of those winemakers that have hydrometers and use them to check. Finally I have used data on the phenolics level of ingredients that I have listed in my data book *Must*; I have also made necessary corrections based on personal experiments which have checked on how the tannin levels of typical wines decrease when the wines are stored for a few months.

These technical aspects will be discussed in more detail in the following chapters.

## Red wines

### Recipe 10.1 Dry Red Table Wine (Beaujolais Style 1)

This is a very simple recipe that makes use of ingredients that can be bought in any home brew shop at any time of year. It is ready for drinking in just a few weeks and is a useful standby as a light fruity wine which has an alcoholic strength of some 11.5%, and an acidity of about 6 grams per litre. The tannin level will not be more than 0.15%, and depending on the concentrate used is likely to be closer to 0.1%. This ensures that the astringent bite that characterises a red wine is kept to a minimum, thus making the wine drinkable at an early stage. It will go down well if served chilled, and is ideal for buffets and picnics.

| Red grape concentrate | 500 ml | (18 fl oz) |
|---|---|---|
| Granulated sugar | 480 grams | (1lb 1 oz) |
| Pectolytic enzyme | 1/2 tablet | |
| Minavit nutrient | 2-3 grams | (1/2 tsp) |
| Gervin No.1 yeast | 1 sachet | |
| Boiled water | to 4.5 litres ( | to 1 gallon) |

The flavour of the wine will depend on the brands of apple juice and grape concentrate that you use, of course, so it will pay you to experiment a little and find which one suits you best. I have selected Gervin No.1 yeast because it settles without difficulty and lets the flavour and aroma of the fruit show through. If you wish you can use Gervin Varietal B yeast, which will impart a more distinctive bouquet to the wine; this yeast is traditionally used for making white wines at relatively low fermentation temperatures, but serves red ferments equally well. For the enthusiasts with hydrometers, the finishing S.G. (specific gravity) is likely to be close to 0.993.

**Recipe 10.2  Dry Red Table Wine (Beaujolais Style 2)**

This is a simple variation of the previous recipe which adds 450 grams (1 lb) of blackberries to the recipe and reduces the red grape concentrate by 50 ml (2 fl oz). If you like, you can make other minor changes by introducing a few raspberries in place of some of the blackberries. I recently made up an experimental gallon using 350 grams of blackberries and 100 grams of raspberries, both from the freezer, with the remainder of the recipe the same, and I was delighted with the result.

The wine in all cases will again contain about 11.5% alcohol.

**Recipe 10.3  Dry Red Table Wine (Beaujolais Style 3)**

This is a more ambitious recipe, which depends upon whether you can get the bilberries that form the bulk of the fruit. While bilberries can be found on most northern moors and in the west country, on Exmoor, where they are known as whortleberries, winemakers in other parts of the country are less lucky. In such instances I suggest that you use a mixture of blackberries, elderberries and raspberries (700 grams, 700 grams and 100 grams respectively), in place of the bilberries.

The recipe is intended to give a wine with 12% of alcohol, an acid level of 6.0 - 6.5 grams per litre and a finishing S.G. of between 0.992 and 0.993.

| | | |
|---|---|---|
| Bilberries | 1.5 kg | (3.5 lb) |
| Grapes | 1 kg | (2 lb 3 oz) |
| Granulated sugar | 650 grams | (1 lb 7 oz) |
| Pectolytic enzyme | 1/2 tablet | |
| Minavit nutrient | 2-3 grams | (1/2 tsp) |
| Gervin No.2 yeast | 1 sachet | |
| Boiled water | to 4.5 litres | (to 1 gallon) |

I have included fresh grapes because I suggest that the wine will be particularly good if the initial fermentation is carried out using the carbonic maceration method (see page 77), and this needs whole fruit, complete with skins. It is normally possible to buy grapes of reasonable quality and relatively cheaply if you have a local market that you can visit near the end of trading. You may be able to find black grapes, but if you can't don't worry if only green ones are available because the bilberries will provide the colour. I have found the sultana (Thompson Seedless) grapes to be especially suitable for this recipe.

Follow the carbonic maceration method described on page 77, putting the fruit into the plastic sweet jar, adding the nutrient, pectolytic enzyme and yeast, and allowing the fermentation to work for up to a week. The fermenting must is then pressed and the sugar added after it has been dissolved in the water. The fermentation is then allowed to go to completion in the demijohn under lock and the wine racked and bottled in the usual way. It should be noted that as with all red wines the addition of stabilising sulphite solution should be only half of that used with white wines.

If you wish, you can use the recipe but crush the fruit and ferment on the pulp in the usual way; the wine will still be good but it is likely to be rather less obviously fruity.

**Recipe 10.4  Dry Red Table Wine (Bordeaux Style 1)**

This is a variation on Recipe 9.1. It will give a rather firmer wine, and needs a few months in bottle before it is drunk. The alcohol level will be close to 12%, and the finishing S.G. close to 0.992. The bananas and pears will give the wine a little extra body, but it will still be on the light-medium side.

| | | |
|---|---|---|
| Red grape concentrate | 500 ml | (18 fl oz) |
| Apple juice | 500 ml | (18 fl oz) |
| Bananas (flesh) | 100 grams | (4 oz) |
| Pears | 450 grams | (1 lb) |
| Granulated sugar | 500 grams | (1 lb 2 oz) |
| Pectolytic enzyme | 1/2 tablet | |
| Minavit nutrient | 2-3 grams | (1/2 tsp) |
| Gervin No.1 yeast | 1 sachet | |
| Gervin maturing solution | 5 ml | (1 tsp) |
| Boiled water | to 4.5 litres | (to 1 gallon) |

The wine has a somewhat blander taste than say a Claret, and more closely approaches the everyday red found in regions such as Bergerac, just to the east of Bordeaux. The No.1 yeast ferments out quickly and settles well. Once the wine is reasonably clear I recommend that you add the maturing solution to round it out. The addition is not essential but it does improve the mouthfeel of the wine to a marked extent.

### Recipe 10.5 Dry Red Table Wine (Bordeaux Style 2)

You will have to go to a little more trouble to make this wine. It lists blueberries amongst the ingredients, although you can use bilberries instead if you can get them. I know that some readers will grow their own blueberries, and I can recommend this fruit as an easy one to grow if your soil is on the acid side, but the alternative is to visit the local freezer shop where New Zealand blueberries can usually be found. They are not cheap but they are good.

Again I am suggesting that you use fresh grapes as a back-up for this recipe, but you can use 200 ml of red grape concentrate instead of the fresh grapes if this is more convenient. Either way you will get an excellent wine of 12% alcohol strength, and an acidity of around 6.5 grams per litre. The tannin level is about right for a wine with this medium depth of body.

| Ingredient | Metric | Imperial |
| --- | --- | --- |
| Blueberries | 450 grams | (1 lb) |
| Elderberries | 680 grams | (1 lb 8 oz) |
| Raspberries | 100 grams | (4 oz) |
| Grapes | 450 grams | (1 lb) |
| Granulated sugar | 700 grams | (1 lb 9 oz) |
| Tartaric acid | 10 grams | (2 tsp) |
| Pectolytic enzyme | 1/2 tablet | |
| Minavit nutrient | 1 gram | (1/4 tsp) |
| Gervin Varietal A yeast | 1 sachet | |
| Gervin oak granules | 5-10 grams | (1/4 oz) |
| Boiled water | to 4.5 litres | (to 1 gallon) |

The oak granules (or oak chips) are quite optional, and you should put them in if you like a hint of oak. I have chosen Varietal A yeast because it is a quality yeast from Bordeaux, but be prepared for the fermentation to take a little longer because this strain of yeast is a little less vigorous than say the Burgundy strain (No.2). I think the extra wait is worth it, but if you are impatient for the fermentation to end then use No.2.

### Recipe 10.6 Dry Red Table Wine (Burgundy)

This wine will be in the style of one of the lighter modern Burgundies, and a feature of the recipe is the inclusion of a small amount of blackcurrants. This flavour is one characteristic of Burgundies, and another is the reasonably high tannin levels and a slightly higher level of alcohol (now 13%). The fruit will not produce sufficient tannin for a true Burgundy, and so for the first time I recommend the addition of some grape tannin. Some writers of recipes recommend adding cold tea, but I must emphasise that the tannin from tea is quite different from grape tannin. Watch out too for weak solutions of "tannin", and avoid it. Go to the trouble of buying true oenological tannin.

| | | |
|---|---|---|
| Elderberries | 600 grams | (1 lb 5 oz) |
| Pears | 750 grams | (1 lb 10 oz) |
| Sultanas | 450 grams | (1 lb) |
| Blackcurrants | 100 grams | (4 oz) |
| Grapes | 450 grams | (1 lb) |
| Granulated sugar | 400 grams | (14 oz) |
| Gervin grape tannin | 4 grams | (1 tsp) |
| Gervin oak granules | 10 grams | |
| Pectolytic enzyme | 1/2 tablet | |
| Minavit nutrient | 1 gram | (1/4 tsp) |
| Gervin No.2 yeast | 1 sachet | |
| Boiled water | to 4.5 litres | (to 1 gallon) |

This should be a pulp fermentation, with not more than 4 days on the pulp, so make sure that you crush the fruit, and chop the sultanas to ensure the extraction of sufficient flavour and sugar. Remember too that No.2 yeast is very vigorous, and is likely to froth a little in the early stages. With this particular recipe, I put all the ingredients except the sugar in the fermentation bin, with just two litres of water and carry out the pulp fermentation without the granulated sugar. Then I remove the spent fruit with a sieve and transfer the fermenting must to the demijohn, adding the sugar at this stage, already dissolved in more water. This "fruit only" fermentation stage is a useful alternative to fermenting on all the ingredients, especially when you want a slightly more delicate flavour.

**Recipe 10.7 Dry Red Table Wine (Loire Style)**

Loire red wines, such as those from Chinon and Samur are not big heavy wines, but they do have a beautifully complex flavour when at their best. As with most table wines the alcohol level is kept to around 12%, but the acid level is deliberately a little higher. Raspberries form a small but vital role in the recipe. The pears (again the Conference variety) should be chopped up small, skins and all.

| | | |
|---|---|---|
| Elderberries | 500 grams | (1 lb 2 oz) |
| Blackberries | 500 grams | (1 lb 2 oz) |
| Apple juice | 650 ml | (23 fl oz) |
| Grapes | 500 grams | (1 lb 2 oz) |
| Pears | 500 grams | (1 lb 2 oz) |
| Raspberries | 100 grams | (4 oz) |
| Granulated sugar | 600 grams | (1 lb 5 oz) |
| Pectolytic enzyme | 1/2 tablet | |
| Minavit nutrient | 1 gram | (1/4 tsp) |
| Gervin oak granules | 3-4 grams | (3 tsp) |
| Gervin maturing solution | 5 ml | (1 tsp) |
| Gervin No.2 yeast | 1 sachet | |
| Boiled water | to 4.5 litres | (to 1 gallon) |

I recommend using a small quantity of oak granules if you have them available because they will add roundness to the wine; at the level recommended, the oak flavour added will be quite small. The maturing solution is another optional ingredient; it will give added mouth feel.

There are many changes that can be rung on this recipe, and readers may like to try adding up to 225 grams (8 oz) of such fruits as blueberries and bullaces, at the same time dropping the level of blackberries by the same amount.

### Recipe 10.8 Dry Red Table Wine (Italian Style)

There are quite a number of different styles of Italian red wines, of course, ranging from the blockbusting Barolo of the north west to the lighter Valpolicella of Venetia, with Cabernet style wines in the north east to the classic Chianti from Tuscany. I have found that the recipe which follows gives a nicely balanced wine with characteristics somewhere between the Chianti and Valpolicella styles. It owes a lot to the red grape concentrate; I use Italian concentrate (Solvino is one brand but there are others equally good) to give some authenticity. Apart from this, the only fruit ingredient is elderberries. If you would like your wine to be heavier in style then add around 500 grams of chopped Conference pears.

| Ingredient | Metric | Imperial |
| --- | --- | --- |
| Elderberries | 250 grams | (9 oz) |
| Red grape concentrate | 750 ml | (27 fl oz) |
| Granulated sugar | 450 grams | (1 lb) |
| Pectolytic enzyme | 1/2 tablet | |
| Minavit nutrient | 2-3 grams | (1/2 tsp) |
| Gervin oak granules | 5 grams | (4 tsp) |
| Gervin No.2 yeast | 1 sachet | |
| Boiled water | to 4.5 litres | (to 1 gallon) |

I have suggested using Gervin No.2 yeast, but Varietal D will produce a better bouquet. If you opt for Varietal D yeast then add 5 grams of tartaric acid to the must to replace the malic acid that will be metabolised by the yeast.

### Recipe 10.10 Dry Red Table Wine (Spanish Style)

My intention is to produce a light Rioja style of wine. I have assumed that readers will be willing to be a little patient in that this wine really needs a year at least in the bottle to reach its peak. In particular the tannin has now been increased to between 0.15 to 0.20%, and there is quite a lot of oak flavour that needs time to integrate with the fruit. To give the wine a little extra body I have put in the minimum of banana flesh; at this level its effect will be noticeable but not its distinctive flavour and aroma. The alcohol level is kept to the normal 12% and the acidity should be close to 6 grams per litre.

| | | |
|---|---|---|
| Sloes | 750 grams | (1 lb 10 oz) |
| Elderberries | 450 grams | (1 lb) |
| Grapes | 450 grams | (1 lb) |
| Bananas (flesh) | 100 grams | (4 oz) |
| Granulated sugar | 600 grams | (1 lb 5 oz) |
| Gervin oak granules | 15 grams | (1/2 oz) |
| Pectolytic enzyme | 1/2 tablet | |
| Minavit nutrient | 2-3 grams | (1/2 tsp) |
| Gervin Varietal A yeast | 1 sachet | |
| Boiled water | to 4.5 litres | (to 1 gallon) |

I must emphasise once again that the sloes must be really ripe before they are to be picked. If they are not, the wine will have an unforgiving "green" taste. I have chosen Varietal A yeast because of its quality, but in my experience No.1 yeast does pretty well with this recipe and has the advantage of fermenting out the must faster.

If you wish, you can replace the sloes with 900 grams (two pounds) of blackberries, or even better with 450 grams each of bilberries and blackberries.

# Rosé Wines

Rosé wines should be easy to drink and accordingly we do not want too much body, tannin should be kept to a minimum, and the overall impression of the wines must be youthful and "fruity", although the fruit must not be excessive. To meet the demands of such wines I have produced these recipes such that the alcohol level never exceeds 11%, and in most cases will be closer to 10%. Nearly all of the ingredients can be purchased at any time of the year. In each case the wine will be ready for drinking just a few weeks after it has finished working. Serve it chilled.

### Recipe 10.11 Medium-dry Table Wine (Rosé 1)

| | | |
|---|---|---|
| White grape juice | 1 litre | (35 fl oz) |
| Elderberries or bilberries | 250 grams | (9 oz) |
| Granulated sugar | 560 grams | (1 lb 4 oz) |
| Pectolytic enzyme | 1/2 tablet | |
| Minavit nutrient | 2-3 grams | (1/2 tsp) |
| Gervin No.5 or Varietal B yeast | 1 sachet | |
| Boiled water | to 4.5 litres | (to 1 gallon) |
| Sugar for sweetening | 100 grams | (4 oz) |

This has the typical light-medium body that is required. It will have an alcohol level of 11% and after sweetening will have an S.G. of between 1.003 and 1.006. If elderberries are your choice for the source of the red colour, then do make sure that the berries have been chosen carefully (see page 37). A further point is that the pulp fermentation should be a short one, since otherwise too much tannin may be extracted from the skins. Either No.5 or B yeast will do, since both are capable of fermenting down to 10-12°C. Try to keep the temperature well below 20°C if you can, so that you get a good yield of fruity esters.

I have recommended ordinary sugar for the sweetening, which means that you will have to stabilise this wine, and indeed each of the four rosé wines. It may be possible for you to get some xylitol, which is a non-fermentable sugar-alcohol, whose sweetening power and taste are identical with those of sugar. It is expensive, and I don't recommend adding more than 100 grams of it to a wine, but at this level it does an excellent job, and there is no risk of refermentation taking place.

**Recipe 10.12 Medium-dry Table Wine (Rosé 2)**

| | | |
|---|---|---|
| Red grape concentrate | 170 ml | (6 fl oz) |
| Gooseberries | 250 grams | (9 oz) |
| Bananas (flesh) | 100 grams | (4 oz) |
| Granulated sugar | 680 grams | (1 lb 8 oz) |
| Tartaric acid | 10 grams | (2 tsp) |
| Pectolytic enzyme | 1/2 tablet | |
| Minavit nutrient | 2-3 grams | (1/2 tsp) |
| Gervin Varietal B yeast | 1 sachet | |
| Boiled water | to 4.5 litres | (to 1 gallon) |
| Sugar for sweetening | 100 grams | (4 oz) |

The juice should be extracted from the gooseberries by the freezer method (see page 51), but the banana flesh should be squashed with a potato masher. If you have no gooseberries in the freezer when you want to start this wine then you can replace the fresh fruit with a 800 gram can of gooseberries. In that case just crush the berries gently without damaging the seeds.

With both this and the previous recipe the amount of solid fruit is quite small, so the fermentation can be carried out in the demijohn. I suggest that you retain say 225 grams of the granulated sugar at the start and add water such that the liquid level is just below the shoulder of the jar. Then after 3 - 4 days you can sieve off the solids, and add the remainder of the sugar dissolved in water, taking the liquid level nearly to the top of the jar.

Sweeten and stabilise in the usual way.

**Recipe 10.13  Medium-sweet Table Wine (Rosé 3)**

This is a very simple recipe whose ingredients can be obtained at any time of the year. The wine it gives is still fairly light in body but it is fruity enough to stand sweetening to the medium-sweet category. When the sweetening sugar is added then the final S.G. is expected to be just over 1.010. The wine will have around 6 grams per litre of acid.

| | | |
|---|---|---|
| White grape juice | 1 litre | (35 fl oz) |
| Apple juice | 1 litre | (35 fl oz) |
| Red grape concentrate | 200 ml | (7 fl oz) |
| Granulated sugar | 480 grams | (1 lb 1 oz) |
| Pectolytic enzyme | 1/2 tablet | |
| Minavit nutrient | 2-3 grams | (1/2 tsp) |
| Bentonite | 5 grams | (1 tsp) |
| Gervin No.5 or Varietal B yeast | 1 sachet | |
| Boiled water | to 4.5 litres | (to 1 gallon) |
| Sugar for sweetening | 225 grams | (8 oz) |

I have put in bentonite as an optional ingredient, since it will ensure a smooth fermentation and helps the wine to clear quickly. Because it takes out yeast protein, there is then much less chance of the wine throwing a light deposit in the bottle a month or so later. But do make it into a smooth slurry before adding it to the must.

**Recipe 10.14  Medium-sweet Table Wine (Rosé 4)**

This wine will have a little more backbone because of the canned peaches and bananas, and the alcohol level may be as high as 12%. But it is a quality wine showing an excellent balance of body, acidity, sweetness and flavour. It can be drunk quite soon after the fermentation is over, but it will improve if kept in bottle for a few months. When the sweetening sugar has been added the S.G. is likely to be around 1.012.

| | | |
|---|---|---|
| Apple juice | 1 litre | (35 fl oz) |
| White grape juice | 500 ml | (18 fl oz) |
| Canned peaches | 800 grams | (28 oz) |
| Blackberries | 225 grams | (8 oz) |
| Blackcurrants | 100 grams | (4 oz) |
| Bananas (flesh) | 100 grams | (4 oz) |
| Granulated sugar | 625 grams | (1 lb 6 oz) |
| Pectolytic enzyme | 1/2 tablet | |
| Minavit nutrient | 2-3 grams | (1/2 tsp) |
| Gervin Varietal B yeast | 1 sachet | |
| Boiled water | to 4.5 litres | (to 1 gallon) |
| Sugar for sweetening | 225 grams | (8 oz) |

The canned peaches will contain a fair amount of syrup and this should be included in the must; it has been allowed for in the recipe. Some readers may like to sweeten this wine up rather more than I have suggested, but if so then do it in small doses because you can't remove the sugar, only blend the wine with another drier one.

# White Wines

### Recipe 10.15 Dry White Table Wine (Alsace/German Style)

This dry white table wine is described as being in the Alsace/German Style because in the dry form it has the characteristics of an Alsace wine but it can be sweetened up with apple juice to produce a medium to medium-sweet wine in the Liebfraumilch style. The basic part of the recipe is the mixture of apple and grape juices with apple dominating but there is the addition of a little Gervin White Wine Improver. This essence contains many of the esters produced during fermentation, plus the substances that are found in the Riesling grape (the king of the Alsace and German wine world). I recommend that you add the essence at the start of the fermentation since it is then well integrated; moreover the yeast is then less likely to produce a lot more of any one of the constituents of the essence, so that the bouquet will not become unbalanced.

| | | |
|---|---|---|
| Apple juice | 2 litres | (70 fl oz) |
| White grape juice | 500 ml | (18 fl oz) |
| Gervin White Wine Improver | 1-2 ml | (1/4 tsp) |
| Gervin oak granules | 1-2 grams | (1 tsp) |
| Pectolytic enzyme | 1/2 tablet | |
| Minavit nutrient | 2-3 grams | (1/2 tsp) |
| Bentonite | 5 grams | (1 tsp) |
| Gervin Varietal B yeast | 1 sachet | |
| Boiled water | to 4.5 litres | (to 1 gallon) |

The recipe will give a wine with an alcoholic strength of around 11%. If you would like to take the level up to 12% then add a further 70 - 80 grams (3 oz) of sugar to the must at the start of the fermentation. On the other hand, if you intend to turn the wine into the Liebfraumilch style, do not increase the sugar level and leave out the oak granules. Add 500 ml of apple juice once the fermentation is over and the wine is clear. The sweetened wine must be stabilised if it is to be bottled. The half litre of apple juice will increase the bulk of the wine and drop the alcohol level to about 10%; if you wish you can add a full litre of apple juice and reduce the alcohol level to nearer 9%, a typical level for this style of commercial wine.

The ferment should be carried out at a relatively cool temperature, say 12-15°C, if possible, in order to enhance the bouquet, and for that reason I have selected Varietal B yeast, which has a German pedigree and will work away happily down to 10°C. As with all the dry white table wines, the finishing S.G. should be between 0.991 and 0.993.

**Recipe 10.16  Dry White Table Wine (Bordeaux Style)**

This wine will have a less floral nose as a consequence of reducing the amount of apple juice and leaving out the White Wine Improver. I have included a small amount of orange juice (freshly pressed for preference) and a very small amount of honey. Do choose your honey carefully to avoid Australian gum notes etc. I suggest that you dissolve the honey in a litre or so of the water and heat this to the simmering point; remove any scum that may form. This treatment is a little more harsh than that which I normally suggest for honey, but we are not especially interested in the floral aroma in this instance, more for the slight extra body.

| | | |
|---|---|---|
| Apple juice | 1 litre | (35 fl oz) |
| White grape juice | 1 litre | (35 fl oz) |
| Fresh orange juice | 250 ml | (9 fl oz) |
| Honey | 30 grams | (1 oz) |
| Granulated sugar | 480 grams | (1 lb 1 oz) |
| Pectolytic enzyme | 1/2 tablet | |
| Minavit nutrient | 2-3 grams | (1/2 tsp) |
| Bentonite | 5 grams | (1 tsp) |
| Gervin No.5 yeast | 1 sachet | |
| Boiled water | to 4.5 litres | (to 1 gallon) |

No.5 yeast has been selected since it is a very clean yeast, of French origin, that ferments readily at temperatures as low as 12°C. As with the previous recipe, and for that matter with all dry white wines, we want the fermentation to take place at a fairly cool temperature. In this way we avoid producing dull, flat, tired-tasting white wines.

**Recipe 10.17  Dry White Table Wine (Burgundy style)**

We are now moving a little "up market", and producing a more complex wine by using a recipe that makes use of quite a mixture of fruits. The result should be a wine with an alcohol level of 13% or so, an acidity of 7 grams per litre, a full body and a complex flavour. Gooseberries are an essential part of this recipe as it will be for the following Sancerre and Chablis ones, and I can't emphasise enough the virtue of extracting the "juice" by the freezing method rather than fermenting on the pulp.

| | | |
|---|---|---|
| Apple juice | 2 litres | (70 fl oz) |
| White grape juice | 1 litre | (35 fl oz) |
| Pineapple juice | 200 ml | (7 fl oz) |
| Gooseberries | 450 grams | (1 lb) |
| Bananas (flesh) | 100 grams | (4 oz) |
| Pectolytic enzyme | 1/2 tablet | |
| Minavit nutrient | 2-3 grams | (1/2 tsp) |
| Oak granules | 1-2 grams | (1 tsp) |
| Gervin No.2 or | | |
|   Varietal D yeast | 1 sachet | |
| Boiled water | to 4.5 litres | (to 1 gallon) |

The choice of yeast will influence the nature of the finished wine since Varietal D will give an even better bouquet than No.2, but it will also destroy a little of the malic acid; this will give you a slightly less acid wine. Should the finished wine then seem a little too low in acid, simply add 5 grams (1 tsp) of tartaric acid.

If, during your search of the shelves of the better health food shops and supermarkets, you come across either a juice or nectar that is rich in passion fruit, do get some and try adding just a little of it to the must. It will have a very positive effect.

**Recipe 10.18 Dry White Table Wine (Sancerre Style)**

While this recipe has quite a lot in common with the previous one, it has reversed the relative amounts of apple and grape juices, and increased the amount of gooseberries. The overall effect will be to enhance the gooseberry note, which is generally thought to resemble that of the Sauvignon Blanc grape, and to give a somewhat more austere wine. It will benefit a lot by a few months in bottle, and after a year will do well on the show bench - if you are prepared to surrender such a precious brew to the judges!

| | | |
|---|---|---|
| Apple juice | 1 litre | (35 fl oz) |
| White grape juice | 2 litres | (70 fl oz) |
| Pineapple juice | 200 ml | (7 fl oz) |
| Gooseberries | 680 grams | (1 lb 8 oz) |
| Granulated sugar | 500 grams | (18 oz) |
| Pectolytic enzyme | 1/2 tablet | |
| Minavit nutrient | 2-3 grams | (1/2 tsp) |
| Oak granules | 1-2 grams | (1 tsp) |
| Gervin No.5 or | | |
|   Varietal D yeast | 1 sachet | |
| Boiled water | to 4.5 litres | (to 1 gallon) |

This wine will also contain 13% of alcohol. The acid level will be around 7 grams per litre if No.5 yeast is used, but will be reduced to 6 grams per litre if you use Varietal D.

### Recipe 10.19  Dry White Table Wine (Chablis Style)

Gooseberries continue to play an important role, backed up now with rhubarb and juices plus an extract from a small addition of whitecurrants. I suggest using sultana grapes (Thompson Seedless) if they are available; alternatively you can replace them with 550 ml (19 fl oz) of a good quality white grape concentrate. I have come across an excellent concentrate which is described as Chardonnay; use this if you can find it in your local homebrew shop.

| | | |
|---|---|---|
| Apple juice | 250 ml | (9 fl oz) |
| Sultana grapes | 2 kg | (4 lb 6 oz) |
| Gooseberries | 500 grams | (1 lb 2 oz) |
| Rhubarb | 400 grams | (14 oz) |
| Whitecurrants | 100 grams | (4 oz) |
| Granulated sugar | 550 grams | (1 lb 3 oz) |
| Pectolytic enzyme | 1/2 tablet | |
| Minavit nutrient | 1-2 grams | (1/4 tsp) |
| Oak granules | 1-2 grams | (1 tsp) |
| Gervin Varietal D yeast | 1 sachet | |
| Water | to 4.5 litres | (to 1 gallon) |

The rhubarb must be used as juice, so you may as well use the same freezing method to extract the juice from the whitecurrants. But I suggest that you simply crush the grapes gently and ferment on the pulp for about 4 days, since you will then get a little extra flavour from the skins. During this pulp fermentation stage the juices will be present as well of course, but you can leave out the granulated sugar until after you have sieved off the grape skins.

I suggest that you use the Varietal D yeast if possible, since this will drop the malic acid level a little and give extra bouquet; alternatively use No.5 yeast. The wine will contain some 12.5% of alcohol and will repay a decent period of bottle storage. It is a wine that is a potential winner.

### Recipe 10.20  Dry Sparkling Wine (Loire style 1)

This recipe will give a suitable base wine for the secondary fermentation that is carried out in the bottle as described on page 80. It is a very simple recipe using gooseberry extract and white grape juice, giving a base wine of 12% alcoholic strength.

Carry out the normal fermentation in the demijohn, and let the wine drop quite clear, fining if necessary to remove any haze. But do not add sulphite at the racking stage. Then dissolve 50 grams (2 oz) of sugar in the wine, add a small amount of rehydrated yeast slurry to each bottle and fit the stopper and wire restrainer. Continue to follow the basic method described for making sparkling wine.

| | | |
|---|---|---|
| Gooseberries | 1 kg | (2 lb 3 oz) |
| White grape juice | 1 litre | (35 fl oz) |
| Granulated sugar | 650 grams | (1 lb 7 oz) |
| Pectolytic enzyme | 1/2 tablet | |
| Minavit nutrient | 2-3 grams | (1/2 tsp) |
| Gervin Varietal C yeast | 1 sachet | |
| Boiled water | to 4.5 litres | (to 1 gallon) |

Readers will have noted that I have specified Varietal C yeast. This is because it is a splendid yeast intended specifically for making sparkling wines; it is said to be used for making around 70% of Champagne. It is capable of bringing about the required secondary fermentation despite the inhibiting influence of the 12% or so of alcohol present. Gervin No.3 yeast is an excellent substitute if you have difficulties in getting Varietal C.

Strictly speaking you could carry out the first stage of the fermentation with another strain of yeast (say No.5), and then use the Champagne yeast only for the secondary stage, but I prefer to use Varietal C all the way through, since then any residual cells in the base wine will be of this strain.

**Recipe 10.21 Dry Sparkling Wine (Loire 2)**

| | | |
|---|---|---|
| Rhubarb | 900 grams | (2 lb) |
| Pears | 450 grams | (1 lb) |
| White grape juice | 650 ml | (23 fl oz) |
| Granulated sugar | 650 grams | (1 lb 7 oz) |
| Pectolytic enzyme | 1/2 tablet | |
| Minavit nutrient | 2-3 grams | (1/2 tsp) |
| Gervin Varietal C yeast | 1 sachet | |
| Boiled water | to 4.5 litres | (to 1 gallon) |

This recipe uses rhubarb (as juice) rather than gooseberries, but adds a little body building by including some pears; extract the juice from the latter rather than fermenting on the pulp.

These days we see on the market an increasing number of sparkling rosé and even red wines. The secret of the success here is to keep the tannin level to a minimum, and use the fruit extract rather than the solid fruit for the red colour.

You can use the rhubarb recipe described in this section, but if so I suggest that you cut the amount of rhubarb down to 700 grams (1 lb 9 oz) and add the juice extracted from 100 grams (4 oz) of blackcurrants. The juice from around 225 grams (8 oz) of redcurrants may be substituted for the blackcurrants, when the wine will have a rather less aggressive flavour and a delicate pink colour.

### Recipe 10.22 Medium-dry Table Wine (Southern France Style)

We have already looked at one way of making a medium-dry table wine, namely taking the dry Alsace style wine (Recipe 10.15) and sweetening it with either sugar or apple juice. This Southern France style uses a related base, but with less emphasis on apple juice, and adds pineapple juice and a can of peaches.

| | | |
|---|---|---|
| Apple juice | 1 litre | (35 fl oz) |
| White grape juice | 1 litre | (35 fl oz) |
| Pineapple juice | 200 ml | (7 fl oz) |
| Canned peaches | 800 grams | (1 lb 12 oz) |
| Granulated sugar | 225 grams | (8 oz) |
| Tartaric acid | 5 grams | (1 tsp) |
| Pectolytic enzyme | 1/2 tablet | |
| Minavit nutrient | 2-3 grams | (1/2 tsp) |
| Bentonite | 5 grams | (1 tsp) |
| Gervin No.5 yeast | 1 sachet | |
| Boiled water | to 4.5 litres | (to 1 gallon) |

Provided the peaches are pureed, the fermentation can be started in the demijohn. I recommend that you leave out the bentonite until after the first racking and then add it as a slurry. Then you won't need the bentonite as a means of reducing the frothing, since the peach particles will provide the necessary surface on which the gas bubbles can form, but the bentonite will remove yeast protein and prevent later deposits in the bottle.

### Recipe 10.23 Medium-sweet Table wine (Bordeaux Style)

Since we are looking for a table wine rather than a social wine, the intention is to keep the alcohol level down to 12% or thereabouts. Of course this can be used for party functions if you want to drink larger amounts and yet not go over the limit.

| | | |
|---|---|---|
| Apple juice | 1.5 litres | (53 fl oz) |
| Grapes | 1.5 kg | (3 lb 5 oz) |
| Canned peaches | 800 grams | (1 lb 12 oz) |
| Bananas (flesh) | 150 grams | (5 oz) |
| Granulated sugar | 350 grams | (12 oz) |
| Pectolytic enzyme | 1/2 tablet | |
| Minavit nutrient | 2-3 grams | (1/2 tsp) |
| Gervin Varietal B yeast | 1 sachet | |
| Sugar for sweetening | 300 grams | (11 oz) |

You can use almost any white dessert grapes, but the sultana ones do especially well in this recipe. Again just crush the grapes and ferment with the skins present for the first few days. The wine can be drunk quite quickly, but if you want to speed it up then add a little Gervin maturing solution to smooth it out.

### Recipe 10.24 Medium-sweet Table Wine (Loire Style)

My aim is to produce a wine in the lighter Bonnezeaux style, with around 13% of alcohol, and a finishing S.G. of 1.015 or thereabouts. To reach its best it needs to be allowed to mature for a year in bottle.

| | | |
|---|---|---|
| Apple juice | 1 litre | (35 fl oz) |
| White grape juice | 1 litre | (35 fl oz) |
| Rhubarb | 450 grams | (1 lb) |
| Gooseberries | 450 grams | (1 lb) |
| Canned peaches | 450 grams | (1 lb) |
| Honey | 50 grams | (2 oz) |
| Granulated sugar | 500 grams | (1 lb 2 oz) |
| Pectolytic enzyme | 1/2 tablet | |
| Minavit nutrient | 1 gram | (1/4 tsp) |
| Gervin Varietal D yeast | 1 sachet | |
| Boiled water | to 4.5 litres | (to 1 gallon) |
| Sugar for sweetening | 225 grams | (8 oz) |

Extract the juices from the gooseberries and rhubarb by the usual freezing method. Varietal D yeast is recommended so as to get the benefit of some reduction in malic acid and the extra bouquet.

### Recipe 10.25 Sweet White Table Wine (Heavy Loire Style)

It is questionable, of course, whether a wine of this weight of flavour and sweetness can be considered as a table wine at all, and drunk with the pudding course, or kept for post-meal slurping. The same problem arises with the next three wines. This recipe certainly gives a lovely wine, and it is about as close as we can hope to get to the fabulous Moulin Touchais, with 14% alcohol, and acidity close to 7 grams per litre and a finishing S.G. of 1.020.

| | | |
|---|---|---|
| White grape concentrate | 350 ml | (12 fl oz) |
| Rhubarb | 600 grams | (1 lb 5 oz) |
| Bananas (flesh) | 200 grams | (7 oz) |
| Canned peaches | 425 grams | (15 ounces) |
| Dried apricots | 100 grams | (4 oz) |
| Strawberries | 200 grams | (7 oz) |
| Granulated sugar | 540 grams | ( |
| Minavit nutrient | 2-3 grams | (1/2 tsp) |
| Gervin No.3 or Varietal C yeast | 1 sachet | |
| Glycerine | 10 ml | (2 tsp) |
| Boiled water | to 4.5 litres | (to 1 gallon) |
| Sugar for sweetening | 340 grams | (12 oz) |

I have included a little glycerine (glycerol) in this recipe. This increases the sweetness a little, but more importantly helps to improve the mouthfeel. It should be added once the fermentation is over. The yeast itself will produce between 5-5 grams per litre of glycerine during the fermentation, so let this take place before we add more. Be very patient with this wine and keep at least a couple of bottles for two years and open them on a special occasion!

**Recipe 10.26 Sweet White Table Wine (Monbazillac Style)**

This wine will be lighter than the previous one, with medium body, 13% alcohol and an acid level of 7 grams per litre. I have found that when this wine has been kept in bottle for a year or two it really does match up with the commercial equivalent, and is as good as all but the very best that this region of France can offer us.

| | | |
|---|---|---|
| Apple juice | 1 litre | (35 fl oz) |
| White grape juice | 1 litre | (35 fl oz) |
| Canned peaches | 800 grams | (1 lb 12 oz) |
| Dried apricots | 400 grams | (14 oz) |
| Honey | 50 grams | (2 oz) |
| Granulated sugar | 525 grams | (1 lb 3 oz) |
| Pectolytic enzyme | 1/2 tablet | |
| Minavit nutrient | 1 gram | (1/4 tsp) |
| Gervin No.3 or | | |
| Varietal C yeast | 1 sachet | |
| Boiled water | to 4.5 litres | (to 1 gallon) |
| Sugar for sweetening | 300 grams | (11 oz) |

**Recipe 10.27 Sweet White Table Wine (Barsac Style)**

| | | |
|---|---|---|
| Apple juice | 1 litre | (35 fl oz) |
| White grape juice | 1 litre | (35 fl oz) |
| Rhubarb | 900 grams | (2 lbs) |
| Dried apricots | 200 grams | (7 oz) |
| Bananas (flesh) | 225 grams | (8 oz) |
| Honey | 100 grams | (4 oz) |
| Granulated sugar | 550 grams | (1 lb 3 oz) |
| Pectolytic enzyme | 1/2 tablet | |
| Minavit nutrient | 1-2 grams | (1/4 tsp) |
| Gervin No.3 or | | |
| Varietal D yeast | 1 sachet | |
| Boiled water | to 4.5 litres | (to 1 gallon) |
| Sugar for sweetening | 340 grams | (12 oz) |

With this recipe and the following one we are moving to the Bordeaux region, this time to try to imitate the lighter Barsac style. The acid level comes out on the high side at 8 to 9 grams per litre; this doesn't worry me since there is ample alcohol and body to allow the wine to be sweetened up to give an S.G. of around 1.025 to 1.030. If you would prefer to have rather less malic acid in your wine then use Varietal D yeast, which should drop the acid level by about one gram per litre.

If the acid really is too high for your palate then you can reduce it by adding sodium bicarbonate (potassium bicarbonate is better still). But be careful and limit the amount of bicarbonate that you add to one heaped teaspoonful. If you use more than this the flavour is likely to be adversely affected. Another tip. Split your gallon of wine into two halves and treat one half with half a teaspoonful of bicarbonate. If the result is what you want then treat the other half; if you think you may have overdone it then mix the treated and untreated wine.

### Recipe 10.27 Sweet White Table Wine (Sauternes Style)

This is a lovely blockbuster of a sweet wine with around 14% of alcohol and an acid level close to 8 grams per litre. The sweetening should bring the S.G. up to around 1.030. Again I suggest adding a little glycerine, and on this occasion I think that the faintest touch of oak will be in order.

| Ingredient | Metric | Imperial |
|---|---|---|
| Apple juice | 2 litres | (70 fl oz) |
| Sultanas | 450 grams | (1 lb) |
| Dried apricots | 100 grams | (4 oz) |
| Canned peaches | 825 grams | (1 lb 11 oz) |
| Rhubarb | 250 grams | (9 oz) |
| Strawberries | 150 grams | (5 oz) |
| Honey | 100 grams | (4 oz) |
| Granulated sugar | 225 grams | (8 oz) |
| Oak granules | 1-2 grams | (1 tsp) |
| Pectolytic enzyme | 1 tablet | |
| Minavit nutrient | 1-2 grams | (1/4 tsp) |
| Gervin No.3 or Varietal C yeast | 1 sachet | |
| Boiled water | to 4.5 litres | (to 1 gallon) |
| Sugar for sweetening | 450 grams | (1 lb) |

I have included the strawberries here, as with the recipe for a heavy Loire wine, even though you might think of this as a "red" fruit. In practice the red colour fades to a light amber which is quite appropriate for this style of wine. In addition the strawberries contain some of the esters found in Sauternes wines, so they make an appropriate fruit when used in small amounts.

Like all full-bodied wines with lots of flavour, this wine will get steadily better in the bottle over a period of up to five years.

# Social Wines

By the term "Social Wine", the amateur winemaker means a wine that can be drunk with friends on a social occasion. And this normally means that the wine will have an alcoholic strength of 13-14%, and a degree of sweetness best described as medium sweet. There are many commercial white wines that fall into this category, and I gave two recipes (10.23 and 10.24) which would produce wines in this style. Many amateur winemakers like to extend their range to include red social wines. And why not? If we can now have red sparkling wines from the commercial world, then medium-sweet red wines would seem to have a place too. Unfortunately, at the moment there are very few commercial models for us to copy, apart from the odd Italian, and possibly the Cypriot Commandaria. So we will have to start a trend for lovers of red wines who have a sweet tooth.

But we must take care because most ingredients that can be used to make red wines will also contain a fair measure of tannin, and it is the mix of sweetness with tannin that sometimes seems a little out of place. From my own experiments I have found that the most acceptable results come from using our fruits in such a way as to reduce the impact of the tannin. I make up my musts by first treating my red ingredients with heat, using either the thermal vinification method (see page 76) or the steaming (Säftborn) process (see page 54). Another important point is that we must use really ripe fruit. The following two recipes have been very successful.

**Recipe 10.28 Red Social Wine 1**

This recipe contains a lot of fruit, the principal "red" ingredients being blackberries and elderberries in a 2:1 ratio. I strongly recommend that you use a steamer on these two fruits if you have the equipment, but if not then put the fruit into a suitable large glass vessel, which is itself inside a larger vessel containing water. The water in the outer vessel is heated to 70 to 80°C and kept there for say 30 minutes. After this time take the fruit out, crush it and press out the juice. Only the juice of the pears should be used so that we can keep the tannin to a minimum.

| | | |
|---|---|---|
| Blackberries | 900 grams | (2 lb) |
| Elderberries | 450 grams | (1 lb) |
| Red grape concentrate | 150 ml | (5 fl oz) |
| Pears | 450 grams | (1 lb) |
| Bananas (flesh) | 150 grams | (5 oz) |
| Granulated sugar | 680 grams | (1 lb 8 oz) |
| Pectolytic enzyme | 1/2 tablet | |
| Minavit nutrient | 2-3 grams | (1/2 tsp) |
| Gervin No.3 or Varietal C yeast | 1 sachet | |
| Boiled water | to 4.5 litres | (to 1 gallon) |
| Sugar for sweetening | 250 grams | (9 oz) |

The banana flesh should be added as pulp in the usual way and not heat extracted. The sweetened wine should have a finishing S.G. of about 1.012, with an alcoholic content of 14%.

**Recipe 10.29   Red Social Wine 2**

This recipe gives less tannin than the previous one, so it can be processed using the usual pulp fermentation for just three days if you wish to avoid the longer and more messy heating approach. The alcohol should again be 14% and the S.G. close to 1.015.

| | | |
|---|---|---|
| Cherries | 900 grams | (2 lb) |
| Elderberries | 450 grams | (1 lb) |
| Raspberries | 100 grams | (4 oz) |
| Sultanas | 500 grams | (1 lb 2 oz) |
| Granulated sugar | 570 grams | (1 lb 4 oz) |
| Pectolytic enzyme | 1/2 tablet | |
| Minavit nutrient | 1-2 grams | (1/4 tsp) |
| Gervin No.3 or Varietal C yeast | 1 sachet | |
| Boiled water | to 4.5 litres | (to 1 gallon) |
| Sugar for sweetening | 225 grams | (8 oz) |

This recipe is much more extravagant than the previous one for most of us because it uses cherries which are less likely to be available except in the greengrocers or orchard shop. But don't be too mean, buy the best ripe black cherries that you can find. It just isn't worth making this wine if you have to settle for Whitehearts. You may find it worthwhile adding 5 ml of Gervin maturing solution to this gallon of wine once the fermentation has stopped, since it will produce an effect out of all proportion to its cost.

If you are quite content to add natural flavourings to your wine, then try adding a small amount of Gervin Superior Port Essence to this one. While this essence is really intended to give that little extra to the simulated Port-style wine, it does an excellent job when added to red social wines, and it can also have a positive impact on full-bodied dry red table wines.

# Aperitif Wines

**Recipe 10.30   Dry Aperitif Wine (Citrus Style)**

In the last chapter I gave two simple recipes for dry aperitif wines, one based on grapefruit (Recipe 9.14) and the other on lemon (Recipe 9.15). The recipe that now follows is a more complex one, but it still depends on grapefruit juice for its aperitif character. I have set out the recipe to give a wine of some 15% alcohol, but with the acidity not exceeding 5 grams per litre.

| | | |
|---|---|---|
| Grapefruit juice | 300 ml | (11 fl oz) |
| Pineapple juice | 400 ml | (14 fl oz) |
| Dried dates | 100 grams | (4 oz) |
| White grape concentrate | 250 ml | (9 fl oz) |
| Granulated sugar | 800 grams | (1 lb 12 oz) |
| Pectolytic enzyme | 1/2 tablet | |
| Minavit nutrient | 2-3 grams | (1/2 tsp) |
| Gervin maturing solution | 5 ml | (1 tsp) |
| Gervin No.1 yeast | 1 sachet | |
| Boiled water | to 4.5 litres | (to 1 gallon) |

**Recipe 10.31 Dry Aperitif Wine (Vermouth Style)**

This is basically a fairly non-descript wine containing some 15% of alcohol and a relatively low acidity. The Vermouth flavour is added after the fermentation is over by means of a commercial essence. I recommend the Gervin brand of essence since it was the best one that I found after trying out the dozen or so different ones I was offered by the flavour houses.

| | | |
|---|---|---|
| White grape concentrate | 500 ml | (18 fl oz) |
| Bananas (flesh) | 150 grams | (5 oz) |
| Dried figs | 100 grams | (4 oz) |
| Granulated sugar | 700 grams | (1 lb 9 oz) |
| Pectolytic enzyme | 1/2 tablet | |
| Minavit nutrient | 2-3 grams | (1/2 tsp) |
| Gervin Vermouth essence | 20 ml | (4 tsp) |
| Gervin maturing solution | 5 ml | (1 tsp) |
| Gervin No.1 yeast | 1 sachet | |
| Boiled water | to 4.5 litres | (to 1 gallon) |

This wine does not have a lot of body but it will stand a moderate degree of sweetening if you want your wine to be just off dry. I suggest adding 100 grams of sugar to the finished wine but not a lot more if you wish to maintain the balance.

You can add the Vermouth flavour to the wine by using a mixture of herbs. Such mixtures used to be available in most homebrew shops, but this is now less likely. If you want to use the dried herbs rather than the essence, then try the mixture that follows on the next page.

| | |
|---|---|
| Sage | 8 parts |
| Wormwood | 8 parts |
| Calamus | 6 parts |
| Coriander | 4 parts |
| Hyssop | 4 parts |
| Bitter orange peel | 4 parts |
| Thyme | 4 parts |
| Mugwort | 2 parts |
| Cinnamon | 1 part |
| Nutmeg | 1 part |
| Vanilla | 1 part |

Take the mixture of herbs and spices and reduce them to a coarse powder by giving them a quick whirl in a coffee mill. Put 2-3 grams (1 tsp) in a muslin bag and suspend it in the finished wine for two or three days, shaking the jar from time to time. If the amount of flavour extracted is not enough then add more mixed herbs to the bag and repeat the extraction.

Many of the herbs can be purchased from health food shops, but if there are difficulties try the mail order company Cathay of Bournemouth. You may not be able to get all of the herbs listed, but in any case you may want to experiment a little and try the effect of adding one or two different herbs or spices. If you want to increase the aromatic character try including angelica, summer savory and camomile.

You can make a red Vermouth, of course, by replacing the white grape concentrate with red. Such aperitif wines are often sold as sweeter wines. If you want a sweet red Vermouth style of wine then I suggest that you cut the Vermouth flavouring down to half in the first instance, since otherwise there may be a clash between the herbal extracts and the tannin. It is very much a matter of trial and error.

Recipe 10.32 Dry Aperitif Wine (Bitters Style)

You can take the same base wine as for the previous Vermouth recipe, but use a mixture of bitter herbs rather than Vermouth ones. The two herbs giving characteristic bitter flavours are cinchona bark (the quinine note) and gentian root, both of which can be purchased from Potters Herbal Supplies of Wigan, if you have local difficulties in purchasing supplies. One simple mix of herbs and spices that I like is:

| | |
|---|---|
| Cinnamon | 1 part |
| Gentian root | 15 parts |
| Bitter orange | 10 parts |
| Sweet orange | 10 parts |
| Wormwood | 5 parts. |

With this bitter mix it is best to extract the flavours by soaking the herb/spice mixture in Vodka for two weeks. You can then add the extract to the finished wine and adjust the level of bitterness to your liking.

### Recipe 10.33  Dry Aperitif Wine (Madeira Style)

It is a matter of opinion whether we include Madeira here as an aperitif or later as a dessert wine. The same goes for Sherry too, of course. In each case I am taking the dry wines to be aperitifs.

| | | |
|---|---|---|
| Dried bananas | 60 grams | (2 oz) |
| Dried dates | 100 grams | (4 oz) |
| Dried peaches | 170 grams | (6 oz) |
| Raisins | 680 grams | (1 lb 8 oz) |
| Demarara sugar | 700 grams | (1 lb 8 oz) |
| Pectolytic enzyme | 1/2 tablet | |
| Minavit nutrient | 2-3 grams | (1/2 tsp) |
| Gervin maturing solution | 5 ml | (1 tsp) |
| Gervin No.3 or  Varietal C yeast | 1 sachet | |
| Boiled water | to 4.5 litres | (to 1 gallon) |

This wine will have an alcohol content of at least 16%. On this occasion I suggest using Demarara sugar simply to get the hint of caramel that we need in the Madeira. The wine has the right sort of base for Madeira but it will still lack the true Madeira nose. I have used an excellent Italian essence which adds just what I want in my Madeira, but unfortunately this could only be bought in large amounts and so it still hasn't reached the British market. Failing the availability of a suitable essence, the best we can do is to "cook" the wine in a way that vaguely resembles the traditional estufa process used in Madeira, where the wines are heated to 40-50°C for three to six months.

One way we can imitate this is to place our gallon jar of wine in a hot place, such as the airing cupboard, or an uninsulated attic during a hot summer. Another way is to put the demijohn of wine outside in the garden during the summer, covering it with a metal bucket. This concentrates the heat of the sun and cooks the wine. Before you give your wine the heat treatment you must take account of the fact that the increase in temperature will cause the wine to expand, so allow for this by leaving sufficient air space in the neck of the jar. Since any water in the trap is likely to evaporate, fill the trap with a 50:50 mixture of water and glycerine; the latter will not evaporate and will provide a protective seal.

For a sweeter Madeira, first increase the amount of flavour in the wine by doubling the amount of dried dates, then sweeten up the finished wine before you give it the estufa treatment.

**Recipe 10.34 Dry Aperitif Wine (Sherry Style)**

Our aim is to produce a wine of 18% alcohol, or as high as possible, keeping the acid level down to 5 grams per litre or less if we can. To get the high level of alcohol it is important to make sure that the yeast is in fine fettle and capable of coping with the inhibiting influence of the alcohol. We can ensure that the yeast is well equipped for this task if we give it an adequate supply of nutrient and prepare it during the rehydration such that the cell membrane is healthy. We shall discuss this again in Chapter 11, but for the moment let me just say that when you rehydrate the yeast, you should stir the slurry strongly to get plenty of air into it.

There are two approaches to making the Sherry. The simplest way is to ferment out the wine to as high a level of alcohol as possible, using a Champagne yeast, and then add a good Sherry essence. Some readers may feel that adding essence is too easy a way, and in this case I recommend that they use a true Sherry yeast. At the time this book is being completed, the only Sherry yeast that is available in dried form is the one sold to amateurs as Gervin No.4 (blue label). This is a Californian Sherry yeast, which under ideal conditions will form a submerged flor. It is unlikely that the typical surface flor will form. Even so the yeast does give the wine a Sherry note. Perhaps the "belt and braces" approach would be to use the Sherry yeast first of all and see what the finished wine is like. If the Sherry note is not pronounced enough then resort to adding the essence.

| | | |
|---|---|---|
| Apples | 900 grams | (2 lb) |
| Bananas (flesh) | 450 grams | (1 lb) |
| Dried figs | 225 grams | (8 oz) |
| Raisins | 225 grams | (8 oz) |
| Granulated sugar | 1050 grams | (2 lb 5 oz) |
| Pectolytic enzyme | 1/2 tablet | |
| Minavit nutrient | 5 grams | (1 tsp) |
| Gervin maturing solution | 5 ml | (1 tsp) |
| Gervin Superior Sherry Essence | 5 ml | (1 tsp) |
| Gervin No.3 or Varietal C yeast (or Gervin No.4) | 1 sachet | |
| Boiled water | to 4.5 litres | (to 1 gallon) |

Make sure that you use a mixture of cookers and eaters and that these apples are free from blemishes. Cut the apples up small, or pulverise them after they have been frozen, and use the pulp fermentation method. If you adopt the essence approach remember that the essence must be added after the fermentation is over.

This Sherry wine can be sweetened if you wish, but don't try to make it into a sweet cream Sherry because it doesn't have enough body for this. If you want to make a sweet Sherry then cut the apples in the recipe to half and replace them with

150 grams (5 oz) of dried dates and 100 grams (4 oz) of dried rose hip shells. The sherry can then be sweetened with up to 340 grams (12 oz) of sugar.

**Recipe 10.35  Sweet Aperitif Wine (Citrus Style)**

This wine can be made from the types of orange used for making marmalade, or indeed from marmalade itself. The easiest way is to take a can of oranges intended for making marmalade, and puree the fruit ( I am assuming that the can contains enough fruit to make two to three pounds of marmalade; if this is not so then take the necessary part of the contents of the large can). Add a kilo of sugar, a whole tablet of pectolytic enzyme and 2-3 grams of minavit nutrient. Dilute the mix down with boiled water and add the rehydrated yeast; I recommend Gervin No.1 yeast for this purpose. When the fermentation is complete, and the wine is clear, sweeten to taste, by adding up to 340 grams of sugar.

If you have some of last year's batch of marmalade left over, use it according to the following recipe:

| | | |
|---|---|---|
| Marmalade | 2 kg | (4 lb 6 oz) |
| Sultanas | 450 grams | (1 lb) |
| Pectolytic enzyme | 1 tablet | |
| Minavit nutrient | 2-3 grams | (1/2 tsp) |
| Gervin No.1 yeast | 1 sachet | |
| Boiled water | to 4.5 litres | (to 1 gallon) |
| Sugar for sweetening | 340 grams | (12 oz) |

# Dessert Wines

These are the wines that must be drunk after a meal rather than during the course of eating it, because they have immense flavour and a high level of alcohol. Most of our dessert wines use lashings of ripe fruits and in that sense they have no real commercial equivalent. One comparison is Port, of course, and I have given a recipe to produce this style of wine.

Commercial white dessert wines are either wines of somewhat lower alcohol content, such as the heavy Loire wines or the late harvest offerings from many countries, or sweeter fortified wines such as Sherry and Madeira.

## Recipe 10.36  Red Dessert Wine 1

| | | |
|---|---|---|
| Cherries | 900 grams | (2 lb) |
| Elderberries | 600 grams | (1 lb 5 oz) |
| Bananas (flesh) | 450 grams | (1 lb) |
| Blackberries | 450 grams | (1 lb) |
| Blackcurrants | 100 grams | (4 oz) |
| Granulated sugar | 700 grams | (1 lb 9 oz) |
| Pectolytic enzyme | 1 tablet | |
| Minavit nutrient | 2-3 grams | (1/2 tsp) |
| Gervin oak granules | 15 grams | (1/2 oz) |
| Gervin Superior Port Essence | 5 ml | (1 tsp) |
| Gervin maturing solution | 5 ml | (1 tsp) |
| Gervin No.3 or Varietal C yeast | 1 sachet | |
| Boiled water | to 4.5 litres | (to 1 gallon) |
| Sugar for sweetening | 450 grams | (1 lb) |

This delightfully full-bodied dessert wine should contain around 17% of alcohol, and the final S.G. after sweetening will be about 1.030. The Gervin Superior Port Essence and Maturing Solution are both optional, since a splendid wine will be produced without them, but they will bring about a further improvement. The acid level, while perhaps on the high side at 7 grams per litre, will be balanced by the body, alcohol and sweetness, and won't seem intrusive once the wine has had a decent period of maturation. The acidity and the strength of fruit flavour guarantees that this wine will have a long, long life - if you let it!

## Recipe 10.37  Red Dessert Wine 2

| | | |
|---|---|---|
| Blackberries | 500 grams | (1 lb 2 oz) |
| Elderberries | 1 kg | (2 lb 3 oz) |
| Plums (blue) | 1 kg | (2 lb 3 oz) |
| Red grape concentrate | 200 ml | (7 fl oz) |
| Granulated sugar | 1 kg | (2 lb 3 oz) |
| Pectolytic enzyme | 1 tablet | |
| Minavit nutrient | 2-3 grams | (1/2 tsp) |
| Gervin oak granules | 15 grams | (1/2 oz) |
| Gervin maturing solution | 5 ml | (1 tsp) |
| Glycerine | 10 ml | (2 tsp) |
| Gervin No.3 or Varietal C yeast | 1 sachet | |
| Boiled water | to 4.5 litres | (to 1 gallon) |
| Sugar for sweetening | 450 grams | (1 lb) |

The main worry is the high level of acidity that is inevitable when such quantities of fruit are used in the recipe. To some extent we can help by making sure that the fruit is really ripe, but even so the acid level is high and this will hinder the fermentation and make it slow, besides giving a somewhat tart wine for most palates. Accordingly I suggest that you neutralise some of the acid by adding two level teaspoonsful of potassium (or sodium) bicarbonate to the crushed fruit just before you add the yeast.

If you can obtain true damsons that are very ripe, then use 500 grams of them in place of the kilogram of plums. I suggest half as much because there will be plenty of flavour in the damsons, but damsons will be more acid than the plums even if they are ripe.

The glycerine and maturing solution should be added after the wine has finished working.

**Recipe 10.38 Red Dessert Wine (Port Style)**

Port is made commercially in a way that would be ruinous to the amateur, in that the fermentation is allowed to proceed only as far as the production of 7 - 8 % alcohol; the fermentation is then stopped by adding grape brandy, the fortification taking the alcohol level up to 20% or so. We can't match this process. And a point to note is that the yeast used in the fermentation is not intended to produce high levels of alcohol. Thus even if an active dried Port yeast were available it would be of no use to us. In fact if you see a dried yeast labelled Port, take the label with a pinch of salt.

The amateur approach has to be to use a yeast that will produce as much alcohol as possible, and to choose the ingredients to give the right sort of flavour. I recommend using Gervin No.3 or Varietal C yeast, which will give 19% and possibly 20% under the right conditions.

The recipe that follows on the next page should produce a wine of 18% alcohol, and a final S.G. of about 1.030. Unfortunately the acid level is likely to be around 7 grams per litre, which is quite a bit higher than that found in true Port wines. Accordingly I suggest that you treat the must with two heaped teaspoonfuls of potassium (or sodium) bicarbonate before you start the fermentation.

I recommend adding oak granules to the must and Gervin Superior Port essence to the finished wine. If you do this, and allow the wine to mature for a year or so it will make the world of difference.

| | | |
|---|---|---|
| Red grape concentrate | 1 kg | (standard can) |
| Pears | 1 kg | (2 lb 3 oz) |
| Bananas (flesh) | 100 grams | (4 oz) |
| Granulated sugar | 450 grams | (1 lb 3 oz) |
| Pectolytic enzyme | 1/2 tablet | |
| Minavit nutrient | 5 grams | (1 tsp) |
| Gervin oak granules | 10 grams | |
| Gervin Superior Port Essence | 5 ml | (1 tsp) |
| Gervin No.3 or Varietal C yeast | 1 sachet | |
| Boiled water | to 4.5 litres | (to 1 gallon) |
| Sugar for sweetening | 450 grams | (1 lb) |

There is a commonly held view that "feeding the yeast", that is adding the sugar (as syrup) in small amounts as the yeast is getting near the end of its tether, will produce much higher levels of alcohol. Indeed I have heard many tales of wine-makers who have done this and persuaded the yeast to consume fantastic quantities of sugar, so much in fact that the wine should contain 25% or more of alcohol. Analysis of wines made this way reveal a disappointing amount of alcohol to be present, typical levels being 16 - 17%. It seems that the sugar is used to produce something other than alcohol, mainly more yeast in fact. It is now well established that if the yeast is in good heart, it will ferment out enough sugar to produce the high alcohol levels even when the sugar is added all at once at the beginning of the fermentation.

If the wine does show signs of sticking near the end of the fermentation, simply pouring it from one jar to another often works wonders. It adds a little oxygen to the wine and revives the flagging yeast.

This is especially important when larger quantities of wine are being made, and the oxygen supply is becoming exhausted, and is good advice to those serious winemakers who will want to make most of the wines in larger amounts of say 20 litres (about 5 gallons). When this is so the ingredients are simply increased accordingly, although 1 sachet of yeast is sufficient for 20 litres. With the heavier, more alcoholic wines like Port, there is a lot to be said for maturing the wines in bulk in oak casks. The wines will then throw out unstable colouring matter and drop clear. My only reservation on the cask maturing method is that it is essential to keep the casks free from bacteria when they are empty, and to keep topping up the wine in the cask as it slowly evaporates. Remember too that the casks will add oak flavour quite strongly for the first and second time they are used, but after that it is the law of diminishing returns. Then it is important to add oak chips or granules for the oak flavour, and to use the casks for the stabilising of the red pigments etc.

**Recipe 10.39  White Dessert Wine 1**

| | | |
|---|---|---|
| Gooseberries | 1 kg | (2 lb 3 oz) |
| Canned peaches | 800 grams | (1 lb 12 oz) |
| Raisins | 450 grams | (1 lb) |
| Dried apricots | 100 grams | (4 oz) |
| Bananas (flesh) | 200 grams | (7 oz) |
| Canned pears | 425 grams | (15 oz) |
| Honey | 100 grams | (4 oz) |
| Granulated sugar | 550 grams | (1 lb 3 oz) |
| Pectolytic enzyme | 1 tablet | |
| Minavit nutrient | 2-3 grams | (1/2 tsp) |
| Gervin oak granules | 2-3 grams | (2 tsp) |
| Gervin No.3 or Varietal C yeast | 1 sachet | |
| Boiled water | to 4.5 litres | (to 1 gallon) |
| Sugar for sweetening | 450 grams | (1 lb) |

This wine should contain at least 17% of alcohol and a final S.G. of 1.030 or more after sweetening. Unfortunately, the concentration of fruit has taken the acid up rather too much, so once again I recommend that you add two heaped teaspoonsful of bicarbonate to the must just before you add the yeast. Stir it well then let fermentation commence. You may wish to speed things up a little by adding the usual amount of Gervin maturing solution to the finished wine, and some 10 ml of glycerine will also smooth out the rough edges of the new wine. If made in quantities of five gallons or more it is worth considering keeping the wine in an oak cask during the initial period of maturation.

**Recipe 10.40  White Dessert Wine 2**

| | | |
|---|---|---|
| Eating apples | 2 kg | (4 lb 6 oz) |
| Dried apricots | 350 grams | (12 oz) |
| Bananas (flesh) | 1350 grams | (3 lb) |
| Sultanas | 450 grams | (1 lb) |
| Granulated sugar | 350 grams | (12 oz) |
| Pectolytic enzyme | 1 tablet | |
| Minavit nutrient | 2-3 grams | (1/2 tsp) |
| Gervin oak granules | 5 grams | (3-4 tsp) |
| Gervin maturing solution | 5 ml | (1 tsp) |
| Glycerine | 10 ml | (2 tsp) |
| Gervin No.3 or Varietal C yeast | 1 sachet | |
| Boiled water | to 4.5 litres | (to 1 gallon) |
| Sugar for sweetening | 450 grams | (1 lb) |

This wine will be another with 17% or more of alcohol, and it will have a very full body. This has been achieved in part by the use of quite a lot of bananas in the must. Although the flavour will be noticeably banana in the early stages, this will become rather less dominant as the wine ages and mellows. Although the acid level may be a little high, the weight of fruit flavour, alcohol and sugar balances it quite well, and so on this occasion I avoid using bicarbonate to neutralise some of the acid.

### Recipe 10.41  White Dessert Wine 3

This final recipe in the dessert section gives a rather lighter style of dessert wine, with the alcohol level around 15-16%, and accordingly somewhat less body. It can be considered as a social wine provided it is drunk in modest amounts.

| | | |
|---|---|---|
| Apple juice | 2 litres | (70 fl oz) |
| Rhubarb | 450 grams | (1 lb) |
| Pineapple juice | 100 ml | (4 fl oz) |
| Strawberries | 225 grams | (8 oz) |
| White grape concentrate | 250 ml | (9 fl oz) |
| Granulated sugar | 800 grams | (1 lb 12 oz) |
| Pectolytic enzyme | 1/2 tablet | |
| Minavit nutrient | 2-3 grams | (1/2 tsp) |
| Gervin oak granules | 2-3 grams | (2 tsp) |
| Gervin No.3 or Varietal C yeast | 1 sachet | |
| Boiled water | to 4.5 litres | (to 1 gallon) |
| Sugar for sweetening | 350-400 grams | (13 oz) |

When you sweeten the wine, start with 350 grams, and leave the wine for a week or so to let the sugar blend in. If the wine is still not quite sweet enough for you then add the other 50 grams of sugar. You can ring the changes on this recipe by including some peaches or canned peaches in place of the pineapple juice. It is also worth experimenting with the addition of some of the nectars and tropical fruit juices now to be found in our supermarkets and health food stores.

# Chapter 11
# Bacteria, Moulds and Yeasts

## Bacteria

These quite tiny single-celled micro-organisms are widely distributed in nature. Typically the bacteria will be either round or rod shaped, with a diameter of the order of a thousandth of a millimetre. From a winemaking point of view, there are two categories of bacteria that interest us, namely acetic acid and lactic acid bacteria.

**Acetic acid producers**

Some acetic acid is always formed during a normal fermentation, of course, the amount produced depending upon a number of factors including the strain of yeast, the speed of the fermentation and the amount of sugar used up. But the amount of acetic acid formed in this way rarely exceeds 0.4 grams per litre. It is only when the level gets much above 0.6 grams per litre that we start to become concerned, and it is of note that the EEC limit is around 1.0 gram per litre. Even at levels of 0.6 grams per litre or so, the volatile acidity is not really noticeable when the levels of alcohol and sugar are fairly high, because of the masking effect.

In passing, note that although we talk of wines as being vinegary, this is not associated with the acetic acid but with ethyl acetate (the ester which is formed between acetic acid and ethyl alcohol). Thus even when the ethyl acetate level is as low as 0.125 grams per litre the affected wine develops a distinctive burning aftertaste, and at a level of 0.165 grams per litre the characteristic "fish and chips" smell becomes noticeable.

The higher levels of acetic acid are formed as a consequence of the oxidation of ethyl alcohol through the agency of acetic acid bacteria. There are two closely related genera of acetic acid bacteria, *Acetobacter* and *Gluconobacter*, both being now placed in the family *Acetobacteraceae*.

Only one species of Gluconobacter is known, the *Gluconobacter oxydans*, but there are many Acetobacter species, the most important being *A.aceti*, *A.hansenii*, *A.liquefaciens* and *A.pasteurianus*. *G.oxydans* oxidises ethyl alcohol to produce acetic acid, but stops at that point. The Acetobacter species, on the other hand, can metabolise the acetic acid too, giving water and carbon dioxide; these species may also metabolise some of the citric, malic and succinic acids that are present.

The acetic acid bacteria are found on the surface of grapes and other fruits, and on the surface of winery equipment, especially wooden casks. They need oxygen to grow, and optimum growth occurs at temperatures between 25 and 30°C, and with the pH around 5.0 - 6.5. The bacteria are susceptible to alcohol levels above 10% and to sulphur dioxide levels above 100 mg per litre.

With these points in mind it is often supposed that bacteria will neither grow nor survive if the wine is sulphited, kept at a cool temperature and with the tank full. Unfortunately, while the bacteria may be kept under control under such conditions, it does seem that they can get their oxygen from other components in the wine. It is found that while *Gluconobacter oxydans* is prominent in the must it will not survive when the alcohol level gets much above 6%. Thus it is the species of Acetobacter that persist in the wine and can cause problems later if the wine is not looked after properly. As always, a sensible use of sulphur dioxide will help to maintain the quality of the wine.

**Lactic acid producers**

Whereas the acetic acid bacteria invariably produce unwanted effects, this is not the case with the lactic acid bacteria. In particular, these bacteria can convert some of any malic acid present into lactic acid. This is represented by the following chemical equation:

$$HO_2C.CHOH.CH_2.CO_2H \rightarrow CH_3.CH_2.CO_2H + CO_2$$

    malic acid                 lactic acid       carbon dioxide

Now malic acid contains two acid groupings ($CO_2H$), and it is changed into lactic acid with only one acid grouping. This results in a lowering of the titratable acidity and a consequent softening of the wine. We will look at acids in more detail in the next chapter.

This conversion of some of the malic acid into lactic acid is practised commercially for red wines in particular, although not all white wines benefit in the view of many authorities. It is always unwelcome in hot countries where the acid levels are likely to be on the low side anyway, so that any further loss may result in a flabby wine. The commercial encouragement of malo-lactic changes can take two routes. First of all the wine can be left on the lees once the fermentation is over, since then the sulphur dioxide level will be low and the nutrient level favourable because of the breakdown of yeast cells etc. The second approach is to deliberately add a culture of a suitable lactic bacteria. The one generally considered most suitable is Leuconostoc oenos.

This addition of bacteria is not an option open to amateur winemakers working on a small scale, because the bacteria are expensive and have to be stored under special conditions. It will also be appreciated that many of our wines will not contain significant amounts of malic acid, since this acid is only found in ingredients such as apples, gooseberries, grapes, pears, plums and rhubarb. On the whole it is perhaps best to discourage malo-lactic changes in case the effect is not beneficial.

Thus there are many species of lactic acid bacteria, and some can attack residual sugars and other wine constituents, producing flavour-influencing substances such as acetoin and diacetyl; in small amounts these substances add to the character of the wine, but at higher levels they are objectionable.

The adverse effects of lactic acid bacteria are fairly complicated and I list only the more common ones under the following four headings.

**Ropiness** (formation of sugar polymers). If the bacteria grow very quickly they can produce a sugar polymer which coats the cells and makes them join up into chains or "ropes" - hence the name. The result may be the wine developing a somewhat oily appearance. This is not a disaster, though, because the wine itself has not suffered, and usually a vigorous shaking (after a protective addition of sulphite) will break up the "ropes".

**Attack on sugars.** These can lead to the formation of excessive amounts of lactic acid and wine taking on more than a hint of "sauerkraut". At the same time acetic acid may be formed thus giving the wine a "sweet and sour" taste. This fault is usually to be found when the temperature gets too high, and the fermentation sticks, giving us a sugar-rich, low-alcohol wine. My advice is to keep your demijohns off the boiler top and out of the airing cupboard, to reduce the chance of this happening.

**Attack on glycerine.** When the acid level of the wine is on the low side, some lactic acid bacteria can attack the glycerine (glycerol), and produce acrolein, with a consequential bitter taste in the wine. So keep the acid level reasonable and do not leave the wine too long on the lees.

**Attack on tartaric acid.** Fortunately this is rare and seems to happen only when our wines suffer the invasion by a mutant strain of Lactobacilli brevis. When it does happen, then the tartaric acid is destroyed completely, leaving a terribly flat wine. We will notice the wine going hazy and even developing a silky sheen if this attack should take place. Prevent it by keeping the acid level up and using the appropriate amount of sulphite.

# Moulds

Moulds form part of the microflora of fruits such as grapes, and grow in wine-making areas, including cellars, and on wine-making equipment, especially wooden casks. Perhaps the best known mould is *Botrytis cinerea*, which plays a very important role in viticulture. It can act in two ways. When the weather is dry and warm, the "noble rot" develops and attacks the skins of the grapes, causing them to lose moisture and shrink. This causes the sugar levels to increase. On the other hand the acidity undergoes a noticeable change in its balance. In particular, gluconic acid is formed, and can reach levels as high as 5 grams per litre. Both malic and tartaric acid are metabolised in part. At the same time the infected grapes are likely to become hosts to both acetic and lactic acid bacteria, so that the levels of acetic and lactic acids are likely to be on the high side in wines made from botrysised grapes.

When the weather is unkind, and rain dominates, then the mould degenerates, and the berries suffer vulgar rot. As a consequence there is even more destruction of malic and tartaric acids and greater formation of gluconic acid.

The two moulds that are more likely to worry the amateur winemaker are species of *Aspergillus* and *Penicillium*. Aspergillus species, and particularly *A.glaucus de Bari*, is to be found on fruits and in the winery. It will attack corks and wooden casks, such that any wine coming into contact with the affected materials will pick up a most unpleasant mouldy taste that is very persistent. *Penicillium glaucum*, one of the more common Penicillium species, attacks fruit, especially if it has been damaged by heavy rain or insect attack, and it consumes some of the acids, sugars and nutrients, producing volatile substances with a mouldy taste. Colouring matter and tannins may be destroyed. Casks and corks that have been badly treated may also be attacked. If the wine is made from the mouldy fruit or comes into contact with affected materials then it will take on the mouldy taint.

The moral for amateurs is to choose the ingredients carefully, throwing out any berries etc. which have mould on them, and practice scrupulous hygiene in the "winery".

# Yeasts

**Introduction**

Yeast is perhaps the most important component of musts because without it there cannot be any fermentation, and because the quality of the wine that is produced depends a great deal on the type and quality of the yeast. Once upon a time, there were home winemakers who firmly believed that it was unnecessary for us to use yeast, because the natural ingredients we used were amply supplied with yeasts on their surfaces. It was this philosophy that gave the believers the sweet, sickly, low alcohol wines that they loved but which were scorned by all who had ever tasted commercial wines. I cannot emphasise too much that the so-called wild (or natural) yeast is a very uncertain quantity, and will not contain any of the true wine yeasts.

The next stage up in sophistication was the introduction of bakers' yeast, which produced a lot of gas but not necessarily a lot of alcohol. And since these yeasts were intended to produce carbon dioxide gas quickly rather than produce alcohol, it is hardly surprising to find stuck ferments when the weather cooled down, and yeasty flavours in the wine because of the breakdown of the yeast cells. I am sad to say that there are still suppliers who package bread yeast and perhaps imply that it is good for winemaking. In these days of trading standards officers the sachets do not say that the yeast is a wine yeast, but the unwary beginner often takes it to be so. The check here is to look at the label and see if it states that the yeast inside is a wine yeast. Then go further and see if the species of yeast is stated; I say this because this is frequently not the case, and sachets of yeast get labels saying that they are Sauternes or Port yeasts, when such yeasts are not available in active dried form!

If the label is misleading, then draw your own conclusion about what is inside the sachet! At all costs avoid using the tubs containing a mixture of dried yeast, nutrient salts and sugar, because such a mixture will pick up moisture every time the tub is opened, and possibly various unwanted bacteria or moulds. Not surprisingly, such mixtures have a relatively short shelf life, so it just isn't economical to buy such packs.

## What are yeasts?

They are part of the fungi family, and consist of single cells that are quite tiny, having a diameter of about 10 mm (where 1 mm is a thousandth of a millimetre). The cells can be readily seen under a microscope if you have facilities to use a magnification of 450. Figure 11.1 shows a very simplified sketch of the main features of a yeast cell. The cell has a wall that is about 0.2 mm thick, and which makes up about 30% of the weight of the cell. This wall has quite a complicated

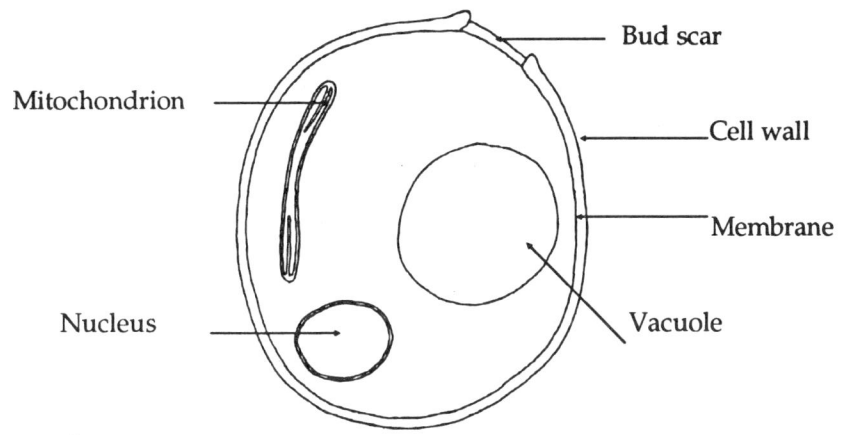

**Figure 11.1**

structure made up from carbohydrates (80%) with smaller amounts of fat and protein. The wall is essentially in two layers, the outer one being made of mannan (a polymer of the sugar mannose) linked with phosphate units, and the inner layer being made of glucan (a polymer of glucose units) plus most of the protein. The outer mannan layer is the active one for absorbing substances from the must, while the glucan layer lends strength and rigidity.

When a substance gets through the cell wall it then meets the very thin membrane (just 0.008 mm thick), which acts as a kind of guardian and protects the cell from unwanted visitors. The health of this membrane is vital to the proper functioning of the cell. Other structures within the cell include the nucleus, the vacuole and the mitochondria, each playing a role in the functioning of the cell.

**Yeast classification**

This is an extremely complicated business. In the early days the yeasts were grouped according to what they looked like and what sort of sugars they fermented. Later on other criteria crept in such as what kinds of substance the yeast could assimilate, its life cycle and "sexual" behaviour, and more recently its DNA make-up. There are many species and sub-species, each described by a double-barrelled scientific name. One familiar example is *Saccharomyces cerevisiae*, where *Saccharomyces* is the genus and *cerevisiae* is the species.

In 1971 Lodder produced his excellent classification, which had some 39 genera and 349 species. Since then the taxonomists who specialise in this type of classification work have increased the genera to 60 and the species to some 500. Unfortunately, this latest version, while satisfying the needs of fundamental scientists, has resulted in the disappearance of familiar names such as *Saccharomyces bayanus*, a name that describes the species of yeast used for making such sparkling wines as Champagne. This, and *Saccharomyces beticus*, the description of the flor yeast from Jerez, are now classified under the *S.cerevisiae* umbrella. Readers who are interested in this classification debate may like to read Volume 1, of the Second Edition of "The Yeasts", published by Academic Press in 1987. The article by N.J.W. van Kreger, which starts on page 5, says it all. A subsequent article by J.P. van der Walt, points out that in the real world where yeasts are used to produce beverages etc., names such as *S.cerevisiae, S.bayanus* and *S.diastaticus* refer to strains with specific fermentation characteristics, and it is recommended that we should retain our "utilitarian classification".

For our purpose it is fortunate that only a few genera are of interest, and in table 11.1 I list those we may come across in our reading, and comment on some of their characteristics. Of the 7 genera listed, 4 belong to the Ascosporogenous group, and the other 3 to the so-called imperfect yeasts.

**Table 11.1 Yeasts of interest to winemakers**

| | |
|---|---|
| Saccharomyces cerevisiae | |
| (S.bayanus) | For sparkling and high alcohol wines |
| (S.beticus) | For flor production |
| (S.diastaticus) | To ferment degraded starch |
| Schizosaccharomyces species | Metabolise malic acid |
| Pichia species | Weak fermenters |
| Kluyveromyces species | Ferment lactose and inulin |
| Brettanomyces species | Spoilage yeasts |
| Candida species | Ferment lactose |
| Kloeckera species | Only ferment glucose and fructose |

## Commercially available yeasts

Yeasts are now produced to a very high level of consistency and viability. The reference strains are kept as cultures on "slopes" of agar agar, or some similarly suitable material, and they are regularly recultured to maintain their life span. These cultures are normally kept in sealed glass containers. Years ago, when a company called Grey Owl was in existence, slopes of this kind (in test tubes) were available to amateur enthusiasts, who then had to take these cultures and use them to grow sufficient yeast for the fermentation. This was time consuming but meant that quality yeasts could be used by amateur winemakers.

These expensive cultures then gave way to suspensions of yeast cells in a medium such as apple juice. Again the amount of yeast provided was quite small, and a starter bottle had to be made. This was inconvenient in that it took a couple of days for enough yeast to grow, and sometimes the ingredients needed more immediate attention.

The liquid suspensions, often mistakenly referred to as liquid yeasts, have now largely been superseded by active dried wine yeasts, because the latter have a much longer shelf life, can be used without first multiplying them, and have at least as good a quality. Over the past 5 to 10 years, the range and quality of active dried wine yeasts have improved a great deal, and they are used by the vast majority of commercial winemakers. They are now available to amateur winemakers and sold under various brand names; the one referred to in all the recipes is the Gervin brand, whose labels specify the strain/origin of the yeast. These yeasts are sold without dilution with either nutrient or sugar, and are supplied in nitrogen-flushed triple-foil sachets to ensure a long shelf life.

Table 11.2 lists the Gervin yeasts that are currently available, with comments on the types of wine for which they are most suitable.

Table 11.2  Gervin wine yeasts

| Yeast | Species/strain | Application and characteristics |
|---|---|---|
| No.1 | S.cerevisiae Narbonne 7013 | General purpose; clears easily |
| No.2 | S.cerevisiae Montrachet Burgundy Davis 522 | Red, fruit-based wines; very vigorous |
| No3. | S.bayanus Pasteur Inst. Davis 595 | Sparkling wines; high alcohol production |
| No.4 | S.beticus Davis 519 | Sherry-style wines; submerged flor possible |
| No.5 | S.cerevisiae GVN | White table wines; ferments down to 12$^{\circ}$C |

**Table 11.2 (contd.) Gervin wine yeasts**

| Yeast | Species/strain | Application and characteristics |
|---|---|---|
| Varietal A | S.cerevisiae SF84 | Bordeaux yeast for "Claret" production |
| Varietal B | S.cerevisiae CC84 | For Rhine-style wines; ferments down to 10°C |
| Varietal C | S.bayanus EC-1118 | For sparkling wines; high alcohol production |
| Varietal D | S.cerevisiae 71B | For fruit wines; excellent bouquet |
| Varietal E | S.cerevisiae K1 | For fruit wines and mead; low nutrient needs |

**Using dried wine yeasts**

Rehydration is the first stage. It may help readers to appreciate just what dried yeasts are if they think of the dried yeast cell in relation to the fresh yeast cell much as they might think of a sultana in relation to a grape. When the yeast is dried, the cells shrink and most of the water is removed, leaving around 5-7% in most cases. The drying has to be done carefully, to make sure that the cell wall and membrane are not broken open; poor drying will mean less active yeasts and an increased likelihood of the wine collecting a yeasty taste. But it is equally important to rehydrate the yeast cells so as to re-establish their membranes and walls.

For the rehydration to be successful, the conditions must be suitable. First of all we must choose whether to rehydrate our yeasts in water, dilute sugar solution or must. If the must contains a fairly high level of sugar (say 18-20%), then the yeast will be reluctant to rehydrate, because of the osmotic pressure that is exerted. On the other hand, with water only, there is a possibility of damage to the sensitive cell wall and membrane. My own experience is that the best bet is to use a 5% sugar solution. This is easily made by dissolving about half a teaspoonful of sugar in 50 ml (say 2 fl oz) of water. Experiments have shown that the addition of nutrients does not improve the rehydration procedure.

The second factor to consider is the temperature of the rehydrating solution. A great deal of work has been done to find which temperature is best, and all the evidence is in favour of it being between 35 and 40°C. If the temperature goes above 45°C the yeast will be severely weakened, whereas below 35°C the rehydration is not as effective as it might be. I emphasise the point that the ideal temperature is just above 35°C because I get countless calls from winemakers who think that this is much too high. They are confusing the temperature of the rehydration with the temperature of the fermentation! Thus the rehydration period is a matter of 15 to 20 minutes only. If the fermentation temperature was in the high 30s then that would be a different matter, and the yeast death rate would mount rapidly.

To illustrate the point I can refer to some experiments carried out in the United States using three of the yeasts in the Gervin range (Nos. 2, 3 and 4), which showed that in every case the yeasts lost more of their cell constituents when the rehydration temperature was lower; with No.2 yeast for instance there was 17.5% loss at 21.1°C but only 10.5% at 40°C. The reason for this appears to be that when the rehydration is slow then the membrane takes longer to re-establish itself, and so allows more solids to pass out into the rehydrating liquid.

**How much yeast?** The level that is recommended by the commercial people is 15-20 grams per 100 litres, which means 3-4 grams for a 5 gallon batch. A standard Gervin sachet contains approximately 5 grams (minimum 4.7 grams). If the yeast you buy is mixed with nutrient/sugar, then very much less than the necessary quantity of yeast will be there and you will have to build up the yeast population with a starter bottle.

A point to note is that if you are too mean with the yeast then the fermentation will be slower and more acetic acid (volatile acidity) will result. Used in the recommended amount, the dried yeast will give a population of around $4 \times 10^6$ yeast cells in every ml of must. During the first few days of the fermentation there will be a significant amount of yeast growth, and the number of cells will increase at least ten times.

**Storage of dried yeast and period of viability.** Provided that you have purchased a multifoil sachet with inert gas flushing, then you can anticipate the yeast retaining its capabilities for several years. If the yeast could be stored at 5°C then it is expected to lose about 10% of its viability each year. I have found that storing the sealed sachets in the butter drawer of the refrigerator preserves the yeast very well, but I suggest that if you use this cool temperature you should let the yeast warm up to room temperature before plunging it into the rehydration liquor at 35°C. Otherwise the yeast gets a little shock and may not respond as well as it might.

Most of us will keep our yeasts in some cupboard or other, and provided this is reasonably cool, we can expect the yeast to retain its viability for at least two years. If you should use only part of the sachet, as might be the case if you are making just a gallon, then the life span of the remainder will be reduced. If you squeeze out all the air in the opened sachet and seal the sachet with sellotape the yeast left in the sachet will still be satisfactory to use for at least several months. There is no problem if you use all of the 5 grams on just 4.5 litres of must, though, and this is the way I normally go about things. The fermentation is then quicker.

**Choosing a yeast.**

I have already drawn your attention to the merits of buying a quality wine yeast with a clearly stated type of yeast. Quality is essential if you are to avoid yeasts that are contaminated with more bacteria than is acceptable, and with a low viability. The sorts of behaviour you look for in a yeast are that:

>    It is capable of fermenting at your chosen temperature
>    It will coagulate well
>    It will give a good level of esters
>    It will give a good conversion of sugar to alcohol
>    It is reasonably tolerant of $SO_2$
>    It gives as little hydrogen sulphide as possible
>    It gives minimum frothing
>    It gives only a low level of volatile acidity

But even when you consider a quality range you may want to select the yeast that is most suitable for your style of wine. Using a yeast such as Varietal B is sensible if you want to make a wine in the Rhine-style, but do remember that it is only one part of the formulation - the choice of ingredients may be even more important.

**For white table wines.** Choose a yeast that will ferment down to low temperatures without going sulky. The two *S.cerevisiae* yeasts No.5 and Varietal B (in the Gervin range) meet this criterion. Both *S.bayanus* strains (No.3 and C) will also go to low temperatures but generate less bouquet; use them when the ingredients have the aroma character that you are looking for.

**For red table wines.** These wines are usually produced at rather higher temperatures. Both the Bordeaux (Varietal A) and Burgundy (No.2) yeasts work well in the 20 to 25°C range, while Varietal D gives an extra bonus on the nose and reduces excessive levels of malic acid.

**For sparkling wines.** Use a yeast that is capable of fermenting easily even when the alcohol level has reached 14% or so. Either No.3 or Varietal C (both *S.bayanus* strains) will do.

**For dessert wines.** High alcohol wines are essential, so use either of the *S.bayanus* strains.

**For Sherry-style wines.** No.4 yeast is the only Sherry yeast on the market at the moment, and while it will only form a submerged flor when the conditions are right, it makes a very suitable base wine with the right character.

## Yeasts other than S.cerevisiae strains

*Schizosaccharomyces strains.* These used to be available to amateur winemakers, but this is no longer the case. Some readers may have access to slopes of such yeasts, and will be interested to know that they destroy virtually all the malic acid present in any must, turning it into alcohol. There is clearly a potential application when the fruit is over-rich in malic acid (as with English grapes in a poor year), but most strains of this yeast produce a rather indifferent wine, so the best bet is to start the ferment with a Schizosaccharomyces strain, let it ferment the must for a day or so, thus reducing the malic level, and then add a S.cerevisiae strain that will take over the fermentation. I know of at least one strain of this yeast that does produce a good wine without adverse organoleptic side effects has been isolated in New Zealand; let us hope that in due course it will join the band of active dried wine yeasts already on the market.

**Spoilage yeasts.** Many of the so-called wild yeasts are unwanted in that they often give high levels of volatile acidity, low levels of alcohol and sometimes distinctly off-flavours. Some species will attack the phenolic substances present in the must to give new substances that have bad flavours. Thus in one fairly recent set of experiments some 32 different "wild" yeasts were examined, and no less than 29 of them produced phenolic off-flavours. Typically, ferulic acid (found in many of our native fruits) was converted into a substance smelling of cloves.

But much worse than this are the effects of contamination of the must or wine with strains of *Brettanomyces* yeast. One disastrous result can be the formation of the infamous "mouse" flavour that may be formed when strains of this yeast attack components of the must. The compound that gives this dreadful taste is 2-acetyl-tetrahydropyridine. It seems that this forms when both alcohol and lysine are present in the wine. As a point of interest, the "mousy" compound is an important part of the aroma of many bread products.

Two other spoilage yeasts that may trouble us from time to time are *S.bailii* and *S.ludwigii*, both of which are resistant to quite high levels of sulphur dioxide; the latter yeast is said to be able to grow even when the $SO_2$ level is as high as 500 mg/litre.

## The rise and fall of the yeast population

There is the substantial increase in the yeast cell count in the early stages of the fermentation, as I mentioned earlier, and the count can reach $10^8$ cells per ml (i.e. one hundred million cells per ml) quite quickly. This is followed by a stationary phase when the cell count remains much the same and most of the conversion of sugar into alcohol takes place. During this period new cells are formed as older ones die. Finally there is the decline phase, when there is no more cell growth and cells continue to die, such that the number of viable cells gets steadily less. This rise and fall is illustrated in Figure 11.2.

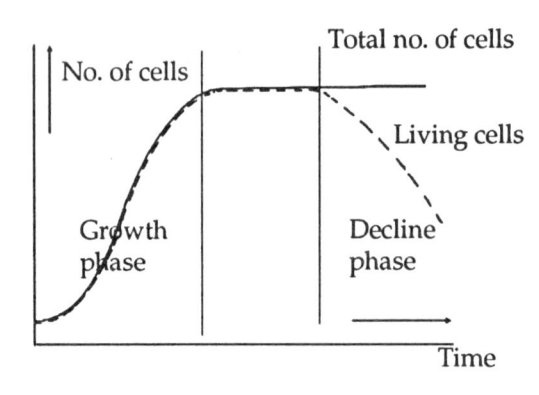

Figure 11.2

The decline phase concerns us a lot, since if this takes place too soon then the fermentation will stick. Some strains of yeast are more capable than others of sustaining growth even when the alcohol level gets quite high and there is still a fair amount of sugar present to add to the difficulties. The reasons for alcohol tolerance are not completely understood, but a major factor seems to be the ability of the yeast cell membrane to be able to cope with the problem of sending out into the bulk of the must the alcohol being formed within the cell. Moreover, when the fermentation is very rapid, the alcohol may build up in the cell and inhibit one or more of the essential enzymes. Sometimes diluting the fermenting must saves the day since it upsets the osmotic pressure and lets the alcohol escape, thus ensuring continued fermentation.

**Yeast inhibition**

Natural causes. We have seen that the fermentation can come to an end prematurely if the yeast is unable to tolerate the level of alcohol. And we have seen that the position is made worse if substantial amounts of sugar remain in the must. Temperature also comes into the equation, since below 15°C or above 25°C most yeasts become less able to grow at the higher levels of alcohol. Figure 11.3, which is based on work carried out in the USA in 1982, illustrates this point

Shortage of essential nutrients is another cause of sticking ferments. This is noticeable if the musts have been clarified too much, with loss of nutrient by fining. Such overclarified musts may also be short of oxygen, and under these circumstances the yeast cells are unable to synthesise the compounds (sterols) they need to strengthen their cell membranes. This is of interest to the amateur winemaker, and I strongly recommend that when the yeast is being rehydrated, it should be given a good stir to get plenty of air into the liquid.

**Stabilisers.** These may be present unintentionally, and may include traces of fungicide that remain from fruit sprays, which can stress the yeast cells. Stabilisers are often deliberately added by food manufacturers to fruit juices and the like to prevent fermentation in the container; this may be preferable to pasteurisation from a flavour point of view. But it can cause we amateurs problems if the

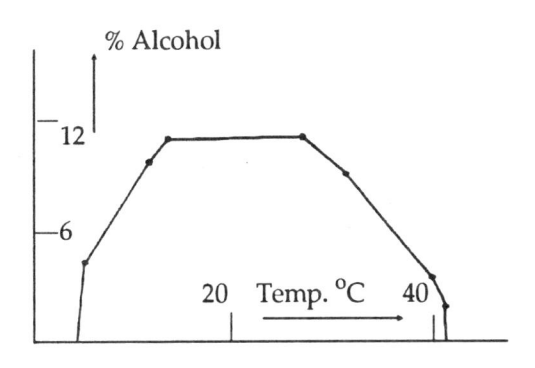

**Figure 11.3**

stabilisers are not easily dispersed. Thus sulphur dioxide is not too bad since vigorous shaking and dilution will reduce the levels well below those that inhibit yeasts. The problem arises with products stabilised with sodium benzoate or potassium sorbate, since these substances are not destroyed by our processing. The moral is to read the label on any bottle, can or carton of fruit or fruit juice, and avoid using them if they contain benzoate or sorbate. The label may not always say which stabiliser is present, but merely quote the E number. Sodium benzoate is E211 and sorbate is E202. Sulphur dioxide is E220, sodium sulphite is E221, sodium hydrogen sulphite is E222, sodium metabisulphite E223, and potassium metabisulphite is E224; none of these (E220 to E224) should cause problems if the must is well aerated.

# Chapter 12
# Acids in wine

### What is an acid?

To most of us the word acid conjures up visions of fuming corrosive liquids that attack metals and produce nasty burns if we get them on our skin. One of the most common acids we are likely to come across is sulphuric acid, which is the acid in car batteries, and we all know what happens to our clothes if we spill battery acid on them. Other common "strong" acids include nitric and hydrochloric. The explanation that follows of the nature of strong acids and the associated alkaline compounds, is a very simple one, and I apologise to those readers who will find it very elementary. It is given to help those readers with little or no experience of chemistry.

Let us take hydrochloric acid as our typical acid for the moment. A molecule of this acid consists of an atom of hydrogen and an atom of chlorine joined together. This is represented with the symbol HCl, H being the symbol for hydrogen and Cl that for chlorine. When hydrogen chloride, as we call this molecule, dissolves in water, the molecule splits, but in doing so forms two ions, $H^+$ and $Cl^-$. The positive and negative charges arise because both of the negatively-charged electrons that form the bond between hydrogen and chlorine are grabbed by the chlorine, so that hydrogen ends up one electron short (and so becomes +ve) while chlorine has one electron more than its fair share and so becomes negatively charged. It is the formation of the hydrogen ion, $H^+$, that characterises acid behaviour.

The "opposite" to an acid is an alkali. A typical example is sodium hydroxide, which is commonly referred to as caustic soda, in recognition of its ability to give us nasty caustic burns should we spill some on ourselves. Sodium hydroxide is made up of one atom each of sodium, hydrogen and oxygen, and is given the formula NaOH. (Na is the chemical symbol for sodium, based on its original name of natrium). When sodium hydroxide is dissolved in water it forms a positive sodium ion and a negative hydroxide ion. This can be symbolised as:

$$NaOH \rightarrow Na^+ + OH^-$$

If we mix hydrochloric acid and sodium hydroxide, there will be a very vigorous reaction indeed, with much generation of heat, and the formation of the salt, sodium chloride, and water. The chemical equation summarising this reaction is:

$$HCl + NaOH \rightarrow NaCl + H_2O$$

We say that the sodium hydroxide has neutralised the hydrochloric acid. The alkali, sodium hydroxide, is more commonly spoken of as a base, so that the equation given above may be described as *"acid plus base gives salt plus water"*.

This neutralisation process can be followed by using an **indicator**. Litmus is an example of an indicator, since it has a red colour in an acid solution and a blue colour in an alkaline solution. A very common example of an indicator is the colouring substance in red and black fruits. Thus blackberry juice is a beautiful red, but when you wash up the blackberry pie dish in an alkaline detergent the colour turns mauve/blue.

## Acids in wine

I am glad to say that our fruits and wines do not contain strong acids that have such unpleasant effects. The acids that are present are said to be **weak acids**. As a simple illustration I will take acetic acid which has the formula $CH_3.CH_2.CO_2H$. The grouping $CO_2H$ is called a carboxylic acid group. This group can lose its hydrogen atom as a hydrogen ion, leaving the group with a negative charge:

$$CH_3.CH_2.CO_2H \rightarrow H^+ + CH_3.CH_2.CO_2^-$$

But the breakdown is very far from complete, and the equation should really be written:

$$CH_3.CH_2.CO_2H \rightleftharpoons H^+ + CH_3.CH_2.CO_2^-$$

where the arrows show that there is an equilibrium between the undissociated acetic acid molecule and the two ions. The equilibrium position is well over to the left and strongly in favour of the undissociated molecule, such that in a weak solution (0.6%) of acetic acid, only one molecule in a hundred is ionised. It is because the breakdown is so incomplete that the acids are called weak acids.

Musts are likely to contain citric, malic and tartaric acids, or some mixture of them, and other acids will be formed in smaller amounts during the fermentation. Table 12.1 gives the formulae for the acids that we are most likely to come across and the amounts likely to be found in musts and wines.

**Table 12.1 Acids in musts and wines**

| Acid | Formula | Typical levels in grape juice (grams/litre) | Typical levels in wines (grams/litre) |
| --- | --- | --- | --- |
| Acetic | $CH_3.CH_2.CO_2H$ | 0 | <0.4 |
| Citric | $HO_2C.CH_2.C(CHOH)(CO_2H).CH_2.CO_2H$ | <0.7 | <0.7 |
| Lactic | $CH_3.CHOH.CO_2H$ | 0 | 0.2-0.4 |
| Malic | $HO_2C.CHOH.CH_2.CO_2H$ | 1.0-8.0 | 1.0-4.0 |
| Succinic | $HO_2C.CH_2.CH_2.CO_2H$ | 0 | 0.5-1.5 |
| Tartaric | $HO_2C.CHOH.CHOH.CO_2H$ | 1.0-4.0 | 1.0-4.0 |

**Acid concentration**

Of the acids listed in the table, it can be seen that there are two (acetic and lactic) with just one carboxylic acid grouping; these are called monocarboxylic acids. There are three dicarboxylic acids (malic, succinic and tartaric) and just one tricarboxylic acid (citric). In Chapter 11 we noticed that there were bacteria that changed malic acid into lactic acid, and reduced the number of carboxylic acid groupings from two to one. As a consequence we said that the wine would be less acid.

However, we should be clear just what we mean by saying a wine is less acid, and remember just how acidity is usually measured. Thus we take a known volume of wine, add an indicator and add sodium hydroxide solution of known strength until the indicator tells us that we have just neutralised the acid that is present. Since this experiment is a titration, the result is expressed in terms of the amount of acid present and said to be the titratable acidity.

If we had only one sort of acid in our wine or must, we would give the result in terms of so many grams per litre of that acid. But as the table shows there will be several acids in the wine, so how do we express the result? In effect we use one acid as our reference and express our results in terms of how much of that acid would be needed to give the titration result.

To explain a little further, let us take one or two examples. Acetic acid has a molecular weight of 60 (i.e. the sum of the atomic weights of the constituent carbon(12), hydrogen(1) and oxygen(16) atoms is 60), so that 60 grams of it would be needed to provide the solution with one gram of hydrogen ion. Lactic acid, on the other hand has a molecular weight of 90, and we need 90 grams of that acid to provide the same one gram of hydrogen ion. It can now be seen that 60 grams of acetic acid are equivalent to 90 grams of lactic acid. In each case the acid would be neutralised by 40 grams of sodium hydroxide.

The dibasic acids contain two acid groupings, so that the molecular weight of the acid in grams will provide two grams of hydrogen ions, and will take 80 grams of sodium hydroxide to neutralise it.

In principle we can choose any acid we like as our reference one. In the commercial world, almost every country uses tartaric acid as the reference because it is the main acid of the grape. The exception is France, where sulphuric acid is taken as standard. This seems rather perverse, in that this is not an acid that occurs naturally in any fruit.

Unfortunately, in the early days of amateur winemaking, sulphuric acid was sometimes used as the reference here too. I am glad to say that knowledgeable home winemakers have seen the light and now use tartaric acid as their reference. This makes sense because if the titration of the must shows it to have too little acid, and more has to be added, it would normally be tartaric acid that we would use. If our titration result was in terms of say sulphuric acid we certainly wouldn't add any of that acid, but would have to look up the tables and find out the tartaric acid equivalent. The list which follows gives the relationship between the common acids:

| Tartaric acid | 1.0 |
| Acetic acid | 0.80 |
| Citric acid | 0.85 |
| Lactic | 1.20 |
| Malic acid | 0.89 |
| Succinic acid | 0.78 |
| Sulphuric acid | 0.65 |

It can be seen that 0.65 grams of sulphuric acid are equivalent to 1.0 grams of tartaric acid, so if you come across acid levels given in terms of sulphuric acid, simply multiply by 1.0/0.65 to get the level in terms of tartaric acid. For all practical purposes this means increasing the figure by 50%.

In Chapter 4 (Table 4.2) I deliberately expressed the likely acid levels in fruits in terms of their tartaric acid equivalents. This means that anyone can calculate how acidic the musts made from such fruits will be. At the same time, I mentioned which acids dominated for each fruit, so that this could be taken into account in producing the best recipes for particular styles of wine.

# pH

This is a subject that is often very confusing to non-chemists. It is another way of saying how acid a wine is, but giving it in terms of the concentration of hydrogen ions that are present. The formal definition is

$$pH = -\log_{10}[H^+]$$

To help those winemakers whose memories of the joys of logarithms are somewhat distant, I will run through a simple example to show how we arrive at a value for the pH of a solution.

Taking first a strong acid such as hydrochloric, we see that its molecular weight is 36.5 (i.e. chlorine and hydrogen have atomic weights of 35.5 and 1 respectively). So if we dissolve 36.5 grams of HCl in a litre of water we get what is described as a molar solution, and written as 1M in shorthand form. If just 3.65 grams of HCl are dissolved in a litre then the solution will be one-tenth molar (0.1M), and since the HCl will be completely dissociated into its ions, there will be just 0.1 gram of $H^+$ in the solution.

Thus the solution is described as 0.1M in hydrogen ion. Now 0.1, or 1/10, can be written as $10^{-1}$, and the logarithm of $10^{-1}$ is -1, so the pH is 1.

If we dilute the solution ten times, the hydrogen ion concentration will be 0.01M, or $10^{-2}$, and the pH 2. Further dilution another ten times, will give 0.001M, or $10^{-3}$ and the pH 3.

It can be seen that we have gone from 0.1M to 0.001M, a hundred-fold dilution, but that this is reflected in the pH changing only from 1 to 3, so that the change of one unit in the pH represents a ten-fold change in the amount of hydrogen ion that is present. Moreover, as the concentration of hydrogen ion gets less, so the pH value increases; it is worth emphasising that a higher pH value corresponds to a lower acidity.

Provided that we are dealing with strong acids, that break down completely in solution, the relationship between the concentration of the acid and the pH of the solution is very straightforward. But when we turn to the acids that interest us as winemakers, then difficulties arise because these are weak acids that dissociate to only a small extent. The case we looked at earlier was that of acetic acid, where I said that in a 0.6% solution only one molecule in a hundred was dissociated. 0.6% is 6 grams per litre, giving a 0.1M solution, but it will not be 0.1M in respect of $H^+$.

We find that such a solution has a pH value of around 2.9, which contrasts with that of 1.0 for 0.1M HCl.

Since winemakers commonly express their acid concentrations as grams per litre, I have made up solutions of each of the three commonly used winemaking acids in distilled water and measured their pH values. These are given in Table 12.2. It can be seen that as the concentration of the acid increases so the pH decreases.

**Table 12.2 pH values for solutions of acids in water**

| Acid | Grams/litre | Strength Molar (M) | Strength Normal* (N) | pH |
|---|---|---|---|---|
| Citric | 3.0 | 0.014 | 0.043 | 2.54 |
|  | 5.0 | 0.024 | 0.072 | 2.42 |
|  | 7.0 | 0.033 | 0.100 | 2.35 |
|  | 10.0 | 0.048 | 0.143 | 2.27 |
| Malic | 3.0 | 0.022 | 0.045 | 2.59 |
|  | 5.0 | 0.037 | 0.075 | 2.47 |
|  | 7.0 | 0.052 | 0.104 | 2.40 |
|  | 10.0 | 0.075 | 0.149 | 2.32 |
| Tartaric | 3.0 | 0.020 | 0.040 | 2.43 |
|  | 5.0 | 0.033 | 0.067 | 2.31 |
|  | 7.0 | 0.047 | 0.093 | 2.24 |
|  | 10.0 | 0.067 | 0.133 | 2.16 |

* The description normal solution, written N, refers to a solution containing the equivalent weight (in grams) of the acid in a litre. Malic and tartaric acids are dibasic, providing two acid groupings, so a molar solution is 2N; citric acid is tribasic so M=3N.

**Buffering**

Our discussion of pH values has been academic in more ways than one, since we have looked at simple solutions of the acids. In real musts, however, made from fruits etc., the problem will be much more complicated because of the presence of other substances, and in particular salts such as phosphates.

One of the common nutrient salts that we use is diammonium hydrogen phosphate (often referred to simply as ammonium phosphate). It has the chemical formula $(NH_4)_2H(PO_4)$. When this salt is added to a solution it breaks down into the ammonium ion ($NH_4^+$) and the hydrogen phosphate ion ($HPO_4^{2-}$). But the latter ion then spots the $H^+$ in the solution and combines with it to form undissociated phosphoric acid:

$$2H^+ + HPO_4^{2-} \rightarrow H_3PO_4$$

In other words, when we add the ammonium phosphate, the effect is to tie up some of the hydrogen ions that are present, and this means that the pH of the solution will increase. Exactly the same effect is produced by salts of other weak acids such as citric, malic and tartaric. If extra acid is added to the solution, some of the hydrogen ions that it provides will be grabbed by the ions of the various salts that are present, and the added acid will therefore not lower the pH as much as might be expected. This stabilising of the solution pH against drastic changes taking place is called buffering.

This effect is quite noticeable in elderberry juice. Thus a titration shows that the juice usually contains as much as 10 grams per litre of acid (expressed as tartaric), yet to our palate the juice may seem much less acid. It is the high level of salts in the juice that fools us by keeping the pH of the juice reasonably high

## The influence of acidity on the fermentation and the wine

Let's now turn away from the necessary but rather dull theories of acidity and pH, and look at how the acid level influences the rate of fermentation, and the taste, colour and stability of the wine.

**Fermentation rate**

There is no doubt whatsoever but that the fermentation will be much slower if the acid level is increased substantially. In some relatively simple experiments we took a 10% solution of ordinary granulated sugar (sucrose) in distilled water, added 4 grams of Minavit nutrient, and the appropriate amount of tartaric acid (our experiments took four levels of tartaric acid, covering the range 2 to 6 grams per litre). One gram of Gervin No.1 yeast was added and the fermentation allowed to proceed at $21°C$ in vessels plugged with cotton wool and protected with cling film. Measurements of S.G. were taken at intervals, with the results shown in Figure 12.1.

It can be seen very clearly that the S.G. drops much more quickly for the lowest acid must than for any of the others, showing that its sugar is being used up faster. These experiments have been repeated many times using citric and malic acids in place of tartaric and at acid levels of up to 8 grams per litre, and always with the same result; increasing the acidity of the must slows down the fermentation.

The reasons for this effect are somewhat complex, and all I will say here is that they relate to the influence of the level of hydrogen ion concentration on the ease with which the yeast cell can take in sugar and expel alcohol.

There is another contributing factor when we consider the practicalities of winemaking. Thus we want to be sure that our equipment is sterile and so we treat it with a sulphite solution. If any sulphite remains in the fermenting jar it will inhibit the yeast, and this inhibiting action is much stronger at higher acid levels. We shall

## Acidity
### Fermentation rate

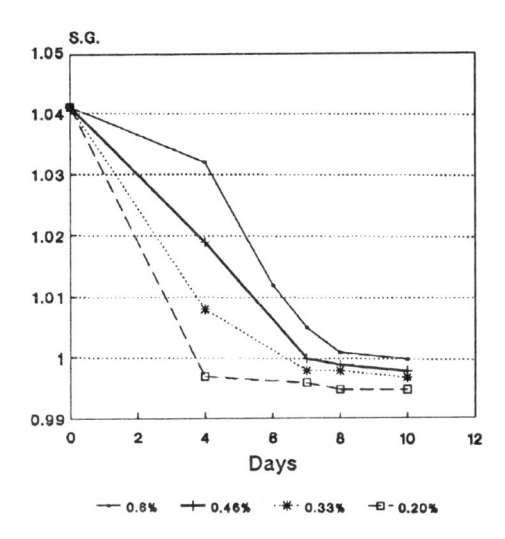

Figure 12.1

look at this later in this chapter; I must emphasise that in our experiments there was no sulphite to complicate the issue.

We also looked at whether the fermentation rate depended on the acid used. We found that the rate was marginally quicker with citric acid than with tartaric with all the yeasts that we tried, but the effect was not huge, and certainly not sufficient to suggest that amateur winemakers should use citric acid in preference to tartaric.

**Acidity and taste**

It is generally accepted that while all the acids have a characteristic "sour" impact on our taste buds, they do show subtle differences. The somewhat derogatory terms used to describe the tastes are sharp or tart for citric, sour but fruity for malic, and hard for tartaric. A fourth acid recommended by some winemakers is succinic. This is not found in the fruits but it is formed in small amounts during the fermentation. It is said to have a salty/bitter taste.

I carried out a series of taste experiments with winemakers at circle meetings and with groups of National Judges, using for my purpose a 10% solution of ethyl alcohol (made by diluting Vodka) plus 4 grams per litre of a specific acid. To round off the rough edges of this synthetic "wine" I also added 1% of sugar.

The taste preferences each time came down in favour of tartaric, followed quite closely by malic, with citric quite a way behind and succinic very much an also ran. The acid strengths chosen were not quite equivalent in their strengths, however, if we want to have solutions with the same titratable acidity. Accordingly we made up solutions in water, where this requirement was met (i.e. tartaric acid 4, citric 4.3, malic 4.5 and succinic 5.1, all as grams per litre). We then considered which solutions seemed the most acid, rather than which one we necessarily liked the best.

We found malic to be the most sour, followed by tartaric and then citric. Similar experiments by oenologists in the USA came out with the same order; they looked at lactic acid as well in their series of experiments and found it to be the least sour. The Americans also looked at acid solutions of the same pH value, and found that while malic still headed the list, lactic now moved up to second position and tartaric was the least sour.

The quality of the acid taste is a very subjective matter, and readers should do some simple tests to see which of the "big three" acids they like the taste of best. Unless you have a major aversion to tartaric acid I suggest you use this when you need to increase the acidity of your must. It is far less likely to be attacked by yeasts or bacteria, and if you should add too much you can always expect to reduce the level simply by chilling the wine.

**An acidity index**

There is often an argument about whether the impact of acid on our taste buds owes most to the amount of acid present (i.e. the titratable acidity) or to the pH of the solution. Readers who own a simple pH meter and make such measurements may like to know of work in the USA which attempted to make use of both titratable acidity (expressed numerically as grams per litre, as tartaric) and pH to develop a so-called acidity index:

$$\text{Acidity index} = \text{Titratable acidity} - \text{pH}$$

They studied a large number of commercial wines and found that the average value for a dry red wine was between 2 and 3 (averaging 2.5), with white wines having a higher average value of 3.8. Wines from different grape varieties had different values, with Chardonnay wines giving an average value of 3.2 and Riesling wines coming out at 4.35.

I looked at a limited number of wines I had made myself from grape concentrates and kits, and wines made from a mixture of apple and grape juices. The values are given in Table 12.3.

**Table 12.3** Acidity index values for amateur wines

| Type | No. of wines | Acidity index Range | Mean |
|---|---|---|---|
| Red | | | |
| Concentrates | 11 | 1.22-4.45 | 2.84 |
| Kits | 6 | 1.49-6.17 | 3.43 |
| White | | | |
| Concentrates | 15 | 0.92-3.56 | 3.26 |
| Kits | 1 | - | 6.13 |
| Juices* | 5 | 3.74-4.90 | 4.3 |

* Fresh apple juice plus grape concentrate.

I was pleased to find that my wines made from apple and grape fell within the approved range, but disappointed to see how wide a spread there was in wines made from kits.

### Acidity and colour

There are two colours that acids have some influence on, namely the red colour associated with the colouring matter found in the skins of red and black fruits, and the brown colour which develops when a wine deteriorates.

The red colour is produced by the so-called anthocyanins in the fruits. It is a bright red in a fairly acid wine but loses its intensity if the pH of the wine rises. The role of anthocyanins and why wines go brown are discussed in Chapter 13.

### Acidity and wine stability

By wine stability I mean the extent to which sulphur dioxide can prevent the wine becoming spoilt through oxidation or bacterial attack. Acidity has a major role to play here because "sulphite" becomes much more effective as the pH is lowered. Thus the active antioxidant and biocidal component is sulphur dioxide, and the amount of this which is present in a solution of sulphite increases as the pH is lowered:

$$SO_2 \rightleftharpoons HSO_3^- \rightleftharpoons SO_3^{2-}$$

$$H^+$$

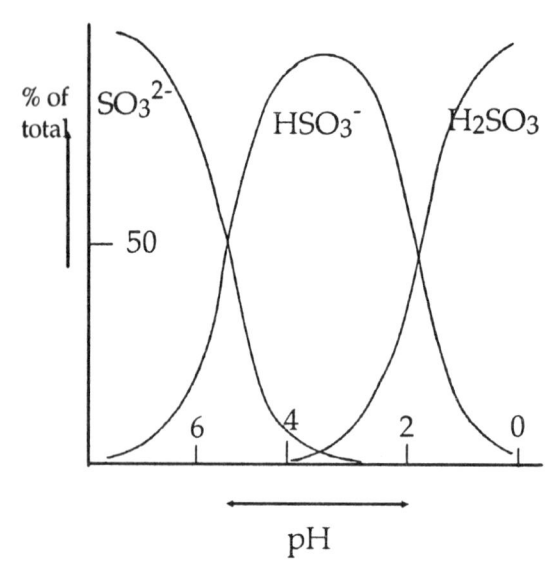

Figure 12.2

Figure 12.2 shows how the percentages of the three species, $H_2SO_3$ ($SO_2$), $HSO_3^-$ and $SO_3^{2-}$, vary according to the pH of the solution. This clearly demonstrates how little active $SO_2$ there will be in the wine if its pH gets much above 3.5. In fact simple calculations show that whereas at a pH of 2.8 (a pretty acid wine!) 10% of the added sulphite will be in the form of active sulphur dioxide, this drops to around 1% when the pH rises to 3.8.

In practice this means that we must use much more sulphite to stabilise our wines if for any reason they have a high pH. All of the recipes I have given should give a wine with a high enough level of acidity, and a pH value of less than 3.6, so that the recommended addition of sulphite solution should be enough to prevent refermentation of a sweeter wine.

Acid changes during the fermentation

This is a much more complicated affair than I once thought, because it depends on so many factors. Let us start by assuming that we will not have any attack on the must or wines by bacteria.

Next, let us deal first with wines based on grape juice or grape concentrate, which will contain only malic and tartaric acids. During a normal fermentation there will be a small loss of malic acid, since most strains of wine yeast metabolise some malic. This loss is unlikely to be more than say 10% of the malic acid in the juice, which will amount in most cases to not more than 0.5 grams per litre. It may be more than this if the juice is from unripe grapes or grapes grown in a cool climate such as the UK, but it will still be less than one gram per litre. If you use Varietal D yeast, the 10% figure is likely to be doubled or even trebled, but even so it would be quite exceptional if more than one gram per litre were lost.

Tartaric acid will not be destroyed in the fermentation, but if the must contains a lot of this acid some may precipitate out as the salt, potassium hydrogen tartrate. This will occur once the alcohol level has built up to 10% or more, and especially if the temperature is on the low side. Indeed, if the wine seems rather acid it makes good sense to chill it, since this reduces the solubility of the salt and makes it come out of solution.

During the fermentation, comparatively small amounts of succinic and lactic acids will be produced, but contrary to what once seemed to be the case the levels will not be more than one gram per litre, taken together. If the fermentation is very slow then acetic acid will be produced at above average levels. A slow fermentation is likely to result if the nutrient level is low and the sugar content high, and it will be made worse if such a ferment is carried out at a low temperature. Acetic acid formation can also result from sloppy winemaking, which allows the wine to be exposed to air for long periods.

If the wines are made from fruits other than grapes, then the only loss likely to occur will be that of malic acid (if the ingredients are rich in this acid). The formation of the new acids (acetic, lactic and succinic) will take place just as with the grape wines. The upshot is that "country wines", based on ingredients other than grapes will be rather more acidic than the musts they were made from, because the gains will be higher than the losses. In round figures we should expect an increase of between 1.0 and 1.5 grams per litre. I have allowed for this in the recipes where it is appropriate.

The unknown quantity is the possibility of bacterial attack. If acetic acid bacteria are present then this acid may be produced in spoilage amounts. If lactic acid bacteria get into the must or wine, then lactic acid will be formed in quite large amounts, and any malic acid is likely to be changed into lactic.

## Acid changes during maturation

Provided that the wines are free from bacteria, the only major loss will be the possible precipitation of potassium hydrogen tartrate; this is likely only when the wine is rich in tartaric acid and stored in a cool place.

A much slower reduction will arise as the acids present react with the alcohols to form esters. I must emphasise that this is a very slow change. Thus the main acid, tartaric, is especially reluctant to form esters, and it has been estimated that a wine of 12% alcohol containing 6 grams per litre of tartaric acid kept at a temperature of 13.3$^{\circ}$C will take 13 years to reach 1.5%. Hence the prolonged storage of such a wine would produce a loss of only 1.5 grams of tartaric acid. Most of the other acids may esterify rather more quickly, but apart from malic acid they will be there in only small amounts. To show the significance of acid loss through esterification, of the acids forming esters, the quickest is succinic, but even here it is only 20% esterified after 5 years. As the amount of succinic acid in wines won't exceed 1.5 grams per litre, the eventual acid loss will be well under half a gram.

Table 12.4 summarises the acid changes likely to occur during fermentation and maturation. I have represented the likely percentage gains and losses with + and - signs respectively, the number of such signs indicating the magnitude of the changes.

**Table 12.4** Acid changes during fermentation and maturation

| Acid | Fermentation (no bacteria) | Bacterial attack | Maturation |
|---|---|---|---|
| Malic | 2- | 3- | - |
| Tartaric | -(2-)* | - | - |
| Acetic | + | 2+ | - |
| Lactic | + | 3+ | 2- |
| Succinic | + | + | 2- |

* The loss will be significant if the initial level is high.

# Chapter 13
# Carbohydrates and Sweeteners

## Introduction

The word carbohydrates is associated with the original idea that these substances were "hydrates" of carbon. We can see how this arises if we look at the chemical formula for glucose, one of the simpler carbohydrates:

$$C_6H_{12}O_6 \quad = \quad (CH_2O)_6 \quad = \quad (C.H_2O)_6$$

The name actually covers a very wide range of substances, ranging from sugars such as glucose to much more complicated molecules like starch.

Because I am writing this chapter for people who are interested in winemaking, I am keeping the chemistry to a minimum and limiting our discussion to those carbohydrates that we are likely to come across in our winemaking. First of all, let us discuss briefly the chemical jargon that is used to describe the principal types of carbohydrate, which includes mono-, di- , tri-, and poly-saccharides.

### Monosaccharides

The two substances that interest us most, and that I have already referred to several times in earlier chapters, are fructose and glucose. They both have the same chemical formula ($C_6H_{12}O_6$), and differ only in the detailed way in which the atoms are linked together. Their structural formulae are given on the next page:

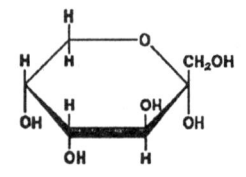

D-fructose 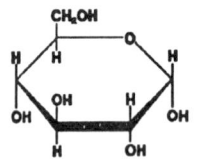                                D-glucose

These two simple sugars are also called hexoses because they contain six carbon atoms. They form the main building blocks for the more complex carbohydrates, together with one other hexose with the same basic chemical formula, galactose. Galactose is not of very great interest to us as winemakers except that it is a component of the milk sugar, lactose, as we shall see shortly.

Before we leave monosaccharides, I should mention that there are other building blocks, such as the pentoses, which contain only five carbon atoms. Common examples are arabinose, ribose and xylose. These occur in various plants, but are not likely to concern winemakers a great deal.

**Disaccharides**

As the name implies, these carbohydrates contain two monosaccharide units linked together. We can represent them simply as:

| | |
|---|---|
| Sucrose | fructose - glucose |
| Maltose | glucose-glucose |
| Lactose | glucose-galactose |
| Inulin | fructose-fructose |

The granulated sugar we use so much of in our winemaking, is sucrose, which is made up of a fructose molecule linked to one of glucose. It has the chemical formula $C_{12}H_{22}O_{11}$. When the fructose and glucose units join up, a molecule of water ($H_2O$) splits off, which explains why the sucrose formula is $C_{12}H_{22}O_{11}$ rather than $C_{12}H_{24}O_{12}$.

Now sucrose is very easily broken down into its components when an acidified solution of it is heated. It is not necessary for the winemaker to do this because the yeast will do it for us. Thus the sucrose molecule gets through the yeast cell wall without difficulty, and while it is in the region between the wall and the membrane it is attacked by an enzyme called invertase produced by the yeast. This enzyme inverts or breaks down the sucrose into fructose and glucose, and these molecules can then pass through the membrane into the interior of the cell, where the fermentation process can take place.

Maltose behaves in a similar fashion, and is broken down into its glucose components by enzymes in the yeast. But this is not the case with lactose and inulin, because our normal winemaking yeasts do not possess the necessary enzymes. The yeasts that can process these two disaccharides are listed in Table 11.1. Lactose is the sugar found in milk. As we shall see later (Table 13.2), this sugar is not anything like as sweet as sucrose, but it is sometimes used for sweetening purposes simply because it cannot cause us problems by fermenting. Inulin is not a sugar that we are likely to come across unless we have a love of Jerusalem artichokes, which contain a few per cent of this sugar.

### Tri- and Tetra-saccharides

When three and four units of glucose are linked together the resulting tri- and tetra-saccharides are called maltotriose and maltotetraose respectively. They may concern some winemakers who use kits containing glucose syrups (see the next section but one). Both of these sugars have to be broken down into the component glucose before they can ferment. This is a fairly slow process for maltotriose, and doesn't normally take place at all in the case of maltotetraose. The consequence is that wines which are made from musts containing these two sugars, will have some residual sweetness and associated body. A snag is that the maltotriose does ferment slowly, which either causes the ferment to dribble on for ages, or else may only become noticeable if it takes place in the bottle when insufficient sulphite has been added.

### Starch

This is the ultimate polysaccharide, in that it consists of many units of glucose linked together. Starch has quite a complicated nature, which varies according to its source, but basically there are two main types, namely amylose and amylopectin. Amylose is the simpler of the two, and consists of long chains of anything between 100 and 300 glucose units joined nose to tail. When this is broken down, it yields the simple disaccharide, maltose.

Amylopectin is a much larger molecule, and contains anything up to 100,000 units of glucose. In this case, however, the structure is not one of straight chains, but has many side branches. When this molecule is broken down by the β-amylase enzyme, the side chains give maltose, but large parts of the structure remain intact, leaving us with the so-called dextrins. This will be very familiar to readers who are enthusiastic brewers, and undertake their own mashing.

When corn starch is hydrolysed, either by acids or enzymes, the mix of sugars and dextrins depends very much on the details of the process. Different types of glucose syrups are listed according to their dextrose (i.e. glucose) equivalent, or D.E. for short. Table 13.1 gives typical values for three of the syrups.

**Table 13.1 Composition of glucose syrups**

| Syrup | 95DE | 63DE | 42DE |
|---|---|---|---|
| Glucose | 85 | 37 | 6 |
| Maltose | 8 | 32 | 39 |
| Maltotriose | 4 | 11 | 12 |
| Maltotetraose | 1 | 5 | 5 |
| Higher sugars | 2 | 15 | 38 |

There is also a syrup that has been produced to give a high level of fructose, but this is not usually used in kits because it has an awkward physical characteristic, being a liquid which is just about turning solid at room temperature.

**Sugar alcohols**

I am sure that all readers will be familiar with glycerine, sometimes spelled glycerin, and usually referred to by scientists as glycerol, in recognition of its hydroxy groups. This substance is produced during the course of fermentation to the extent of 5 grams per litre or thereabouts. In practice winemakers welcome a yeast that will give above average yields of glycerol, which within limits is considered a quality factor. In certain circumstances, such as with grapes that have been infected with the mould Botrytis cinerea, the glycerol level in the wine will be much higher than average, and in the better Sauternes is likely to be around 10 grams per litre.

In recognition of this, we often add glycerol to our wines in the belief that it adds a little sweetness, a fair amount of mouth feel, and a rounding out of the wine. Personally I think that we may overestimate the benefit of adding glycerol, especially in the case of dry wines, since it has rather a "hot" taste that is not really desirable in a dry wine. I use it regularly in my sweeter wines, and particularly those that have real dessert character, and add up to 5 ml (roughly a teaspoonful) to a litre of these heavier wines.

Glycerol is really the first of a series of sugar alcohols, the other ones that may interest us being sorbitol and xylitol. The chemical formulae of these three substances are:

```
    CH2OH              CH2OH              CH2OH
      |                  |                  |
   H-C-OH             H-C-OH             HO-C-H
      |                  |                  |
    CH2OH             HO-C-H             HO-C-H
                         |                  |
                      H-C-OH             H-C-OH
                         |                  |
                       CH2OH             HO-C-H
                                            |
                                          CH2OH

   Glycerol            Xylitol            Sorbitol
```

Sorbitol is found naturally in a number of fruits, including cherries, pears, plums and rowan berries, where levels of up to 2% may be reached. It is accordingly found in amateur wines made from these ingredients and in commercially made perry. It is widely used as a substitute for sugar in a range of products made for people suffering from diabetes. It is not fermented by yeasts and it has the effect of smoothing out the rough edges of young wines. For these reasons, rather than for the sweetening effect, it is added to amateur wines. I emphasise that sorbitol is not ideal for use as a sweetener. Used in excess it could have unfortunate consequences because of its laxative properties!

I find that added at the level of one to three grams, say half a level teaspoonful, to a litre, it is very useful as a smoothening agent.

It is of interest to note that sorbitol cannot be added legally to commercial wines, being banned by the European Community Wine Regulations, but that a recent analysis of wines from Chile by MAFF found that 22% of the 62 wines examined contained sorbitol at levels in the range 1.3 to 6.5 grams per litre. The inescapable conclusion is that either sorbitol was added to the wines, or juices beside those of the grape were used in the must. Such additions are not in the least harmful, as far as we know, and there has been no complaint about the quality of the wines. Amateurs take note!

Xylitol is a more interesting proposition for the amateur winemaker than sorbitol, since it is much sweeter, and has a taste indistinguishable from that of sucrose. Again it is not metabolised by yeasts, and it is used commercially in such items as cool mints. This use arises because when we taste the xylitol it gives us a cooling effect as well as a sweetening one. Technically this is explained by saying that xylitol has a high negative heat of solution, which means that when it dissolves it absorbs a lot of heat from its surroundings.

Xylitol is found in small amounts in such fruits as raspberries, strawberries and yellow plums, but the amount found is only of the order of one gram per kilo of fruit. This means that even if we used two kilos of fruit to 4.5 litres of must, we would be adding only two or three grams of xylitol.

Xylitol is made commercially from a naturally occurring polymer of the sugar xylose; this polymer, xylan, is quite commonplace, and makes up 25-40% of agricultural wastes such as corn cobs and peanut shells.

Besides offering us a non-fermentable sweetener, xylitol has the bonus offering of not undergoing browning reactions (see Chapter 14). Has it any associated health problems? Well it is fully approved for use in foodstuffs, and the only snag seems to be the slight laxative effect; this varies from individual to individual, and it is said that the body rapidly accustoms itself to xylitol, so that it is a "one-off" effect if it occurs at all; and in any case the effect is much smaller than that of sorbitol.

It has been tried experimentally as a sweetener for commercial wines, and the verdict of the tasters was favourable. Unfortunately, xylitol is not always easy to come by and is fairly expensive. If you can get it I suggest that you limit its use to a maximum of 40 grams to the litre (about 6 oz per gallon).

**Sweeteners**

**Table 13.2 Relative sweetness of sugars and sugar alcohols**

| Substance | Relative sweetness (sucrose = 1.0) |
| --- | --- |
| Fructose | 1.5 |
| Sucrose | 1.0 |
| Xylitol | 1.0 |
| Glycerol | 0.8 |
| Sorbitol | 0.6 |
| D-galactose | 0.6 |
| Maltose | 0.5 |
| D-mannose | 0.4 |
| Lactose | 0.2 |

Table 13.2 gives the comparable sweetness of the various sugars we have mentioned so far. The values I give are taken from a very extensive review which appeared in Food Reviews International in 1987, but the question of how sweet is a particular substance is rather subjective, especially since our judgement may be influenced by just how the experiment is carried out. Even so the figures are a very useful guide. Sucrose is taken as the reference sweetener with a value of 1.0.

### Artificial sweeteners

Winemakers sometimes use artificial sweeteners in their wines to make sure that their sweet wines will not referment. Saccharin is still the most commonly used sweetener for soft drinks, but sensitive palates can detect a hint of bitterness behind the sweetness, and this suggests that it is not the ideal sweetening agent for winemakers.

Two comparative newcomers to the sweetener market are aspartame and acesulfame K, both of which are roughly 200 times as sweet as sucrose. Aspartame is sold under a number of labels including Nutrisweet and Canderel. Experts in the sweetener field feel that aspartame has an excellent flavour profile which is similar to that of sugar, being clean with no aftertaste. Some tasters argue that acesulfame K has a slight aftertaste that is undesirable, and suggest that it is best used together with another sweetener.

Experiments using aspartame with soft drinks suggest that malic acid is preferable to citric acid as the acidulant, since the balance of acidity and sweetness then holds on better. With citric acid, the acid taste falls away before the sweet one, leaving the drink oversweet. As far as I know no-one has tried this out with wines.

## Practical aspects of sweetening

There is always the problem of how much sugar we should add to sweeten up a wine to medium or sweet etc. It is impossible for me to be too specific because the amount you need will depend on the composition of the wine. Generally speaking, any wine can stand higher levels of sweetening if the levels of acidity, alcohol and flavour are on the high side. By contrast, a light wine of moderate flavour intensity will not stand the addition of too much sugar.

As a guideline, I have given in Table 13.3 suggestions for the amount of sugar that needs to be added to a dry wine to sweeten it up to meet the requirement of different wine styles. But this is a guide and not a set of firm rules. Thus if you sweetened up a dry table wine to a specific gravity of 1.030 (suggested as suitable for a dessert wine), it would be very unbalanced and seem incredibly over-sweet. So sweeten according to the weight of the wine.

**Table 13.3 Adding sugar to sweeten wines**

| Type of wine required | Suggested SG | Extra sugar needed Grams to 1 litre | Ounces to 1 gallon |
|---|---|---|---|
| Dry | 0.990-0.993 | 0 | 0 |
| Dry-medium | 0.995-1.000 | 10-30 | 2-4 |
| Medium-sweet | 1.005-1.010 | 40-50 | 6-9 |
| Sweet | 1.015-1.020 | 65-80 | 11-13 |
| Dessert | 1.025-1.030 | 95-110 | 15-18 |

For the benefit of winemakers who want an easy life and prefer to work in ounces and gallons, try the simple rule of thumb, and add sugar at the level of 4, 8, 12 and 16 ounces to the gallon, to get respectively medium-dry, medium-sweet, sweet and dessert styles of wine.

I know that many readers will be fully experienced with the use of the hydrometer, and for their benefit I include the data in Table 13.4, which lists the S.G. of sugar solutions in water at 20°C. The information is given in terms of the amount of sugar dissolved in water, with the volume of the solution either one litre or one gallon. It is **not** the amount of sugar added to one litre or one gallon of water.

**Table 13.4 Specific gravity of sugar solutions in water at 20°C**

| S.G. | Sucrose concn. (g/l) | (oz/gall) | S.G. | Sucrose concn. (g/l) | (oz/gall) |
|---|---|---|---|---|---|
| 1.005 | 12.9 | 2.1 | 1.065 | 169.3 | 27.1 |
| 1.010 | 26.0 | 4.2 | 1.070 | 182.3 | 29.2 |
| 1.015 | 38.8 | 6.2 | 1.075 | 195.3 | 31.3 |
| 1.020 | 51.9 | 8.3 | 1.080 | 208.5 | 33.4 |
| 1.025 | 64.8 | 10.4 | 1.085 | 221.8 | 35.5 |
| 1.030 | 77.9 | 12.5 | 1.090 | 235.0 | 37.6 |
| 1.035 | 91.2 | 14.6 | 1.095 | 248.2 | 39.7 |
| 1.040 | 103.8 | 16.6 | 1.100 | 261.4 | 41.8 |
| 1.045 | 117.0 | 18.7 | 1.105 | 274.6 | 43.9 |
| 1.050 | 130.0 | 20.8 | 1.110 | 287.7 | 46.0 |
| 1.055 | 143.1 | 22.9 | 1.115 | 301.0 | 48.2 |

From time to time readers will come across other ways of describing the density of sugar solutions, since the "trade" talks in terms of °Brix and °Baume. Table 13.5 gives an abbreviated list showing the values corresponding to various S.G. values. The values are rounded off.

**Table 13.5 Density scales for sugar solutions**

| S.G. (20°C) | °Brix | °Baume |
|---|---|---|
| 1.000 | 0.0 | 0.0 |
| 1.040 | 10.0 | 5.6 |
| 1.083 | 20.0 | 11.0 |
| 1.129 | 30.0 | 16.6 |
| 1.179 | 40.0 | 22.0 |
| 1.232 | 50.0 | 27.3 |
| 1.289 | 60.0 | 32.9 |
| 1.350 | 70.0 | 37.6 |
| 1.414 | 80.0 | 42.5 |

**Making sugar syrup**

Many readers like to dissolve their sugar in water to give a concentrated syrup which they can then add to the wine or must when needed. I suggest making up a 60% solution, and storing it in a screw-capped glass or plastic bottle. The solution will keep for some time, especially if it is stored in a cold place and not opened too often. But remember that even the cleanest of wine rooms will contain yeast spores and moulds too, so that sooner or later the solution will start to grow micro-organisms. At the first sign of mould growth throw away the remains of your syrup.

To make the syrup take 600 ml (21 fl oz) of water that has been recently boiled, place it in a saucepan or Pyrex vessel, and add to it 600 grams (21 oz) of granulated sugar. Heat the mixture, stirring it regularly with a wooden spoon until the sugar has dissolved completely; this is important if you want to prevent the sugar sticking on the bottom of the vessel that is being heated, and turning into caramel. Once the solution is complete, raise the heat and bring the solution to a simmering temperature; simmer for 5-10 minutes, then allow the syrup to cool to room temperature before you put it in the storage bottle. Label it 60% sugar syrup. And don't forget the label!

**The volume occupied by sugar**

If you use a sugar syrup then you will know how much more liquid you have added and can make allowances for this. Many of us prefer to take some of the wine and dissolve the sugar in the wine rather than add a syrup. The advantage then is that we are adding only sugar, and no more water, so that we keep the dilution of the wine to a minimum.

Even so, the wines will increase in volume when the sugar dissolves. In round figures, adding 100 grams of sugar will increase the volume of the wine by 65 ml. This may be important if you have a completely full demijohn of wine that you want to sweeten up by the addition of say 200 grams of sugar. This sugar will take up about 124 ml of volume, so make sure that you take out more wine than you need to dissolve the sugar, make up your solution in some of the wine, add it to the wine in the demijohn and top up the jar with some of the remaining unsweetened wine. This will leave you with a glass or so for tasting.

# Chapter 14
# Colour of Wines

## Introduction

White wines are rarely colourless, but if so they are generally pretty miserable specimens. The very young white wines often have a pale yellow colour with a hint of green, but older ones, and wines made from really ripe grapes, have a much deeper yellow colour, sometimes with a touch of gold. By contrast, wines made from black grapes have a deep red colour, ranging from a very purple red in young wines to a more gentle red after the wine has aged for a little while. Gradually the red colour begins to fade and by the time the wine is well past its best it will have developed a distinctly brown hue. This sign of old age is seen most clearly if the glass of wine is held at an angle, and the thin edge of the wine (its robe) is studied.

Amateur wines are made from ingredients other than grapes, of course, and these may add their own colour, although the substances that give the colour will be close cousins of those in the grape. An exception is the red colour found with beetroot, which is caused by the presence of a substance called betanin, which is but a very distant relative of the substances in fruits. Some fruits, such as oranges, and related citrus fruits, have an orange/yellow colour, because they contain rather complex substances called carotenoids. These substances are found in other fruits and vegetables as well, including bananas (skins), carrots, peaches, rose hips and tomatoes. They will add a yellow-orange colour to our wines

## Causes of red colour

Pigments called anthocyanins are the cause of almost all of the red-violet colours found in fruits and flowers. One of the principal pigments found in the red/black fruits used by amateur winemakers is cyanidin, the formula for which is as follows:

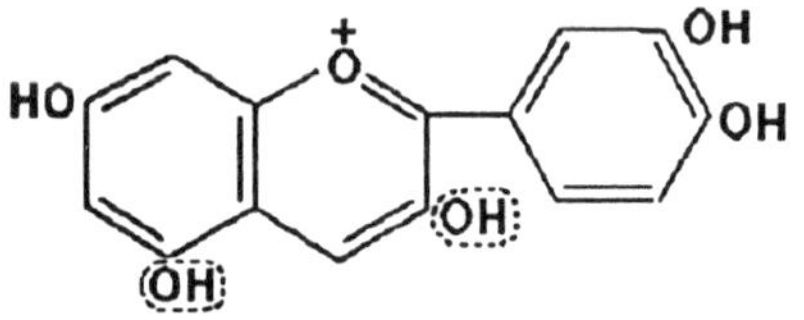

This formula is incomplete as it is shown, because glucose groups are normally attached to one or both of the hydroxy (OH) groups that I have ringed. If the glucose residues are removed, then the basic unit is said to be a anthocyanidin. The two class names, anthocyanin and anthocyanidin, are very similar and this can cause confusion; just remember that the longer name refers to the smaller molecule without the sugar residues. I say sugar residues rather than glucose residues since sugars other than glucose can be found attached to the basic units.

Whereas we describe the colour of the anthocyanins as red-violet, the exact hue depends both on the nature of the sugar side chains and on the relatively minor changes in the chemical composition. Thus the benzene ring shown on the right hand side of the formula contains two hydroxy groups in cyanidin, but there are five other basic anthocyanidin units which differ only in respect of chemical groups associated with this ring. This is shown in Figure 14.1 (only this right hand

**Figure 4.1**

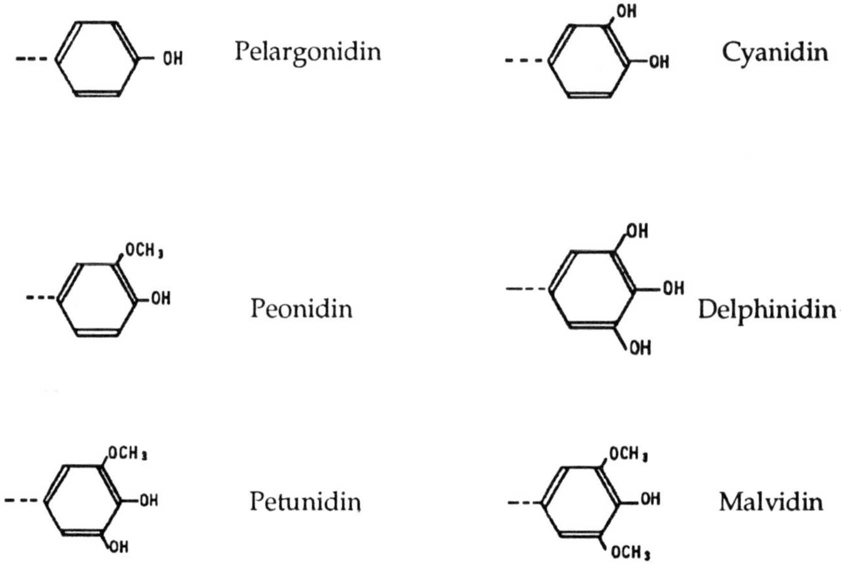

ring is shown). It can be seen that in nature there can be one, two or three hydroxy groups, and in some cases, either one or two of the groups are methylated (i.e. we find methoxy groups (OCH$_3$) rather than hydroxy). As the number of groups on the ring increases, so the colour of the compound changes from an orange-red, through magenta to mauve.

The colour of any one of the anthocyanins depends a great deal on the pH of the fruit or juice. To illustrate the point perhaps I can again remind readers of what happens when a dish containing the remains of blackberry pie is washed up in an alkaline detergent; the clean red colour changes into a mauve. This point is important, because the colour of our red wines will depend a lot on their pH values.

It may help a little if we digress for a moment to see just how the colour is measured. This is done by putting the wine into a quartz cell with parallel sides and then passing light through it. For this purpose we use an instrument called a spectrophotometer. We measure the extent to which the wine absorbs light at different wavelengths, and the result is plotted in graphical form. Figure 14.2 shows a typical plot for the spectrum of the juice extracted from black grapes, using the Säftborn steamer. It can be seen that the "juice" absorbs a lot of the light in the higher end of the spectrum (the ultra-violet region down below 400 nm), then lets through the blue light, absorbs most of the green light in the 520 nm region, and lets through most of the yellow to red light. The combination of the blue and yellow-red light which passes through gives us the characteristic red/purple colour of a fresh grape skin extract, or of a young wine.

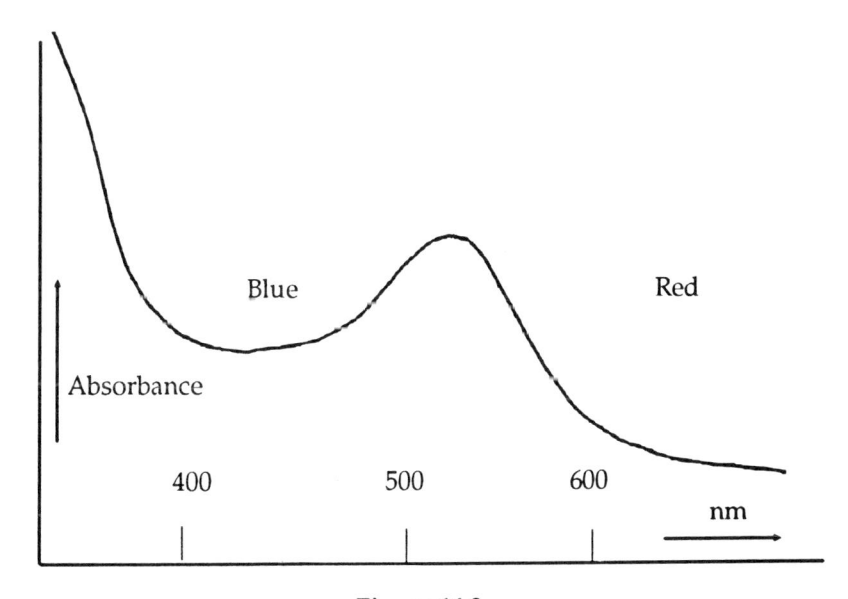

**Figure 14.2**

The intensity of the colour is related to the height of the peak at 520 nm. This increases quite sharply as the pH is lowered. Figure 14.3 shows this very clearly for the spectrum of elderberry juice; I adjusted the pH by adding more acid.

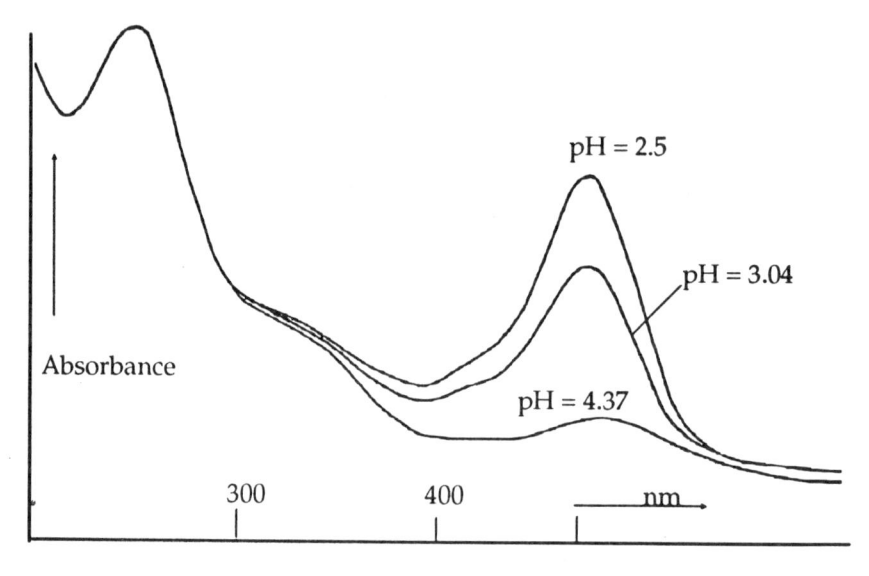

Figure 14.3

### Colour intensity and skin contact

It is often believed that if the fruit pulp and skins are allowed to remain in contact with the fermenting must for really long periods, more red colour will be extracted. Experiments with grapes have shown that this concept is rather over-simplified. Experiments with several varieties of grapes, including Cabernet Sauvignon and Pinot noir have involved carrying out fermentations with varying grape skin contact time. The colour density did not go on rising as we might have expected, but peaked at between 3 and 6 days.

It is interesting to note that allowing the skins to stay in contact with the fermenting must resulted in a steady rise in the pH. This is thought to be a result of the extraction from the skins of potassium salts. The buffering action of these salts causes the pH to rise.

The maximum colour intensity may peak after a skin contact time of just a few days, but the total phenolics content (i.e. anthocyanins and tannins) goes on increasing. While we must avoid such a long contact time that the tannin extraction makes the wine too harsh, it has been shown that when the tannin is present the colour intensity increases during the storage of the wine. If the tannin is too low, then the red colour fades significantly. A study of red wines made by different periods of skin contact has shown that a period of 6-7 days results in the wine having the highest colour intensity after five months or more. The speculation is that the tannin molecules link with the anthocyanin molecules by means of acetaldehyde.

Further experiments have shown that much the same effect can be achieved if the skin contact is for a fairly short period, but oenological tannin is added to the ferment. Enthusiastic readers may like to experiment along these lines by adding 1-2 grams of tannin to their red wines that have had a short time "on the pulp".

**Effect of sulphur dioxide**

Winemakers will know that the colour of red musts is often bleached quite a lot when sulphite is added to sterilise them. This is because the bisulphite ion ($HSO_3^-$) combines with the anthocyanin to form a colourless compound. Fortunately, this process is reversible and most of the colour will return as the sulphite gets used up during the storage period.

**Losses during fermentation**

The red colour of the must often pales during the fermentation, because of temporary changes to some of the anthocyanin molecules, but once again the loss of colour is largely temporary, and it returns to a large extent after a period in cask or even bottle.

# Other wine colours

The tannins found in the skins of grapes and other fruits, have a yellow-brown colour, and it is the presence of these substances that modify the rather stark red-purple colour of anthocyanins. As the wine ages, so some of the anthocyanins polymerise, joining up with the tannin molecules, so that the purple colour fades and is replaced by the more gentle red colour we find in a mature wine. If the skins of white grapes are left in the must, the tannin molecules will contribute a yellow colour to the wine.

If the wine gets oxidised, either by exposure to the air, or heat, then browning will take place at the same time as the taste and smell deteriorates. This question of why wines go brown is covered in the next section.

# Why do wines turn brown?

Both beverages of all kinds and solid foods can go brown for a number of reasons. All of the causes are relevant to winemaking, either because they affect the ingredients or because they have a direct impact on the must or wine. So before we deal with the specific problems found with wines, let us take a brief overall view of browning causes.

Browning may involve enzymes, but this is not always the case. Some fruits and vegetables go brown very easily during processing; apples, for instance turn brown quite quickly once they are cut, but rhubarb does not. The difference is that apples contain an enzyme called polyphenoloxidase, and if air (i.e. oxygen) is present the enzyme will act on any phenolic compounds present, polymerising them and hence turning the fruit brown. The name given to the enzyme, polyphenoloxidase, aptly describes its function, the poly part signifying the polymerisation and the oxidase part the oxidation that takes place.

Although the process is quite well understood, it is quite complicated, and all I need say is that the phenolic substance that is present is first oxidised to a quinone (the OH groups are changed into =O groups) and then polymerisation takes place producing the brown-coloured compounds. For the technically minded readers I will just mention that it is the phenolic compound chlorogenic acid in fruits such as apples and peaches that is the source of the trouble. Potatoes also brown very easily when peeled, but here it is another substance tyrosine that is oxidised and polymerised into the brown-black pigment. As a point of general interest, it is tyrosine that is converted into melanin, the dark pigmentation of the hair and skin of animals (including humans).

It must be emphasised that the browning will only take place if both the enzyme and oxygen are present, together with the phenolic substance. If the phenolic substance could be removed, browning could not take place. Unfortunately it is difficult to remove the phenolic substances from fruit juices (and even more so from solid foods) without altering the character of the product. Accordingly the approach is to either deactivate the enzyme or restrict the access of oxygen. Heat is used to destroy the enzyme, and freezer owners will do this regularly by blanching the fruit and vegetables before freezing them. But, as we have seen, too much heat will alter the flavour of the ingredients.

The simplest approach is to add something that the oxygen will combine with in preference to the phenolic compounds. The answer is sulphur dioxide, or salts such as sodium or potassium metabisulphite. We say that these substances are antioxidants. They also offer us a bonus in that they will destroy invading bacteria.

There are several ways in which foods can go brown without the help of enzymes. The first of these is the so-called *Maillard reaction*, named after a French chemist who found that some sugars could react with aminoacids, with the eventual formation of hydroxymethylfurfural (HMF), which then rapidly polymerised to give a brown-black pigment. Not all sugars can react in this way; thus glucose can but sucrose cannot. But since sucrose breaks down quite readily into glucose and fructose, sucrose solutions too will sooner or later produce glucose that will react with amino acids.

Another browning process is that of caramelisation. We all know that if we cook up a strong sugar syrup then it will gradually take on the colour and flavour of caramel/toffee. The browning process does not need the sugar solution to be boiled, of course, but at lower temperatures the reaction will be much slower; however, it will be speeded up in the presence of salts of the acids commonly found in fruit juices (citrates, malates, phosphates and tartrates).

Finally I should mention the possibility of browning taking place when ascorbic acid (vitamin C) is present. As vitamin C is present in many fruit juices, there is the potential for browning to occur if the juice is cooked for any length of time. During the fermentation any vitamin C will be destroyed and cause no further problems. Unfortunately this vitamin is a good antioxidant (like sulphur dioxide) and there is an increasing practice of adding it to a young fruity wine to keep it nice and fresh. My advice is to use ascorbic acid as an additive only when the wine is going to be drunk relatively young; I don't use it for wines I intend to lay down for a number of years.

Turning now to wines, we shall see that any of the mentioned browning processes could contribute to the development of a brown colour in a wine. Let us look at in turn the ingredients, their processing and the treatment of the finished wine.

Concentrates and dried fruit

When fruit juice is concentrated it is heated under a partial vacuum and the water removed; the desirable volatiles that are lost will be trapped out and returned to the concentrate if the processing is done properly. Even so, there is bound to be some browning. Indeed a look at any grape juice made from concentrate will show that it is quite a lot darker than fresh grape juice. This also applies to other fruit juices such as apple. In the chapter on Curing Faults (Chapter 17), we shall consider how we can reduce the level of this colour, should it be enough to spoil the look of the wine.

Dried fruit will also contain brown colouring substances. This is not surprising since heat has to be applied to remove the water. This heat may be in some sort of commercial drier, or the producer may use nature's bounty (the sun) in a suitable climate. After all we do read about the virtues of sun-kissed raisins etc.

### Fresh fruit

Two possible sources of browning are to be found here. The fruit may be under-ripe or badly bruised. Bear in mind that fruit that is already brown because of poor handling will never recover its true colour completely, even though treatment with a little sulphite may help.

### Processing the ingredients

What has to be watched is exposure of the fruit to too much heat and too much air, especially if the fruit has been cut up or pulped. Prevention is the watchword here. A little sulphite added in time works wonders. I must again warn readers against over-enthusiastic use of a steamer such as the Säftborn on "white" fruits. The heating is sufficient to give the extract both a brownish colour and a slightly cooked taste.

Last, but by no means least, make sure that all the vessels you use for holding the ingredients are made from materials other than metal. Traces of metals such as iron and copper will speed up the browning process; in addition they may also form coloured hazes with phenolic compounds in the must (see Chapter 15).

### Fermentation and storage

The initial must has to have a reasonable level of dissolved oxygen in order for the yeast cells to prosper, but for winemaking on the small scale we shouldn't need to add a lot more air during the fermentation. If I am making just a gallon of wine, I carry out the whole fermentation with the demijohn fitted with a fermentation lock, and I have not had a stuck ferment yet. It is only when really large vats of wine are being made that it may be necessary to rouse the yeast by pumping the wine from one tank to another. This refreshes the yeast if it is flagging.

During the fermentation period, the wine is protected from the air by both the fermentation trap and the atmosphere of carbon dioxide gas that has been generated during the fermentation. When the fermentation is complete and you rack the wine for the first time, then you are exposing the wine to more air. With red wines this doesn't matter quite so much because the tannins and colouring matter are antioxidants and will give the wine some protection.

It is a different story with white wines, though, especially those which are more delicate. The racking should be carried out with the minimum of splashing, and as soon as the wine has been transferred to a clean jar the usual amount of sulphite solution should be added, and the fermentation lock refitted. The demijohn should be filled as far as it is possible. If necessary add a little of another finished wine to top up the jar. If only a little topping up is necessary you can add a little boiled water. In fact all the recipes that I have given in this book assume that boiled water will be used for topping up. The levels of flavour, alcohol and acid should be quite high enough for the wine to stand a small amount of dilution with water.

I recommend bottling as soon as the wine drops clear, and corking with a proper straight-sided wine cork. The bottles should be allowed to stand upright for a day or so after corking, to give the cork a chance to expand fully and effect a good seal, and then the bottles of wine should be placed in a horizontal rack. If the wine is stored this way, it keeps the cork wet. If the bottles are stored upright, the corks will dry up and air will be able to find its way down the sides of the cork and the wine will become oxidised.

Ideally the wines should be stored in a cool place because heat is the enemy and speeds up unwanted changes. It is tempting to have a fancy rack in the centrally heated living room or kitchen, but this should be for short periods of storage only. I built a special store outside for my wines, but I also keep quite a lot in cases, stored horizontally on shelves in the garage. While the temperature there is by no means constant, it very rarely falls below $0^{\circ}C$, and even during the hottest summer keeps reasonably cool. But do not use the attic or roof space other than in the winter, since even in a typical British summer it can get far too hot. The only exception to this is when you want to mature your Madeira style wines, when the baking serves a purpose.

## Summing up

**Ingredients**

> Use good quality- not under-ripe and not bruised fruit
> Do not use old concentrate
> Avoid dried fruit for light table wines
> Do not use fruit rich in phenolics to make white wines

**Must preparation**

> With white wines use juice rather than fruit pulp when possible
> Extract juice without using heat
> Use sensible levels of sulphur dioxide
> For white wine ingredients avoid both heat and too much air
> Do not use metal vessels or utensils

**Fermentation**

> Keep the demijohn full once the primary fermentation is over
> Avoid excessive aeration
> Do not place the demijohn in the sunlight or on a hot surface

**Storage**

    Use good quality straight-sided corks
    Store in cool, dark place
    Store in "laid down" corked bottles
    Do not use thin plastic containers for lengthy storage

# Chapter 15
# Cloudy Wines

## Introduction

Commercial winemakers go to a great deal of trouble to produce a wine that is "star bright". Indeed, if this wasn't so, we would be most reluctant to taste it, let alone buy it. I believe that the amateur winemaker should try to match his commercial counterpart and produce his wines to a similar standard of excellence. In saying this I recognise that we have a much harder job to achieve a near perfect clarity because we work with a much wider range of winemaking ingredients, and will experience greater problems.

When the wine has just finished working, it may well be a little murky because it will contain various particles in suspension, ranging from particles of the ingredients to spent yeast cells. But much of this material settles down to the bottom of the fermenter after the first racking and sulphiting, and can be removed at the second racking. The problem isn't with this material, but that which stubbornly refuses to sink to the bottom, and leaves the wine with a persistent haze that just won't clear.

This becomes obvious when we hold up the bottle of wine to a strong light, and the light rays have to pass through the walls of the bottle and the wine before they reach our eyes. If the wine contains tiny particles in suspension, the light rays will bounce off them and become scattered; as a consequence we shall see a bright haze. Another example, though not concerning wine, is cigarette smoke. The particles of smoke hang in the air and once again the deflected light rays create the haze effect.

Water shells

Hydrophilic particles

Protective coatings

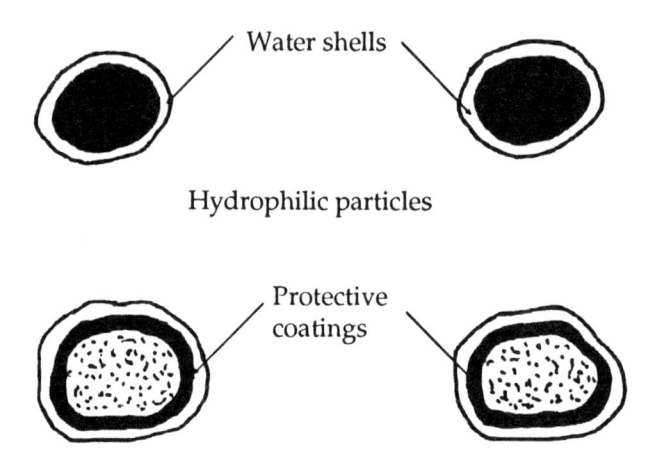

Coated hydrophobic particles

**Figure 15.1**

This light scattering is known as the Tyndall effect. It is observed only when the suspended particles have diameters in the size range 1 - 100 mm ($10^{-7}$ to $10^{-5}$ cm). To put this size into perspective, we would have to line up end to end some ten million of the smallest particles to stretch to one centimetre.

These small particles, which are called colloidal particles, move constantly through the solution; the movement, called "Brownian movement", keeps the particles in suspension and prevents them from settling.

As we shall see in the section dealing with the source of the particles, the commonest ones are those coming from the ingredients, such as gums, pectic substances, proteins and starch. All of these materials contain hydroxy (OH) or similar groups that can interact with water. In this way the water-loving particles (called hydrophilic) can acquire a surrounding water shell, which gives them some stability against aggregation. Another stabilising factor is the tendency of many particles to become either positively- or negatively- charged by absorbing an ion from solution.

Even particles that are not hydrophilic can become so by acquiring a protective coating of either pectin or starch; we then say that there is a protective colloidal solution. Figure 15.1 illustrates the point.

# Sources of colloidal particles

The plant material used to make the must is likely to be the main source of colloidal particles, although the way in which the fruits etc. are selected and handled often determines whether or not the particles are of the crucial size. Poor processing methods can introduce metallic impurities or facilitate oxidation, either of which can play a part in the formation of hazes. Particles of colloidal size can also be formed from the yeast or by action of bacteria. In some cases haze can develop in a clear wine during the process of maturation. We will now look at these various sources in more detail.

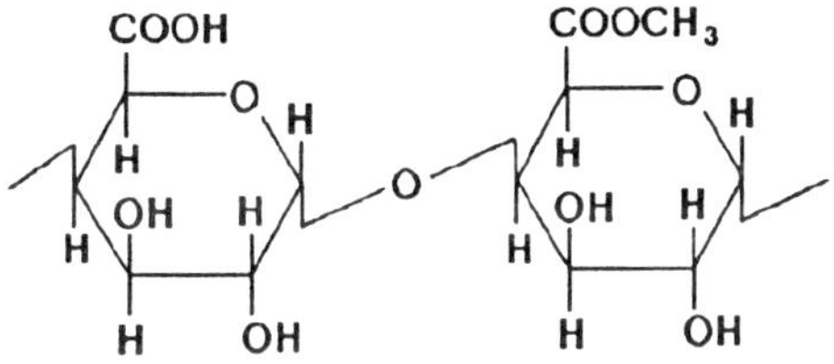

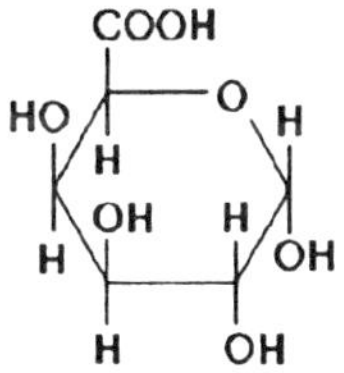

Figure 15.2

## Materials used in the must

Pectic substances are found in fruits and most vegetables. They occur in the cell walls and spaces between the cells, where they act as a kind of cement that holds the cells together and keeps the plant firm. The words pectic substances really describe a range of substances, but in each case the pectic substance will be a polymer based on units of galacturonic acid joined together in a long chain. Figure 15.2 shows a section of a typical pectic substance, together with the formula of galacturonic acid. For the information of the more scientifically minded readers I should add that galacturonic acid closely resembles the sugar galactose that was mentioned in Chapter 13; it differs only in that galacturonic acid contains the carboxylic acid group ($CO_2H$) while galactose has an alcohol grouping ($CH_2OH$).

Some of the carboxylic acid groups may have reacted with methyl alcohol and become methylated, giving the methoxy group (OCH$_3$). The extent to which this occurs varies according to the source of the pectic substance. Thus apple pectin will have at least 60% of its carboxy groups esterified in this way, but the figure for strawberry pectin is only 10%.

I have used the general name pectic substance for simplicity. In practice, three names are used which describe the structures more closely. Thus the name protopectin is used to describe the highly polymeric substances which are insoluble in water. When this is partially broken down it becomes soluble in water, and then it is called pectin. In both protopectin and pectin a fairly high proportion of the carboxy groups are methylated; some material may be virtually free from this methylation and it is then called pectic acid. To avoid unnecessary hassle I shall continue to use the general name of pectic substance to cover all the possibilities.

I have deliberately oversimplified the nature of the pectic substances since in reality their long chains are usually broken up by blocks of sugar units, and there may also be side chains of sugars such as arabinose and galactose.

**Starch** can be another source of colloidal particles. As we saw in Chapter 13, starch is a polymer of glucose units. It is to be found in all root vegetables, and in fruits that are under-ripe.

**Gums** are to be found in a number of fruits. A good example is the plum, which when ripe can split and exude gum; more gum is found close to the stone. Gums are complicated polymers made up from a variety of sugar units linked together. Thus in plum gum the component sugars are arabinose, galactose, mannose, rhamnose and xylose; this is truly a fiendish mixture, and it can be a major problem with plum wines.

**Waxes** are also a source of difficulty with plums, but they are also found on the surface of other fruits, including apples and grapes. These waxes, contain substances called lipids, which have carboxy acid groups linked to long hydrocarbon chains. The layer of wax is quite thin, and if looked at under a microscope can be seen as a series of overlapping plates. It seems to be produced by the plant as a device to prevent the fruit from losing too much moisture.

**Protein** is a general name used to describe the substances that are formed by the joining together of aminoacids. It is found in all grain to the extent of 10-15%, with around 2% in most root vegetables, and rather less than 1% in the majority of fruits. It is produced by yeast cells and enters the wine when the cells die and autolyse.

## Metallic contamination

Musts and wines can become contaminated with traces of such metals as copper and iron. Thus copper is used as a part of the make-up of some fruit sprays such as Bordeaux mixture, and residues can get into the must. Iron is more likely to contaminate the must because of careless processing, though, and I can illustrate the point by referring to a real problem that I was asked to solve by an English vineyard. The problem was that our analysis showed that the wine contained over 20 milligrams per litre of iron, which is well above the limit and likely to cause haze problems. The iron, I found, contaminated the grape juice because the winemaker had left his press out in the open over the winter and it had gone rather rusty! The smaller presses that we use can rust in much the same way so do make sure that you treat the equipment to prevent this.

The metals are a nuisance because they may form coloured hazes by reaction with any phenolic compounds present in the must; typically a blue haze of "ferric tannate" will form in red wines. Even if the phenolic compounds are present at too low a level to produce a haze with the iron, as with white wines, hazes can still form. Thus when the must rich in iron is aerated there may be a precipitation of milky-white iron phosphate.

## Oxidative casse

When wines are exposed to excessive amounts of air, oxidase enzymes may initiate the formation of brown polymeric materials (see Chapter 14); and sunlight also contributes to the formation of such casses.

## Attack by micro-organisms

We have noted that yeasts will release proteins into the wine once the fermentation is over; they will also hand over various polysaccharide substances such as mannan. It is said that the colloidal particles produced by the yeast are 30% proteins and 70% polysaccharides.

If the must or wine is attacked by bacteria the side effects may include the formation of hazes, but fortunately these afflictions are unlikely to trouble the amateur winemaker who follows the normal hygiene rules. Just in case the unexpected should happen, the signs to look for are:

**Oiliness.** A viscous oily appearance will be noticeable in the wines are attacked by Bacterium gracile; carbon dioxide gas will be formed at the same time.

**"Lactic".** This is attributed to some strains of lactic acid bacteria, and shows itself as a turbidity in the wine, together with conversion of malic acid into lactic and some evolution of carbon dioxide.

**Mannitol formation.** *Bacterium mannitopeum*, fortunately a rather rare breed, can attack the wine turning it cloudy and depositing cells. At the same time the wine develops a sweet-sour taste.

**Tourne.** This is characterised by a haze that gives a silky sheen with iridescence when the wine is agitated. It results from an attack by *Bacterium tartarophthorum* on the glycerine or tartaric acid in the wine, and the wine then tastes sour and insipid.

**Storage and maturation**

We have seen that hazes can disappear if the particles in suspension can join together to get bigger and heavier, when they will settle to the bottom of the wine. Unfortunately this "growing bigger" phenomenon can result in the slow formation of colloidal-sized particles during storage. It seems especially likely to happen in white wines when protein hazes can develop.

A haze that may afflict amateur winemakers is that produced by the formation of calcium tartrate. This can only form if the must or wine contains both calcium ions and tartaric acid, and it is very difficult to predict just when it is likely to occur. As a guide line, it seems that levels of calcium tartrate below 200 milligrams per litre for white wines and 300 milligrams per litre for red wines will not cause problems unless the wine is well chilled.

Simple calculations suggest that this is likely to happen only when really hard water with high calcium levels is used together with fruits that are rich in calcium. Such fruits include blackberries with a typical calcium level of 400-500 mg/l. This illustrates the importance of reducing the calcium level in the water by boiling it.

# Prevention of hazes

The first rule of the game is that prevention is better than cure; it is certainly a lot easier. With this in mind, let us quickly run through the causes of hazes and see what we can do to avoid them.

**"Pectin" hazes**

We can prevent these hazes forming if we treat the must with a good quality pectolytic enzyme. Such enzymes are available in several styles and strengths. Remember that the enzyme will not take kindly to heat, and will lose its activity fairly quickly if you store it at high temperatures. The refrigerator is much more suitable than a cupboard above the radiator! When you purchase the enzyme, try to get it from a shop that has a regular turnover, and one where the containers of enzyme materials are not stored in the window or on shelves in full sunlight. The good home-brew shop proprietor will make sure he stores it properly.

The other point is that the way in which the enzyme is presented is important; thus liquid suspensions are likely to have a rather shorter shelflife than the enzyme supplied on a powder support. I recommend the Gervin tablets, because they are much richer in the enzyme than the solutions or powders, and have a long shelf life since the enzyme is protected inside the tablet.

## Starch hazes

If you restrict your winemaking to fruits and flowers you are most unlikely to come across a starch problem; the only possible source will be under-ripe fruits. Both grains and root vegetables do contain quite high levels of starch, so take care if you use these ingredients in your winemaking.

With luck you may not get a problem even with grain, since a lot of the starch that you will have added to your must will interact with other substances and precipitate out. Don't stew up grain, and to be sure, omit grains altogether.

One vegetable that can cause a lot of problems is the parsnip. Reduce your chances of getting a starch haze as much as possible by using parsnips that have been exposed to the frost, when the starch will have turned into sugar, and very little is left behind to trouble us.

## Gums

The solution here is quite simple. If the plums etc. have split and exude gum then do not use them for winemaking. Eat them or make jam with them!

## Waxes

It is only with the plum family that we seem to have a wax problem that does not resolve itself. I suggest that if you use plums in your winemaking it is best to remove any wax by washing the fruit with hot water (say 60°C). Provided that the plums are not really soggy and broken open, but firm, then you can make sure that all the wax is removed by adding a little mild detergent to the wash liquid. Use something like Fairy Liquid, and wash away all traces of suds with cold water before you process the fruit further.

The detergent treatment may seem drastic, but I can assure readers that it works and that your wine will not end up with a "soapy" taste, provided that the fruit is whole and given a very thorough final wash.

**Protein hazes**

There is little we can do to prevent protein getting into the wine from the ingredients. The choice of a good quality wine yeast will reduce the amount of protein that is present in the wine, and racking the wine from the lees as soon as the fermentation is over will keep the protein release to a minimum.

The sure way of solving the problem is to add bentonite to the must at the start of the fermentation. If this is done, it will "collect" the protein and carry it down to the bottom of the fermentation vessel. It is important to use a bentonite of wine quality, and to rehydrate it fully before adding it to the must. The bentonite gives us an added bonus since it provides a surface on which the bubbles of carbon dioxide gas can form, thus preventing gushing and loss of desirable volatile compounds.

**Pulp hazes**

Up until now I have deliberately characterised each of the likely causes of hazes by writing of pectic substances, starch etc., but nature is rather more complicated than this, and the polymeric compounds produced in the fruits etc. will often be a combination of various chemical substances. These may not always respond to specific treatments. We can restrict the amounts of uncharacterised particles by making sure that we do not reduce our fruits to exceptionally fine particles.

Of course fruit juice manufacturers often go out of their way to give us a cloudy product, and they do this by the process of homogenisation, in which the pulp particles are reduced to a very tiny size. This makes them less likely to settle out of the juice. A cloud stabiliser may then be added to make sure.

In practical terms this means that we should not be too mean and try to get out the last drops of must by giving the press that final turn or the straining bag that last squeeze. It is this last effort to increase juice yield that pushes through the smallest particles.

**Metallic casse**

The remedies are fairly clear. Avoid spraying the fruit with copper- and iron-containing compounds if this is possible. If you must use Bordeaux mixture, then wash the fruit well before processing it.

Avoid using metal containers and don't heat your fruit in aluminium containers. Make sure that any equipment you use doesn't have any rusty iron parts. This means looking carefully at the metal strips that link the wooden slats in the press, and removing any rust from metal presses before using them. Look at this sort of equipment well before the time you expect to use it, and give it a coating of protective "varnish" if it is needed.

If you use cans of fruit or fruit juice concentrate, look out for the badly dented cans and reject them. While they may be alright, there is a possibility that the damage may have cracked the layer of tinplate and exposed the iron underneath.

## Oxidative casse

Just take care of the causes, namely too much air and heat, and keep the fermentation vessel well away from the sunlight. Probably the worst place to put a demijohn is on the top of the boiler which is in direct sunlight. In any case keep the jar out of the sun, and do not place it directly on a hot surface. The hot surface will give the yeast a "hot foot" and may weaken it sufficiently for it to give up the ghost and stop working. If your yeast is a suitable one you do not need to supply a lot of heat to ensure a fast fermentation!

## Calcium tartrate

If you live in a hard water area, boil the water and let it cool down before using it. Some of the calcium in the water will precipitate out (the calcium bicarbonate that causes the so-called temporary hardness will be converted into insoluble calcium carbonate).

## Hazes caused by micro-organisms

Destroy any unwanted bacteria in the ingredients, if necessary, by washing the fruit well and then using a little sulphite. If you have frozen the fruit and process it by pouring boiling water over it, then the microbial level remaining will not be menacingly high. Provided that you start the fermentation fairly soon with a really active wine yeast, then the fermentation will get under way quickly, and the increasing level of alcohol will put paid to any bacteria that remain.

Once the fermentation is over, the wine must be protected at all costs from bacteria attack by adding the appropriate amount of sulphite solution and keeping the wine under lock.

# Curing specific hazes

In this chapter we will deal with the problem of getting rid of hazes caused by specific substances such as pectic substances. When such methods fail, then we have to go for more general methods such as fining and filtering; these will form the subject matter of the next chapter.

### Testing for the causes of hazes

It is possible to test for pectic substances, starch, protein, casse and microbial attack, although I suspect that most readers will not wish to bother. I would suggest that they should at least check their wines for starch before they start trying to remove it with a specific enzyme. This is a rare problem and the enzyme is expensive (if you can get it).

**Testing for starch.** Take a white saucer and place on it a few millilitres of the suspect wine. Now add a couple of drops of tincture of iodine solution and stir the mixture. If the wine contains any starch the mixture will go either deep-blue (amylose present) or a red-brown (amylopectin).

**Testing for pectin.** Take about a fluid ounce of the suspect wine and add to it about three or four times its volume of methylated spirits. If the wine is rich in pectin it will be precipitated in strings or curds. Of course this test relies entirely on the assumption that pectin will be insoluble in the added methylated spirits but that nothing else will come out of solution. In practice this test is far from perfect since other substances may precipitate, and the pectin precipitation is not always convincing. My advice is to assume that the haze problem may be caused by pectin and add the enzyme; if the haze doesn't clear then look for other causes.

**Testing for protein.** This, and the following two tests, are only for the real enthusiast. To check for protein, take 95 ml of the wine and add to it 5 ml of cold saturated solution of ammonium sulphate. Keep the wine at a temperature of around 55°C for 7 hours and then put it into an ice bath for 15 minutes. If protein is present in troublesome amounts a haze will develop.

**Testing for casse.** Heat a sample of the wine in a Pyrex flask for 3-4 minutes at 85°C, and then cool it under the tap. Half fill a bottle with this pasteurised wine and cork it loosely. Half fill a second bottle with unheated wine. Leave both bottles for 3-4 days. If the casse gets worse in both bottles then the cause is likely to be an iron casse; if it gets worse only in the unheated wine then the cause is enzymatic.

**Testing for micro-organisms.** Filter a small sample of the wine to clarify it. Now treat one sample with heat and not a second, just as for the casse test. If the haze develops again but only in the unheated sample, then the casse has been caused by microbial action.

# Treating specific hazes

### Enzyme treatments

As I mentioned in the previous section, because there is quite a good chance that the haze will be caused by some pectic substance, and because the test is not always conclusive, I recommend treating any hazy wine with pectolytic enzyme in the first instance. But you must use an enzyme preparation that is capable of working under the level of alcohol found in the wine. Thus alcohol deactivates the enzyme, so that you need to add around four times as much to a wine containing 15% alcohol than you do to a must. In practice you may find that the less potent bran-supported pectolytic enzyme is not able to carry out ist allotted task. The enzyme in the Gervin tablets is said to work even if the alcohol level is 16-17%, but no enzyme preparation available to the amateur winemaker can be guaranteed to work in fortified dessert wines.

If the ingredients were likely to have contained starch, then it is possible that the starch has caused the haze. But test the wine first by the iodine method. If starch is the cause then try to obtain the starch reducing enzyme (amylase) and use according to the instructions provided.

### Bentonite for protein hazes

Bentonite will take out most of the protein from the wine. It is a clay, and consists of calcium or sodium aluminium silicate, which has a layer structure (see Figure 16.1). If it is to work, the bentonite must completely take up all the water it needs to separate the layers in the clay. Then the proteins can move into the structure, between the layers, and are accordingly removed from the wine. I cannot emphasise enough that the bentonite must be given enough time to absorb all the water it needs before it is added to the wine.

If you are lucky, you may be able to get a specially prepared granular bentonite, specially prepared that is for the wine industry. The granules break down almost immediately in water, and if the resultant slurry is stirred vigorously and then allowed to stand for 30 minutes, it will do a splendid job.

If you can obtain only the powdered bentonite, then you will find the business of hydrating it quite tedious, because it is likely to form large sticky lumps that are rather difficult to break up. Some winemakers like to use a blender or kitchen whisk for this purpose; an alternative method is as follows:

Take a clean bottle and partly fill it with water. Place a funnel in the neck of the bottle and pour through it a little of the bentonite powder. Now remove the funnel, cork the bottle and shake it vigorously until the lumps have gone. Now repeat the process, adding the bentonite in small amount, dispersing it by shaking after each addition. Finally, leave the bentonite slurry for at least a day before you use it.

**Casses and unidentified hazes**

The time has come for broader approach, that of removing everything that is in suspension, by either filtering or fining the wine. This is the subject of the next chapter. Before we move on, though, I should just comment that even if we can remove casse particles by filtering or fining, the wine may still not be up to standard because it may be oxidised. We shall discuss the problem of treating an oxidised wine in the final chapter.

# Chapter 16
# Fining and Filtering

## Introduction

Many amateur winemakers are reluctant to fine or filter their wines because they feel that such treatments will remove some of the "body". While there may be some basis for this argument, it should be appreciated that with white wines, the professional winemaker almost always uses both of these processes, starting with fining and following it with filtering. This way they can make sure that the wines will be star bright when they are purchased by the customer.

In my experience, excessive use of these general methods of clearing a wine can make the wine a little dull, but used sensibly it is to be recommended. Thus these techniques will take out of the wine some of the substances that may cause problems later, and in particular they reduce the chance of the wines darkening prematurely. It is impossible to lay down hard and fast rules that have to be followed, but I offer the following guidelines.

1. As soon as the fermentation is complete, rack the wine from the deposit of spent yeast cells and general "debris", add the usual amount of sulphite solution and shake or stir the wine well. The shaking or stirring is to release any carbon dioxide gas bubbles which will otherwise inhibit the settling of lighter particles.

2. Now leave the wine for one to two months to see if it clears naturally.

3. If a haze persists, treat the possible specific causes along the lines suggested in the last chapter. First of all add pectolytic enzyme, and later use bentonite to remove protein; the bentonite treatment is only necessary if you did not add it to the must at the start of the fermentation.

**4. With white and rosé wines**, I believe in fining my table wines as soon as I have carried out treatment with pectolytic enzyme/bentonite. I then make any minor adjustments to the wines and filter them before bottling. Care has to be taken with these more delicate wines, as we shall see when we look into fining and filtering in more detail.

If the white wine is a heavy one, and particularly if it is a dessert wine, then I leave it alone after a second racking and sulphiting (say two months after the first racking). I rarely fine a really heavy wine, but if there is a persistent lack of real clarity I filter it carefully before bottling it.

**5. Red wines** tend to clear naturally if they have been made properly, because the tannin has a clarifying role as we shall see in the section dealing with fining. If the red wine contains far too much tannin, then some can be removed by the addition of gelatine solution, and the gelatine-tannin precipitate that forms will carry down with it other troublesome substances in suspension. Because fining can remove some of the red/brown colour I am reluctant to fine my red wines unless they stubbornly refuse to drop clear. If you cask-age your red wines then this process will yield a clear wine almost every time.

# Fining

The underlying principle of fining is the treatment of the wine with a material that will interact with the colloidal particles in some way and persuade them to settle out of solution. As we saw in the last chapter, the colloidal particles may be protected with a layer of pectin, which prevents them from joining together and settling out, and this is normally taken care of by adding the pectolytic enzyme.

But the particles are further stabilised by carrying either a positive or negative charge. If we add a fining agent that has the opposite charge, then the particle's charge is neutralised and it can be removed from suspension much more easily.

The fining agents also have a second mode of action by forming a network of flocculent material, that traps out the particles by adsorbing them.

To start with, I will list the more commonly used fining materials according to their compositions, putting them into one or other of the two broad categories of organic and inorganic fining agents:

**Organic fining agents**

        casein
        chitin
        egg white
        gelatine
        isinglass
        polyvinylpyrrolidone (PVP)
        sparkolloid

**Inorganic fining agents**

        bentonite
        kieselguhr
        silicic acid (kieselsol)


**Organic fining agents**

**Casein** is the main protein that is found in milk, and it is normally prepared commercially by acidifying skimmed cows' milk until the pH reaches 4.6. Milk also contains a second protein, whey protein, but this is not precipitated under these conditions. Casein is built up from a lot of aminoacid residues linked together, the main ones being glutamic acid, leucine, isoleucine and valine. It is virtually insoluble in water, but you can get it to dissolve if you add a little sodium bicarbonate. It is best to make up a 2% solution in 100 ml of 0.5% sodium bicarbonate solution; for most purposes it is good enough to take one eighth of a level teaspoonful of sodium bicarbonate and dissolve it in 5 fluid ounces of cold water, and then add two teaspoonsful of the casein. Shake or stir the mixture until the casein has dissolved. Use the solution within two or three days because it will deteriorate fairly quickly.

Casein dissolves in sodium bicarbonate solution because it then forms the soluble sodium salt, sodium caseinate. These days you may find it easier to buy this soluble form sodium caseinate or the potassium equivalent. The potassium caseinate is used in the commercial field primarily for fining white wines that have a little too much colour (i.e. slight browning), but it serves a double purpose because it will also remove some of the astringency that we associate with a wine that has been made from over-pressed grapes. Potassium caseinate is sold for use by amateur winemakers under the Gervin label.

To use the potassium caseinate, take around 50 ml of cold water and add a teaspoonful of the caseinate a little at a time. Stir gently to get the mixture into a smooth slurry and then add a further 50 ml of water. Stir well until the caseinate dissolves. You should really use demineralised or distilled water for dissolving the caseinate because hard water contains a lot of calcium and this will produce a precipitate of insoluble calcium caseinate. If such "soft" water is not available use boiled tap water.

This caseinate solution is then added to the hazy wine (or the wine that has too much astringency or colour) and the mixture shaken well. The caseinate precipitates out from the wine and will gradually sink to the bottom, but because the caseinate forms low density flakes, there is a tendency for one or two of the flakes to float. Be patient and use gentle persuasion to encourage settling. If the odd flake stubbornly refuses to settle it will be necessary for you to carry out a final filtering.

You may come across account in some older books written for amateur winemakers that recommend the use of powdered milk for fining. Please ignore this advice. Milk powder contains the whey protein and a fair amount of milk sugar (lactose), neither of which we want in our wines.

**Chitin (chitosan)** is the basis for the material that is sold for fining under a variety of names, including Wine Cleer. Chitin is a natural polymer that forms the skeleton structure of shell fish such as lobsters and crabs. Indeed the waste products from the shell fish industry contain some 20% of chitin. The chitin is extracted from the waste by treating it first with caustic soda solution to dissolve up the protein, and then with hydrochloric acid to dissolve up the chalk, leaving the chitin.

But just what is chitin? It is a polysaccharide not too far removed from cellulose. The basic units are glucose molecules in which one of the hydroxy groups has been replaced by an aminoacetyl ($NHCOCH_3$) group. When the chitin is treated with a strong solution of caustic soda, this side group is modified to give a simple amino ($NH_2$) group, and giving us chitosan. It is chitosan that is used for fining. It is a rather expensive fining agent, despite its humble origins, but is effective in clearing most types of haze.

**Egg white**, which contains albumin, has been used for many years to fine stubborn wines, but at the rate of half a dozen egg whites to 100 gallons of wine. I do not think it is a practical proposition for amateur winemakers, but if you want to try it out, take the appropriate amount of egg white and whisk it well in say half a pint of the wine. Then add the suspension to the rest of the wine, shake the mix well and wait for the wine to clear.

While we are on the subject of eggs, I should mention that crushed egg shells can be used to clear wines; at the same time they remove a very small amount of the acid in the wine because the shells contain chalk.

**Gelatine** is manufactured from many animal sources such as bones, and it too consists of various aminoacid building blocks linked together. In this case the amino acids are hydroxyproline, proline and glycine. There are many commercial grades of gelatine, and only the purest should be used for fining wines. These days amateur winemakers are fortunate in that high quality gelatine has been processed and made into a solution ready for use in our wines. Generally speaking you can get either a 15% or a 30% solution, and these solutions keep well provided that they are not left exposed to possible attack by airborne bacteria and moulds. Remember that gelatine is an excellent source of food for these invaders and take precautions to ward them off. I always add a little sulphite to my gelatine stock, and this does the trick. If you let the gelatine solution get very cold, it will go almost solid, but it will soon be back to normal if you warm up the bottle under the hot tap.

Gelatine is not normally used on its own for fining, unless the intention is to take out some of the tannin; it is usually taken as one part of a two-component fining system, in which silicic acid is the other component.

Originally the two component system used was gelatine and tannin, which interact to give a precipitate which falls to the bottom of the demijohn, bringing with it any haze particles that it picks up on the way. It was for this reason that tannin used to be added to white wines; it didn't stay there of course but was removed by the action of the gelatine. Unfortunately some writers of books for amateur winemakers still tell us to add tannin to white wines but don't realise that it is needed only if it is to be used as part of the fining system.

It is more convenient for us to use silicic acid in place of the tannin. This is essentially silica (or sand) that has been hydrated and made into a colloidal solution. This solution is usually sold to amateur winemakers as Kieselsol. When it is used in conjunction with gelatine, both solutions are of comparable strengths, and they must be added to the wine in equal quantities. I recommend that you add the silicic acid first and then give the wine a very good shake to remove any gas bubbles and disperse the silicic acid throughout the wine. Now add an equal amount of the gelatine and again shake or stir well. The success of the fining depends on removing the gas bubbles, which would otherwise slow down the settling of the gelatinous precipitate that forms, and ensuring a complete reaction between the two fining agents.

The silicic acid solution can grow moulds just like gelatine, so keep it in a screw-capped plastic bottle. But do not let it get too cold, because then some of the silica may come out of the solution and it will be less effective.

For the benefit of interested winemakers, I can say that the silicic acid technique was developed in Germany, as an alternative to using the difficult to get tannin; it was made from either sodium silicate (water glass) or hydrolysed silicon tetrachloride.

**Isinglass** is used more by brewers than winemakers, although some kit manufacturers like to use it for their wines as well. It is another protein, obtained this time from the dried inner membrane of the swimming bladder of the sturgeon. It has a similar make-up to gelatine. Although isinglass works reasonably well, it gives a much "fluffier" deposit that is easily disturbed, and this makes the subsequent racking process a little more difficult.

Isinglass is used at about half a gram to the gallon, being first dissolved in cold water.

**Polyvinylpyrrolidone (PVP)** is a polymeric material which is used to take out phenolic substances (tannins). It is an excellent material but very expensive and really of academic interest only.

**Sparkolloid** is a man-made polysaccharide fining agent that has been developed by wine chemists in the USA. It is made in two forms, a so-called cold-mix, which is used at room temperature, and the normal type which has to be heated in water at 80°C for 20 minutes or so before use. The cold-mix is much easier to use but is less certain to work. This material was marketed in the UK a little while ago, but I have not seen it in home-brew shops recently.

Inorganic fining agents

Bentonite is the clay that we have referred to several times before. It is found in many parts of the world, but the best known source is Wyoming. This material does not have a precise chemical formula, although the commonest form is usually referred to as a calcium aluminium silicate. It has a structure of sheets of aluminium and silicon oxides linked together, and carrying a negative charge, with the calcium cations (+ve ions) in between the layers; these cations are surrounded with a sheath of water molecules. Figure 16.1 shows this in diagrammatic form.

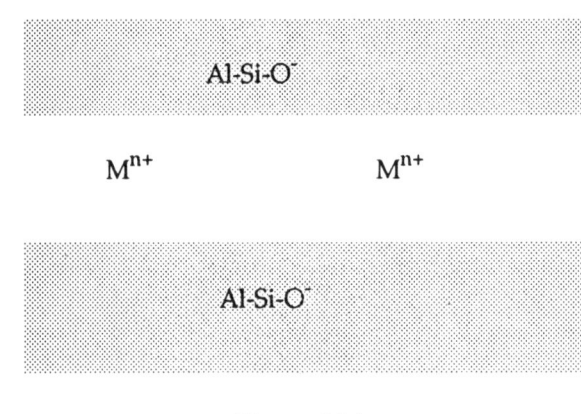

Al-Si-O$^-$

$M^{n+}$   $M^{n+}$

Al-Si-O$^-$

Figure 16.1

As we have seen already, bentonite fining helps to remove unwanted protein, gives a smoother fermentation, and it ensures that the lees are compacted. Grape wine makers have found that bentonite serves another purpose in helping to remove any traces of spray residues that were on the surface of the grapes and are transferred to the juice at the pressing stage. In experiments I have carried out with elderberries picked on very busy roadsides, I have found that fermentation in the presence of bentonite is useful because a lot of any lead compounds (deposited from the exhaust gases of passing cars) are removed by adsorption on the surface of the bentonite.

Other experiments I have carried out have shown that the fermentation is marginally faster when bentonite is present, and it gives a wine with a better bouquet; both of these effects are relatively small, but they are definite benefits. The bentonite we normally use is the calcium bentonite, which collects the positively-charged protein in between the layers, the protein displacing the calcium ions. If you should come across the sodium form then use it because it removes the protein better. Kieselguhr is another mineral that is essentially porous silica; it is sometimes known as diatomaceous earth. It is not used as a fining agent in its own right, but when it is added to the cloudy wine it helps with the fining action. It is used most frequently in filtering, though, where it is one of the materials used to coat the filter plates. Any reader who has used a Harris filter will be familiar with the method of use.

# Filtering

Until a few years ago there were no really good filters that the amateur winemaker could use, and some resorted to the old-fashioned "jelly bag"; this might give a clear wine, but almost inevitably the wine suffered from prolonged exposure to air. Some of the earlier models of filters that were on offer provided a decent filter pad, but the wine was transported to the pad by a syphoning action, and this could be rather a nuisance when gas bubbles still in the wine came out of solution and the syphon action stopped.

Readers may like to know something of the theory behind filtering and a little about commercial developments before we get down to how we can make the best use of any scaled down filter.

There are really two ways in which a filter works, namely by adsorption of the solid particles on to the surface of the filter medium, and the sieve-like action, whereby the bigger particles are unable to pass though the smaller holes in the filter.

**The adsorption process**

Figure 16.2(a) represents the cross-section of an idealised filter pad which contains fairly large pores. In theory the pores are large enough for the particles to pass through, but as they pass down the pores so they get attracted to the surface of the filter material by chemical forces, and remain there. Naturally there is a limit to how much material can be adsorbed, and eventually all the trapping sites will become occupied and further batches of wine will then pass through the filter still in a cloudy state.

In practice this adsorption of the solid particles inevitably causes some of the pores to become partially blocked and then the filter works on the basis of a simple sieve

(a)            (b)

**Figure 16.2**

and just holds back the larger particles. Figure 16.3 shows in close up what a typical filter pad of the adsorption type looks like. It may be made of cellulose fibres which have a natural attraction for the particles of yeast cells and other debris, and continues to pull them out of suspension until the fibres become saturated.

### The sieving mechanism

It is possible for filters to be manufactured so well that all the pores are of the same size and very regular in shape. This means that only particles that are smaller than the pore diameter can pass through. Figure 16.2(b) shows the principle of the sieving action.

**Figure 16.3**

The best known type of such filters is the membrane filter, which can be made from a variety of polymeric materials including cellulose esters. Figure 16.4 shows a somewhat idealised sketch I have made, from which you can see that all the pores are roughly of the same size. Membranes such as millipore can be obtained in several pore sizes, and used according to the size of particles that have to be removed.

I have small membrane pads that I use for filtering relatively small amounts of wine for experimental purposes. My three types of pad have respective pore sizes of 5.0, 1.2 and 0.2 µm (where 1 µm is one millionth of a metre). I use the coarsest one when I want to prepare a bottle of really sparkling wine for a show, and this always guarantees that my wine will at least get maximum points for clarity! The two other sizes are for removing yeast cells (1.2 µm) and bacteria (0.2 um).

### Relative merits of the two types of filter

Membrane filters are normally used only for the final polishing and sterile filtering stage, and are used on a wine that is already clear. Otherwise the filter would become blocked quite quickly. For the basic filtration it is the adsorption type of filter that is commonly used, and it is especially useful in the removal of colloidal substances that would clog up a sieve-type filter. The efficiency of the adsorption filter can be adjusted by changing the type of material that is used and its thickness. Thus with cellulose filters we can get the coarser ones made from long, loosely packed fibres, or finer ones for which shorter, more tightly packed fibres are used.

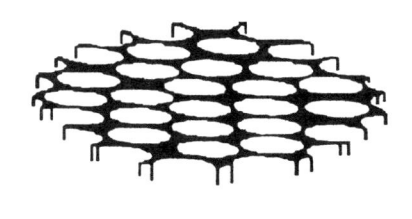

Figure 16.4

Commercial practice is to use either preformed filter sheets, or an inert porous support coated with a filter medium such as kieselguhr. The inert support may be made from a natural or synthetic fibre or from stainless steel mesh. The whole filter has to stand up to being washed and sterilised, and it must be neutral and not add any taste to the wine.

Asbestos was used for filter pads, and it gave excellent results. Unfortunately there were fears that the filtered beverage would contain fibres that would be a possible cause of abnormalities of the gut or intestines. The fear arose because there is a mass of evidence to show that fibres of blue asbestos can cause the lung disease asbestosis when taken into the lung over a long period. In case any winemaker has used asbestos in the past, I offer the reassuring comment that asbestos pads were made from white asbestos, whose fibres are a different shape and that there is no convincing evidence that they can cause problems if swallowed.

## Filters for the amateur winemaker

The filter which I like best and which has served me well over a long period is the one shown diagrammatically in Figure 16.5. The pads, which are made of cellulose (and obtainable in several grades of porosity), are housed in a stout plastic pair of disks, that are held together with a set of easily removable butterfly nuts. The wine is forced through the pads under positive pressure, supplied by means of a hand operated pump, the contraption being much like the garden spray.

**Figure 16.4**

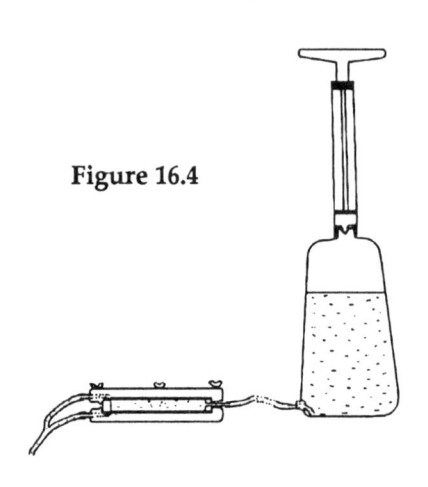

The first point I want to emphasise is that the filter should be assembled with its two pads, and washed first with a gallon of tap water to which a teaspoonful of 10% sulphite has been added. Then at least another gallon of water should be passed through the pad. I continue to wash the pads until I cannot tell any difference between the taste of the water straight from the tap and that coming out the end of the filter. As the washing proceeds, so the pads settle down and the butterfly nuts have to be tightened to prevent the filter from leaking.

Once the filter has been sterilised and washed, then it is time for the wine to be added to the 5-litre container. It should be treated with 5 ml of 10% sulphite solution, or one Campden tablet, since the wine needs some protection from the small amount of air it will inevitably come into contact with. The pressure is then applied to the wine which is forced through the filter pads. Initially it will be diluted with the water that is in the pads, and I usually let about half a bottle of filtrate pass through without saving it.

The wine is collected in a suitable glass container, care being taken not to let it splash as it enters the vessel. I find it best to hold the filter exit tube in position with a little cotton wool plug in the neck of the receiving vessel. I also take care to make sure that the exit of the tube is right against the side of the container, so as to reduce splashing. If the wine is to be bottled straight away, then I put the required amount of sulphite solution in the receiving vessel before I start pumping the wine through.

Although the present day cellulose pads are nothing like as efficient as their asbestos predecessors, they do a reasonable job, and generally will be good for the filtration of 10 - 15 gallons of wine; there will be a little mixing of the wines at any change-over point, of course, so it is sensible to choose wines of a similar nature for each set of pads. A last point is that if I am filtering a non-dry wine, I stabilise it with potassium sorbate before it is filtered.

Winemakers often talk of a wine being "filter-tired" or "filter-sick", which is another way of saying that it has been affected by a hint of oxidation. When sulphited it recovers in a week or so. If you add sulphite before you filter the wine, then you will usually find that this prevents the development of the tired taste.

# Chapter 17
# Curing Faults

## Introduction

Once again I must emphasise the first rule of winemaking:

*Prevention is better than cure*

What this means is that if we follow the normal procedures and adopt good winemaking practice we will have relatively few problems, and the vast majority of our wines will be sound and acceptable. I have suggested the most suitable ways of choosing and processing ingredients, together with the fermentation techniques, in the earlier chapters. All that I need do now is to draw together some of the main points in summary form.

**Ingredients.** Choose them carefully for their quality and level of ripeness as well as for their suitability for a particular style of wine. Don't go for the cheapest - get the best!

**Processing ingredients.** Follow the guidelines given in Chapter 5, and whenever possible avoid using excessive amounts of heat and don't reduce the ingredients to such small particles that pulp hazes are inevitable. Keep metallic containers away from your ingredients as much as possible. Use sulphur dioxide as a sterilant for the ingredients where this is necessary.

**Must requirements.** Make sure that you add pectolytic enzyme and sufficient nutrient to every must, and choose a top quality wine yeast; choose the yeast to suit the sort of fermentation conditions you are using, and don't be sucked in by misleading labels such as Sauternes and Chablis.

**Equipment.** This should be cleaned and sterilised after use, and sterilised again immediately before it is used again.

**Temperature.** Do not put your demijohn on the boiler, in the airing cupboard, or in the attic during the summer. These high temperatures will result in poor aromas and sometimes stuck ferments.

**Sulphur dioxide.** Use this in sensible amounts in your finished wines (especially whites) to prevent oxidation and attack by micro-organisms.

**Stabilising.** Sulphur dioxide is fine for dry wines, but sweet wines need the extra protection of sorbate - but use with sulphite and maintain a reasonably high level of acidity.

**Maturation and storage.** Keep demijohns full and under lock. Use standard straight-sided corks for bottles, and store the full bottles horizontally in a cool place.

## The general approach

The three senses we use in turn are those of sight (i.e. appearance), smell and taste. In the following review of the likely faults and how to cure them we will follow the sequence of appearance, smell and taste, although it should be appreciated that these are inter-related. Thus we can tell that a wine is likely to be oxidised from its appearance, and it will be very evident to both our nose and our taste buds.

In each section I will consider the more general faults first, and then go on to discuss more specific faults that can be linked to particular chemical or microbiological causes. Sometimes the "faults" are a matter of opinion, such as whether the wine is too sweet or too acid. Then you must decide whether to adjust the wine or not. Often such adjustments are best carried out by blending two or more wines, so I will digress for a moment to review the gentle art of blending.

### Blending

If we can, we select all our ingredients and put them together in the must before fermentation, but sometimes one or more of the ingredients may not be immediately available, and then we can make two separate wines at different times and mix or blend them later. We can also blend wines that have one of their characteristics a little too dominant. Typically we might have an excellent wine that used elderflowers, but which turned out to have rather too much aroma. Such a wine is invaluable for blending with other suitable wines that are somewhat lacking in aroma and bouquet.

The first rule of blending is to choose wines that are compatible. As an example, we might have a wine based on apple and grape juices bought in supermarket cartons. The wine may not have enough aroma in some cases, and then it is an ideal candidate for blending with the one with too much elderflower aroma. But never add a flower wine, with the characteristic floral nose, to a red fruit wine. This may seem common sense, and it is, but I have come across quite a few wines on the show bench where elderberry and elderflower wines have been mixed!

The next point to appreciate is that when two wines are mixed, chemical changes can take place, and such changes may occur over a period of several weeks. This means that blended wines should be given a resting period before they are bottled. Typical examples of the consequences of blending are:

The wine produces a **haze**. This can happen overnight, so never blend a wine the night before you are going to enter it for a show. Give it at least a week.

The wine produces a **precipitate**. Again this can happen quite quickly, but it can be a slower process.

The wine starts to **referment**. This can happen only if one of the wines has some residual sugar in it. The act of mixing means that air gets into the wine and activates the few yeast cells that will always be in our wines. If sweeter wines are involved in blending then the mixture must be stabilised.

Winemakers are often given the advice of testing small quantities of the mixture before blending the bulk wines. While this is sensible, it is not practical for wines to be mixed in odd ratios, because it will leave us with partially filled demijohns and the creation of new problems of oxidised wines or the necessity of making unsuitable blends just to use up the oddments. I try out mixtures with small amounts, but I only blend whole gallons or bottles of wine.

The "bottom line" is to blend the wines after an initial tasting of a sample mix, add sulphite (and sorbate if needed), and put the wine back into bulk storage for at least three weeks before bottling it. Last, but by no means least, never try to cover up a really faulty wine by blending it with a good wine. The taste of acetification or mouse will carry through and ruin the good wine as well.

## Appearance

Here we look for colour and clarity.

**Colour**

The main fault is likely to be that the colour is unsuitable. Thus a white table wine should not have a brown hint, although this may be quite acceptable in a heavy white or amber dessert, and looked for in a Madeira-style wine. Rosé wines do not want too much colour, and generally speaking we try to avoid too much orange or too deep a purple.

The biggest problem is likely to be with wines that are too brown, and while browning is less likely to happen if the advice given in Chapter 14 is followed, there is always going to be some wine that has more brown colour than we can accept. If we are dealing with white wines, then we must take care not to use methods that will mar the smell or taste. My advice is to use as gentle a method as possible, and this means using caseinate to lower the brown colour. If the colour is in the must (if the juices are rather brown for instance) then put the caseinate in when you start the fermentation. If the colour has developed because of lack of attention then add the caseinate to the finished wine as recommended on page 205. This treatment will not remove all of the brown colour but it should reduce it quite a lot; it is unlikely to reduce the flavour other than taking out some unwanted astringency.

If the brown colour is really bad and offends you beyond measure, then you can use charcoal to take out the colour. You must find a good source of wood charcoal and not use the materials supplied for barbecues, though, and I'm afraid that few home brew shops now stock a suitable charcoal. A chat with a friendly technician at your local college or university may give you a source. If you are really stuck, you could try to make your own by partially burning some oak, then treating the charcoal with hot water to wash out the minerals; now break up the lumps and heat them strongly in the cooker. Keep the charcoal in an airtight bottle or tin. Take care when you use it because most charcoals will remove colour, aroma and flavour. If the worst happens and you end up with a pale wine that is rather lacking in bouquet and taste, then you can always rescue it by blending it with a suitable wine with lots of bouquet and taste. It can also be used as part of the make-up of liqueurs (see my *Straightforward Liqueurmaking*).

It is difficult to improve the colour of a red wine by taking out the brown tinge, because chemical removal of the brown usually results in a loss of red as well. The casein treatment helps a little, and fining with bentonite usually improves matters. You can add extra red colour, of course, by using the extract of black grape skins (there is a Gervin extract available for amateur winemakers), or you could consider adding a small amount of a young elderberry wine if the flavour consequences are acceptable.

**Clarity**

Your wine really must be clear if you want to offer it to your friends, and a sensible application of the approach given in Chapter 15 will ensure that you are not troubled with hazes or worse. Our big problem is that we make our wines from so many different types of ingredients that there is always the chance of an unpredictable haze developing.

Follow the suggestions given in Chapter 15 for removing hazes, starting with the use of pectolytic enzyme, and then try first fining and finally filtration. I strongly advise using two-part finings for white wines, since this will deal with over 90% of hazy wines. The worst haze of all to clear is the stubborn one that is found with old plum wines. This never seems to clear on its own. My approach is to first blend it with an apple wine, which at least lightens the haze. Then I try out two-part finings. My old friend, John Harrison, tells me that he has used these finings on a soup-like 20-year old plum wine with success. He did it in two stages, each time using at least a double dose of finings. The first dose gets rid of the worst of the haze, and after racking a second fining does the trick.

# Aroma and bouquet

The smell of a wine tells us a great deal about its quality, and the nose will pick up most of the worst defects that we are likely to come across; the major exception is the defect of "mouse", which we shall discuss in the section on taste.

To start with we may have a wine with simply too little smell. This is much better than having one reeking of vinegar, of course. We cure this fault in the obvious way by adding a source of a suitable aroma. This can be an essence, such as that supplied for the manufacture of liqueurs, or a more general aroma source such as Gervin White Wine Improver, which contains a blend of the esters produced in a normal fermentation, plus the esters of maturation, and a selection of the compounds found in the Riesling grape.

Alternatively, for a white wine, you can add a wine such as elderflower or some other flower wine, if a floral note is what you want, or add a fruit juice such as freshly pressed apple. But if you add any fruit juice, remember that you are also adding sugar and diluting the wine; do stabilise it. For red wines I recommend adding a little blackcurrant or raspberry juice, but don't overdo it.

**More specific bouquet faults**

**Hydrogen sulphide.** This is a dreadful smell that is rightly associated with that of rotten eggs. It can be formed in a number of ways. If the must is sulphited very strongly, the excess of sulphur dioxide can be reduced by some strains of yeast to give $H_2S$, and the formation of this horror is made more likely if the wine is allowed to stand on the lees for too long, or if the nutrient content of the must is deficient in some components (especially pantothenic acid). If you pick up this problem at a very early stage, then it can be taken care of by racking the wine and sulphiting it. The chemistry behind this is that hydrogen sulphide and sulphur dioxide react together to produce water and elemental sulphur:

$$H_2S + SO_2 \rightarrow H_2O + 2S$$

The sulphur precipitates and is removed by filtration.

If the defect is not spotted early on, it can get much worse, and we will also get the formation of thiols or mercaptans. This means that one or both of the hydrogen atoms of H₂S will be replaced by a methyl or ethyl group. These thiols and mercaptans are not removed by the sulphite treatment. In the severe cases, when simple sulphiting doesn't work, the best approach is treatment with copper. You can add some newly cleaned strips of copper foil or wire, but I find it best to add a good pinch of copper sulphate to a gallon of wine. The copper reacts with the sulphur compounds to form insoluble copper sulphide. I then fine the wine with bentonite to take out any residual traces of copper.

**Oxidation.** This is very obvious on the nose, and gives us an unmistakable reminder of the worst type of so-called British Sherry. What we smell is the acetaldehyde that has been produced because of the oxidation of some of the alcohol in the wine. Fortunately there is a very simple way of removing the worst aspects of oxidation, and that is the refermentation of the wine. Thus when yeast ferments sugar to produce alcohol, the penultimate compound in the fermentation chain is acetaldehyde. This means that yeast cells are capable of turning acetaldehyde into alcohol.

The problem then resolves into one of how to set up this further fermentation, especially if the wine is a dry one. The technique I recommend is as follows. If the wine is a white one, take a litre of apple juice or white grape juice and add to it a full sachet of No.3 or Varietal C yeast (other makes of a S.bayanus - Champagne yeast will do) that has been rehydrated. This juice will soon start to ferment vigorously. At this point take the oxidised wine and shake it well to get some air into it, and add to it the fermenting fruit juice. The fermentation will then continue as usual and convert the acetaldehyde into alcohol.

**Sulphur dioxide.** If you have been very heavy handed when sulphiting the wine then the effect on the nose will be unmistakable. If the overdose is a relatively moderate one, then you can take care of it simply by shaking the wine well and then letting nature take care of the problem over a decent period of time. If you really have grossly exceeded the dose, such as adding a teaspoonful of the solid sodium metabisulphite rather than one of 10% solution, then heroic measures are called for. But use the following method only in such a very extreme case.

Take your wine and add to it dropwise 5 ml of "10-volume" hydrogen peroxide (buy it from the local pharmacy). This will react with the sulphur dioxide to form water and harmless sulphate:

$$[SO_3^{2-}] + H_2O_2 \rightarrow [SO_4^{2-}] + H_2O$$

sulphite    hydrogen    sulphate    water
            peroxide

This is a really drastic treatment because there is a real risk of oxidising the wine unless the addition of hydrogen peroxide is carried out dropwise with thorough dispersal after each drop. The 5 ml of hydrogen peroxide will remove about 70 - 80 mg/litre of sulphur dioxide. Bear in mind that 5 ml of 10% solution of sulphite will correspond to around 60 mg/litre of sulphur dioxide when added to a gallon of wine.

The hydrogen peroxide treatment is probably of more use when the must has been over-sulphited and won't ferment, because should you accidentally partially oxidise the must, the fermentation may rescue it from your recklessness.

**"Geranium"**. This is the name given to the characteristic smell that is sometimes produced when a wine has been stabilised with potassium sorbate and is then attacked by strains of lactic acid bacteria. It is said that the bacteria attack the sorbate to produce the compound 2-ethoxyhexa-3,5-diene. In principle this shouldn't happen if you sulphited the wine at the same time as you added the sorbate, because the sulphite should kill the bacteria. The problem usually arises when both sulphite and sorbate have been added but the wine is low in acid and the sulphite not very effective. I must emphasise that this defect is rare, since it needs an attack by bacteria, the presence of sorbate and the lack of sulphite. Try to avoid it because the smell is not easily removed. The only way I have managed it is by using a heavy dose of charcoal, and then blending the resulting neutral wine with fruit juice.

**Acetification.** We have seen that this defect occurs when the wine is attacked by acetic acid forming bacteria (see page 154). It can also be formed if the wine gets excessive exposure to air, but the more obvious oxidation then dominates the wine. Once again I must point out that the smell we get is not that of acetic acid itself, but its ester, ethyl acetate.

There is no known safe cure for this defect. My old (nineteenth century) winemaking books do give a cure, which takes the form of advice to the innkeeper. This advice is to add to a barrel of vinegary wine a lump of lead the size of your fist. It goes on to say that when the lead has dissolved the vinegar taste will have gone and been replaced with a sweetness. An alternative way of achieving the same result is to add red lead (an oxide of lead). The reaction that takes place is the formation of lead acetate, known as sugar of lead because of its sweet taste. It is unlikely that you would prefer to suffer lead poisoning to drinking a vinegary wine I feel!

I suggest that if the wine is only just "over the taste and smell limit", you should blend it with a little fruit juice and drink it up quickly. It can only get worse. If you love wine vinegar, and this is a very expensive commodity, then let your gallon of wine go all the way to vinegar, but keep it isolated from your other wines.

**Medicinal.** This is a rather vague term which describes wines that have been made from musts containing too little acid, such that the yeast produces side products reminiscent of out childhood medicines. Adding more acid, even at the finished wine stage may help a little, as will masking by blending, but you cannot hide the taste completely. The choice seems to be between taking out the smell and taste with charcoal or using the wine as a basis for a winter warming mulled wine.

**Green.** This term reflects a wine made from unripe fruit; it is even more obvious to our taste buds. If it is a red wine, it will have been spoilt by the uptake of unripe tannins. In this case fine the wine with gelatine. But the moral is to use ripe fruit.

## Taste

There are three general taste faults that emphasise the lack of balance in a wine. These are the tastes associated with either too much or too little acidity, sweetness and tannin.

### Acidity

If the acidity is on the low side then simply add the required amount of tartaric acid. Adding one level teaspoonful to 4.5 litres of wine increases the acidity by one gram per litre. Try adding half this amount first to half of the wine, then you can blend the two halves together if you added too much to the first half. Of course a wine made from really low acid must may suffer from the medicinal taint I referred to earlier, and the addition of acid will not remove this, only perhaps making it a little less obvious.

When we know that a must is likely to be on the high acid side, and some of the ingredients will be contributing malic acid, then use Varietal D yeast to metabolise some of this acid. Otherwise you have three choices with an overacid wine. You can blend it with a wine that rather lacks acid. If the wine is rich in tartaric acid, then put it in a cold place and wait for some of the potassium hydrogen tartrate to precipitate out. If neither of these methods is appropriate then you can only neutralise some of the acidity by adding a base.

Chalk is often recommended for this purpose, but this means chemically pure calcium carbonate, of course, and not chunks from the South Downs. I am not enthusiastic about using calcium carbonate, since it leaves a lot of calcium ions behind which have an effect on the flavour that I don't like. The alternative is to use a carbonate or bicarbonate of either sodium or potassium. I prefer to use potassium bicarbonate (potassium hydrogen carbonate).

As we have seen, there is a limit to how much the acidity can be reduced. In practice, for table wines, I recommend reducing the acidity by not more than 2 grams per litre, or three at the outside. It takes 100 grams of potassium hydrogen carbonate to neutralise 75 grams of tartaric acid or its equivalent, so adding 5 grams of potassium hydrogen carbonate will take out a little less than 4 grams of acid. In round figures this is about one gram per litre. As a simple guide, I suggest adding one level teaspoonful of potassium hydrogen carbonate to 4.5 litres of wine in the first instance. If the reduction is not enough then use a second teaspoonful. It may be that you will want to reduce the acidity by only a small amount, and my advice is to play safe by splitting the gallon of wine in half and treating it with half a teaspoonful of potassium hydrogen carbonate powder. If your taste buds tell you that you have taken out too much acid then blending the treated and untreated half gallons will put matters right.

There is a second reason for treating just half a gallon first, because when the potassium hydrogen carbonate is added to the wine, quite a lot of carbon dioxide gas will be liberated, and the froth that forms needs a little room. After you have treated your wine in this way, put it on one side in a cool spot, so that any precipitation of potassium hydrogen tartrate that is going to take place can do so before you bottle the wine. This precipitation means a further reduction of acidity, so don't overdo the reduction in the first instance. If you try to take out too much acid you will load the wine with various salts, which will create a characteristic and rather unpleasant earthy sort of taste.

Potassium hydrogen carbonate is the best base to use, but it may not be easy to purchase in all areas. In this case use sodium hydrogen carbonate (sodium bicarbonate) in its place but use just a little bit less. Remember too that there will be no further loss of acidity in this case when the wine is chilled because sodium hydrogen tartrate is much more soluble than potassium hydrogen tartrate.

### Sweetness

If the wine is not sweet enough then either blend it or add extra sugar. Fruit juice or concentrated grape juice can be used for this purpose if you prefer it. Dealing with an oversweet wine is rather more of a problem, especially if it is low in alcohol as a consequence of the fermentation sticking. Blending is then less appropriate because the final product will still be short of alcohol. For this reason I recommend that you referment the wine using the technique I suggested for removing the taste and smell of oxidation.

Ideally I like to make up a gallon of must, add the yeast and make sure that the fermentation is very vigorous. Then I mix the gallon of oversweet wine with the fermenting must and end up with two gallons of dry wine. If you are too mean with the amount of fermenting must, the amount of active yeast present may not be enough to ensure complete fermentation.

## Tannin

Tannin gives stability to a red wine, but its astringency can be a little overpowering in a heavy young wine. Time usually solves the problem, since the harsh young tannins polymerise with time, and soften in the process. At the same time some tannin interacts with the anthocyanin colouring matter and precipitates out of the wine. This can take a long time, though, and we sometimes find that the fruit has "died" before the tannin drops to an acceptable level.

Elderberry-based wines are classic examples of wines that will benefit enormously by a few years in the bottle, and provided the fruit was really ripe, periods of 5 - 10 years are worth considering. But just in case things are not quite as we would hope, I suggest that you open a bottle every year after year 2, and check the taste. If it becomes really smooth after just three years, drink the lot except for one bottle that you put away for another three to five years just to see how the wine changes.

Many readers will want to drink their wines well before this, though, and fining with gelatine may be the answer, since it will reduce the tannin level and soften the wine for earlier drinking.

If the wine is clearly much too low in tannin then add the required amount of true oenological tannin, and give the wine a few weeks for the new tannin to blend in. Buy the powdered tannin and make it into a strong solution when you need it. Avoid using the very weak solutions sometimes offered on sale to winemakers, because their tannin content is too low to have enough effect on the wine

## Other general taste faults

**Filter paper taste**, or filter pad taste, is a sign of inadequate washing of the paper or pad. Prevention is the answer, but you may be able to remove the worst effects by gentle fining with caseinate.

An **aftertaste of astringency** in a white wine is often the sign of over-vigorous pressing. Fine with caseinate to reduce this unwanted taste.

**Roughness** or harshness arises from a variety of causes, but generally reflects youthfulness, especially if sloes have been used in the recipe. Time usually smoothes out the wine, but a fining with caseinate will offer a quick partial solution. The alternative, if the roughness is fairly mild, is to add a teaspoonful of sorbitol to each litre of wine, and the mouthfeel will improve even more if you add a little Gervin Maturing Solution. This is a solution of French oak extract in alcohol, plus maturing esters, and really does take off the rough edges of a young wine. Provided that you like your wine to have a touch of sweet oakiness, try treating the wine with oak chips or oak granules (see page 75).

A **hot taste** is often found in wines made from grain and vegetable ingredients, and is usually an indication that the wine contains more higher alcohols than usual. These fusel oil components cannot be removed without ruining the wine, and I find that turning the wine into a sweeter social style disguises the hot taste fairly well.

## Specific taste faults

We have already considered acetification, oxidation and geranium formation under bouquet defects, so I will not look at these again. The major defect that can occur with a wine is the formation of the infamous **mouse** taste. Perhaps fortunately, about ten per cent of folk are quite unable to taste mouse, while at the other end of the scale, ten per cent of us are ultra sensitive. Regrettably I fall into the latter category.

The taste is one that comes after the wine has been swallowed, when a most unpleasant taste arises in the throat. It is like a super yeastiness. We now know that it is the consequence of an infection by either Brettanomyces strains of yeast, or possibly some strains of lactic acid bacteria. The offensive taste is produced by a chemical named 2-acetyl-tetrahydopyridine, and only the minutest amount of this chemical is required to produce the effect. It is by no means limited to wines but can be found in beers too, and forms a tiny part of the taste of newly baked bread.

We are not sure why some of us are sensitive to this substance and some not, but simple tests suggest that it is to do with the pH value of our saliva. Thus in an acid medium such as wine, the compound forms a salt which is non-volatile - which is why we do not smell it. When it gets into our mouths it meets the saliva, and if this is fairly acid, the compound remains in its salt form and passes down the throat without our noticing it. If we have rather alkaline (higher pH) saliva, then this liberates the free base, which is volatile, goes up into our nostrils, and then tells us it is there.

It is a horrible defect, and at the first sign the affected wine should be put into isolation. If the wine is given a treble dose of sulphite and put away for six months or a year, the mousey flavour often goes, although the wine that is left never goes back to its original quality. Moreover, the mousiness often returns once the air gets at the wine, so drink it up quickly.

The only way I have ever got rid of it in an economical fashion is by treating the wine with a large dose of charcoal, filtering it, and blending the characterless result with fruit juice.

# Microbial disorders

We have already come across the effects of a variety of attacks by bacteria, including acetification, malo-lactic changes (which can sometimes generate a "sauerkraut" flavour), and mouse. Generally speaking, a sensible use of sterilisation procedures will prevent really serious problems arising. Keep all the equipment clean and sterilise it before it is used again, and make sure that all the bench surfaces are wiped down regularly. I know that it is often tempting to leave the cleaning up to the next day or not bother to wipe up the spillages of wine and sugar solutions. Such rich feeding grounds will be pounced on by bacteria and moulds, and once they get really established it is much harder to deal with them.

I used to keep my spare fermentation locks and bungs in a solution of sodium metabisulphite, but I have found that when such solutions are left for a long time they do become contaminated by persistent moulds. When that happens I sterilise with a solution of hypochlorite and this has taken care of the problem up until now.

**Flowers of wine** show up as a very thin off-white surface film on the wine. The film is of a surface growing yeast Candida mycoderma, which grows in the presence of air and gradually consumes the alcohol in the wine turning it into water and carbon dioxide. If it is allowed to grow long enough, the wine will have lost all its life and become flat and undrinkable.

If this film of yeast does develop in one of your wines, treat the wine with a double dose of sulphite, and shake the wine well to break up the film. After a few days filter the wine through a fairly fine filter, sulphite it again and store it in demijohns filled to the brim. Top up the wine in the demijohn with boiled water if you don't have quite enough wine to fill the jar. Keep an eye on this wine because the film producing yeast is quite persistent and a further treatment may be necessary.

Other microbial problems, which we noted earlier (see page 156), include ropiness. Try the action of sulphite, which normally works with ropiness, but if in doubt, put it down to experience and throw the wine down the sink.

# Index

| | | | |
|---|---|---|---|
| Acesulfame K | 187 | Aspartame | 187 |
| Acetic acid | 154, 169, 229 | Astringency | 232 |
| Acetic acid bacteria | 154 | | |
| Acetobacter | 155 | | |
| Acetoin | 156 | | |
| Acid changes | 178 | Bacteria | 154 |
| Acidity | 230 | Banana | 30, 59 |
| and colour | 177 | Banana wine | 102 |
| and fermentation rate | 170 | Barley | 143 |
| and maturation | 179 | Barsac | 140 |
| and wine stability | 177 | Base | 169 |
| Acidity index | 176 | Baume | 188 |
| Acids | 23, 121, 168 | Beaujolais style | 124, 125 |
| in canned fruit | 28 | Beetroot | 40 |
| in dried fruit | 27 | Bentonite | 14, 75, 122, 211, 218 |
| in fruit | 29 | Betanin | 191 |
| in fruit juices | 29 | Bilberry | 34 |
| Acid taste | 70, 175 | Birch sap | 44, 120 |
| Acrolein | 156 | Bitters style | 145 |
| Adsorption | 219 | Blackberry | 35, 102, 103 |
| Alcohols, higher | 41, 42, 71 | Blackberry wine | 102, 103 |
| Alcohol yield | 23, 68 | Blackcurrant | 35, . |
| Alkali | 168 | Blackcurrant wine | 103 |
| Alsace style | 133 | Blending | 224 |
| Amygdalin | 49 | Blueberry | 34 |
| Amylase | 184 | Boiling | 55 |
| Amylopectin | 183 | Bonnezeaux style | 139 |
| Anthocyanins | 9, 177, 191 | Bordeaux style | 126, 127, 134, 138 |
| Antioxidants | 10, 196, 197 | Botrytis cinerea | 157 |
| Aperitif wines | 40, 143 | Bottling | 87 |
| Appearance | 224, 225 | Bouquet | 66, 227 |
| Apples | 29, 48 | Brettanomyces | 165 |
| Apple wine | 99, 100 | Brix | 188 |
| Apricot | 30 | Brownian movement | 202 |
| Apricot wine | 101 | Browning | 196 |
| Arabinose | 204 | Brush | 20 |
| Aroma | 56, 66, 67, 227 | Buffering | 174, 194 |
| Artichoke | 40 | Bullace | 117 |
| Artificial sweeteners | 187 | Burgundy style | 127, 134 |
| Asbestos | 221 | | |
| Ascorbic acid | 197 | | |
| Aspergillus | 157 | | |

| | | | |
|---|---|---|---|
| Calcium tartrate | 72, 209 | Demijohn | 19 |
| Canderel | 187 | Dessert wines | 148 |
| Canned fruit | 28, 60 | Destemming | 9 |
| Caramelisation | 197 | Dextrins | 184 |
| Carbonic maceration | 77, 125 | Dextrose | 184 |
| Carbohydrates | 181 | Diacetyl | 156 |
| Carotenoids | 191 | Diatomaceous earth | 219 |
| Carrot | 40 | Dicarboxylic acid | 170 |
| Carrot wine | 115 | Disaccharide | 182 |
| Casein | 215 | Dried flowers | 57 |
| Cask maturation | 151 | Dried fruit | 48, 60, 197 |
| Casse | 212 | | |
| testing for | 210 | Egg white | 216 |
| Cecil press | 52 | Elderberry | 36 |
| Centrifuge | 53 | Elderberry wine | 105 |
| Cereals | 42, 61 | Elderflower | 44 |
| Cereal wine | 115 | Elderflower wine | 116 |
| Chablis style | 136 | Enzymes | 10, 211 |
| Chalk | 230 | Equipment | 18 |
| Cherry | 30 | Estufa | 146 |
| Cherry Laurel | 45 | Ethyl acetate | 154, 229 |
| Cherry wine | 104 | | |
| Chitin | 216 | Faults | 223 |
| Chitosan | 216 | Fermentation | 8, 11, 86 |
| Citrus fruit | 30 | rate | 174, 179 |
| Citrus wines | 143, 148 | temperature | 11 |
| Clarification | 13, 87, 226 | trap | 20, 85 |
| Cleaning ingredients | 47 | vessel | 18 |
| Cloudy wines | 201 | Filtering | 213, 219 |
| Colloidal particles | 203 | Filter paper taste | 232 |
| Colour intensity | 194 | Filter-sick taste | 222 |
| Colour of wines | 191, 225 | Fining | 87, 213, 214 |
| Commercial winemaking | 9 | Flavour | 62, 90 |
| Concentrates | 197 | Flowers | 44, 56 |
| Corking | 88 | dried | 57 |
| Corn | 43 | Flowers of wine | 234 |
| Country wines | 96 | "Folly" | 120 |
| Cranberry | 36 | Food processor | 52 |
| Crushing | 8, 9, 49, 50 | Freezing | 47, 52 |
| | | Fruit | |
| Damson | 36 | canned | 60 |
| Damson wine | 104 | citrus | 58 |
| Dandelion | 43 | dried | 60 |
| Dandelion wine | 117 | hard | 58 |
| Deadly nightshade | 45 | juice | 61 |
| Delphinidin | 192 | soft | 59 |

| | | |
|---|---|---|
| Fruit, stone | 58 | |
| Fruit preparation | 47 | |
| Funnels | 20 | |
| Fusel oil | 42, 71, 233 | |
| | | |
| Galactose | 204 | |
| Galacturonic acid | 203 | |
| Gelatine | 216 | |
| Geranium flavour | 92, 229 | |
| German style | 133 | |
| Ginger wine | 120 | |
| Gluconobacter | 155 | |
| Glucose syrup | 184 | |
| Glycerine | 88, 184 | |
| Glycolysis | 8 | |
| Gooseberry | 3, 57, 59 | |
| Gooseberry wine | 105, 106 | |
| Grape | 32, 59 | |
| Grape concentrate | 94 | |
| Grapefruit wine | 107 | |
| Greengage | 33 | |
| Greengage wine | 106 | |
| Green taste | 230 | |
| Gums | 204, 207 | |
| | | |
| Hawthorn berry | 39, 59, 119 | |
| History of winemaking | 3 | |
| Home winemaking | 15 | |
| Honey | 44, 58, 134 | |
| Honeysuckle | 43 | |
| Honey wine (mead) | 118 | |
| Hydrogen peroxide | 228 | |
| Hydrogen sulphide | 227 | |
| Hydrophilic particles | 202 | |
| Hydrophobic particles | 202 | |
| | | |
| Indicator | 169 | |
| Ingredients | 121, 223 | |
|   processing | 46 | |
|   selection | 22 | |
| Inulin | 183 | |
| Invertase | 8, 183 | |
| Isinglass | 217 | |
| Italian style | 129 | |
| | | |
| Jelly bag | 219 | |

| | | |
|---|---|---|
| Kieselguhr | 219 | |
| Kieselsol | 217 | |
| | | |
| Lactic | 205 | |
| Lactic acid bacteria | 155 | |
| Lactose | 183 | |
| Leaf vegetables | 42, 120 | |
| Lemon wine | 107 | |
| Leucine | 41 | |
| Leuconostoc oenos | 156 | |
| Liebfraumilch style | 133 | |
| Loganberry | 38 | |
| Loganberry wine | 108 | |
| Loire style | 128, 136, 137, 139 | |
| | | |
| Madeira style | 146 | |
| Maillard reaction | 196 | |
| Malo-lactic change | 155 | |
| Maltose | 183 | |
| Maltosetetraose | 183 | |
| Maltosetriose | 183 | |
| Malvidin | 192 | |
| Mannitol | 206 | |
| Marrow rum | 41 | |
| Maturation | 13, 89 | |
| Mead | 44, 118 | |
| Medicinal taste | 230 | |
| Melon | 60 | |
| Membranes | 220 | |
| Metallic casse | 208 | |
| Metallic contamination | 205 | |
| Méthode champenoise | 80 | |
| Methylation | 204 | |
| Microbial disorders | 140 | |
| Micro-organisms | 205, 209 | |
|   testing for | 211 | |
| Millipore pads | 220 | |
| Mincer | 50 | |
| Mock orange | 43 | |
| Monbazillac style | 140 | |
| Monocarboxylic acids | 170 | |
| Monosaccharides | 181 | |
| Moulds | 157 | |
| Mouse | 233 | |
| Mulberry | 38 | |
| Mulberry wine | 108 | |

237

| | | | |
|---|---|---|---|
| Neutralisation | 169 | Protein | 204 |
| Nouveau Beaujolais style | 65, 77 | Protein haze | 208 |
| Nutrients | 12, 24 | Pulp fermentation | 13 |
| Nutrisweet | 187 | Pulp haze | 208 |
| | | | |
| Oak granules | 64, 65, 75, 94 | Quince | 33 |
| Oats | 43 | | |
| Oiliness | 205 | Racking | 86 |
| Orange wine | 91, 109 | Raspberry | 38 |
| Oxidation | 14, 228 | Raspberry wine | 111 |
| Oxidative casse | 205, 209 | Red colour | 191 |
| | | Redcurrant | 38 |
| Parsley | 42, 61 | Redcurrant wine | 112 |
| Parsnip | 40 | Rhubarb | 34, 52 |
| Parsnip wine | 116 | Rhubarb wine | 112, 113 |
| Pasteur | 4 | Ribena | 36, 93 |
| Peach | 33, 48 | Rice | 43 |
| Peach wine | 109 | Rohament P | 56 |
| Peapod | 42 | Root vegetables | 40, 61 |
| Pear | 33 | Ropiness | 156 |
| Pear wine | 110 | Roses | 43 |
| Pectic substances | 204 | Rose hip | 39 |
| Pectin | 203 | Rose petal wine | 117 |
| testing for | 210 | Rosé wines | 93, 130 |
| Pectolytic enzyme | 52, 55, 56, 71, 206 | Roughness | 232 |
| | | Rowanberry | 39, 60, 119 |
| Pelargonidin | 192 | | |
| Penicillium | 157 | Saccharin | 187 |
| Peonidin | 192 | Säftborn steamer | 59 |
| Petunidin | 192 | Sancerre style | 135 |
| pH | 172 | Sauerkraut flavour | 150 |
| Phenolic compounds | 9 | Schizosaccharomyces | 165 |
| Phenoloxidase | 10, 196 | Sherry style | 147 |
| Pineapple | 33, 60 | Sieving mechanism | 220 |
| Pineapple wine | 110 | Silicic acid | 217 |
| Plum | 33 | Skin contact | 194 |
| Plum wine | 111 | Sloe | 38 |
| Poisonous plants | 45 | Sloe wine | 113 |
| Polyvinylpyrrolidone | 218 | Social wines | 142 |
| Port essence | 95 | Sorbitol | 185 |
| Port style | 66, 150 | Spanish style | 129 |
| Potassium caseinate | 215 | Sparkling wines | 13, 65, 79, 136 |
| Potassium hydrogen tartrate | 178 | Sparkolloid | 218 |
| | | Specific gravity (S.G.) | 188 |
| Potato | 40 | Spoilage yeasts | 165 |
| Pressing pulp | 51, 52 | Stabilisers | 92, 122, 166 |
| Protected colloid | 207 | Starch | 183, 204 |

| | | | |
|---|---|---|---|
| Starch haze | 207 | Whitecurrant | 34 |
| testing for | 210 | Whitecurrant wine | 114 |
| Steamer | 54 | White Wine Improver | 67 |
| Storage | 89 | Wine colour | 191 |
| Strawberry | 37 | Wines, red | 64, 124 |
| Strawberry wine | 114 | Wines, white | 64, 133 |
| Stuck ferments | 86 | Wine styles | 63, 123 |
| Sucrose | 182 | | |
| Sugar | 16, 23, 67, 121 | Yeast | 158 |
| solutions (SG) | 188 | available strains | 161 |
| syrups | 189 | cell | 158 |
| volume of | 181 | choice | 11, 13, 73 |
| Sugar in canned fruit | 28 | classification | 159 |
| in dried fruit | 27 | inhibition | 166 |
| in fruit juices | 28 | rehydration | 162 |
| in fruits | 25 | | |
| Sulphur dioxide | | Xylitol | 185 |
| (sulphite) | 177, 195, 196, 228 | Xylose | 186 |
| Swede | 40 | | |
| Sweeteners | 181, 186 | | |
| Sweetening wine | 89, 122, 187 | | |
| Sweetness | 231 | | |
| Syphoning | 86 | | |
| Syphon tube | 19, 86 | | |
| | | | |
| Tannin | 9, 195, 232 | | |
| Taste | 175, 230 | | |
| Tetrasaccharides | 183 | | |
| Thermal vinification | 72 | | |
| Tourne | 206 | | |
| Tricarboxylic acids | 170 | | |
| Trisaccharides | 183 | | |
| Tropical fruits | 40 | | |
| Turnip | 40 | | |
| Tyndall effect | 202 | | |
| Tyrosine | 196 | | |
| | | | |
| Vegetables | 40, 42, 61 | | |
| Vermouth | 65, 66, 144 | | |
| Vine leaves | 44 | | |
| Vitamin C | 197 | | |
| | | | |
| Walker-Desmond press | 50 | | |
| Water | 57, 72 | | |
| Wax | 204, 207 | | |
| Wheat | 43 | | |